RESTORATIVE JUSTICE

Restorative Justice

Philosophy to practice

Edited by

HEATHER STRANG
JOHN BRAITHWAITE
The Australian National University

Ashgate

DARTMOUTH

Aldershot • Burlington USA • Singapore • Sydney

Published by
Dartmouth Publishing Company Limited
Ashgate Publishing Ltd
Gower House
Croft Road
Aldershot
Hants GU11 3HR
England

Ashgate Publishing Company
131 Main Street
Burlington VT, 05401-5600 USA

Ashgate website: http://www.ashgate.com

British Library Cataloguing in Publication Data
Restorative justice : philosophy to practice
   1.Restorative justice 2.Victims of crimes - Legal status,
   laws, etc.
   I.Strang, Heather II.Braithwaite, John, 1951-
   344'.03288

Library of Congress Control Number: 00-134012

ISBN 0 7546 2147 2

Printed in Great Britain by
Antony Rowe Ltd, Chippenham, Wiltshire

Contents

Acknowledgements

Our greatest debt in making this book a reality is to Alison Pilger, who was the organisational backbone of the conference where the papers were first presented and who prepared the manuscript in camera ready copy. Alison also applied her sophisticated understanding of restorative justice to the preparation of the index. Chris Treadwell and Mary Hapel were also of great assistance in organising the conference in 1999. That conference was funded by the Reshaping Australian Institutions Project and supported by the Law Program in the Research School of Social Sciences at ANU. We thank their heads, Frank Castles, Geoffrey Brennan and Peter Cane for their support.

Finally we wish to thank our colleagues at Ashgate Dartmouth, especially Tom Campbell, for the efficiency with which this book has proceeded to publication.

Heather Strang
John Braithwaite

List of Contributors

Christine Alder is an Associate Professor in the Criminology Department at the University of Melbourne. Her teaching and research interests have been predominantly in juvenile justice and youth offending and in violence. Her particular focus is an enduring concern for the situation of women and girls. Her publications include co-edited volumes on working with young women in juvenile justice and on family group conferencing.

Charles Barton lectures in ethics at the New South Wales Police Academy and is Program Director for Criminal and Restorative Justice Ethics in the Centre for Professional and Applied Ethics at Charles Sturt University, New South Wales. He is a former Postdoctoral Research Fellow (Philosophy) at Massey University, New Zealand, and a current Visiting Fellow in the Key Centre in Ethics, Law, Justice and Governance at Griffith University, Queensland.

John Blackler served with the New South Wales Police Service for 27 years and is a holder of the Australian Police Medal. Currently he is a researcher with the ARC Commonwealth Special Research Centre in Applied Philosophy and Public Ethics at Charles Sturt University, New South Wales. He is co-author (with Seumas Miller and Andrew Alexandra) of *Police Ethics* (1997).

John Braithwaite is a Professor in the Research School of Social Sciences of the Australian National University. He is active in the Restorative Justice Group there. He does research on business regulation as well as criminal justice. Recent books include *Corporations, Crime and Accountability* (1993) (with Brent Fisse), *Global Business Regulation* (with Peter Drahos) (2000) and *Regulation, Crime, Freedom* (2000).

Valerie Braithwaite is a Fellow in the Research School of Social Sciences of the Australian National University. She has published in the areas of human values, trust relationships, stress and coping, and social change. She is Coordinator of the Program of Reintegration and Individual Shame Management (PRISM), which has developed an anti-bullying program for use in primary schools.

Kathleen Daly is Associate Professor in the School of Criminology and Criminal Justice, Griffith University, Queensland. Her book, *Gender, Crime and Punishment* (1994) received the Michael Hindelang Award from the American Society of Criminology. She edited (with Lisa Maher) *Criminology at the Crossroads: Feminist Readings in Crime and Justice* (1998). During 1998/99 she directed a major research project on restorative justice in South Australia.

Mark Findlay teaches and researches at the Institute of Criminology, University of Sydney. He also holds a research Chair at the Centre for Legal Research, Nottingham Trent University. During his time at the University of the South Pacific, Mark explored his interests in customary justice in transitional cultures, resulting in *The Globalisation of Crime* (1999).

Sir Anthony Mason AC KBE is a Non-Permanent Judge of the Hong Kong Court of Final Appeal. He has been National Fellow in the Research School of Social Sciences of the Australian National University, Chancellor of the University of New South Wales and Chief Justice of the High Court of Australia.

Gabrielle Maxwell is Senior Research Fellow at the Institute of Criminology, Victoria University of Wellington. She has previously held positions in Psychology at the University of Otago, in the New Zealand Department of Justice and at the Office of the Commissioner for Children. Her research and publications focus on children's needs and issues, youth justice, family law, legal services and victims.

Seumas Miller is Professor of Social Philosophy and Director of the ARC Commonwealth Special Research Centre in Applied Philosophy and Public Ethics at Charles Sturt University, New South Wales. He has authored over one hundred academic papers and a number of books, including *Police Ethics* (1997) (with John Blackler and Andrew Alexandra) and *Social Action* (forthcoming).

Allison Morris is Professor of Criminology and Director of the Institute of Criminology, Victoria University of Wellington. She has previously taught at the University of Edinburgh and the University of Cambridge. Her main research and teaching interests are youth justice, victims and restorative justice.

Philip Pettit is Professor of Social and Political Theory in the Research School of Social Sciences of the Australian National University. He is the author of a number of books on philosophy and political theory, including (with John Braithwaite) *Not Just Deserts: A Republican*

Theory of Criminal Justice (1990), *The Common Mind: An Essay on Psychology, Society and Politics* (1993) and *Republicanism: A Theory of Freedom and Government* (1997).

Heather Strang is Coordinator of the Restorative Justice Group and a Research Fellow in the Research School of Social Sciences of the Australian National University. Her research interests are in victims and restorative justice. She directs the Reintegrative Shaming Experiments, evaluating the effectiveness of restorative conferencing compared with criminal processing through the courts.

Lode Walgrave is Professor of Juvenile Criminology at the Catholic University of Leuven, Belgium, and has published a number of articles and books on restorative justice. He is also Coordinator of the International Network for Research on Restorative Justice for Juveniles.

Warren Young is Professor of Law at Victoria University of Wellington. Prior to that he was Director of the Institute of Criminology and Assistant Vice Chancellor (Research). His recent publications include *Juries in Criminal Trials: A Summary of Research Findings* (1999) and the *New Zealand National Survey of Crime Victims* (1996).

Preface

This volume is the outcome of a conference conducted in 1999 by the Restorative Justice Group in the Research School of Social Sciences, Australian National University. The conference was sponsored by the Reshaping Australian Institutions project and opened by the former Chief Justice of Australia, Sir Anthony Mason, whose remarks are the first chapter in the volume. Sir Anthony comments on the difficulties of distinguishing and balancing restorative and retributive traditions in our history. He uses the *Clotworthy* case to reveal the difficulties the judiciary will increasingly confront in the future: this was a case where the New Zealand Court of Appeal overturned a non-punitive remedy favoured by the victim and other stakeholders following a restorative justice conference.

In Chapter 2 Allison Morris and Warren Young provide an overview of the development of restorative justice and the contrasting values, processes and outcomes it involves compared to traditional criminal justice. The main lines of critique are also discussed.

Kathleen Daly in Chapter 3 challenges the widely promulgated view among restorative justice activists that restorative justice is defined in distinction to retributive justice. Punishment, Daly argues, is an inevitable and important part of restorative justice. Criminal justice is centrally about the public denunciation of criminal wrong and punishment is essential to that.

In Chapter 4 Charles Barton works a similar theme, taking the argument one step further. Barton contends that, contrary to the implied suggestion in many restorative justice critiques of the status quo, the chief strength of restorative interventions lies not in their rejection of punitiveness and retribution, but in the empowerment of communities of care who are most likely to respond effectively to both the causes and consequences of criminal wrongdoing. Thus, it is the empowerment of affected stakeholders on both sides that is the crucial feature of restorative justice for Barton, and the feature whose absence causes both conventional and restorative justice to fail.

Seumus Miller and John Blackler in Chapter 5 seek to locate certain contemporary restorative justice mechanisms, such as youth conferencing, in relation to the ancient institution of confession. They offer a critique of some of the more ambitious claims made in relation to these mechanisms, including the claim that such mechanisms obviate the need for punishment.

In Chapter 6 Gabrielle Maxwell and Allison Morris reveal an important set of new research findings from New Zealand on when Family Group Conferences succeed and fail in reducing recidivism. This study considers a wider range of explanatory variables than any previous published study. It is based on six and a half years of reoffending follow-up. Some of the findings provide support for a variety of key claims of restorative justice theory.

Christine Alder in Chapter 7 articulates a challenging set of feminist concerns about restorative justice, especially in relation to young women as offenders. At the same time, Alder sees potential in the kind of informal spaces restorative justice provides for social support that might encourage young women to speak in their own voice.

In Chapter 8 Valerie Braithwaite explores empirically the relationship between basic value structures of parents and support for restorative resolution of school bullying problems. She finds stronger support for restorative than for punitive justice, but stronger support still for a hedged combination of the two.

John Braithwaite and Philip Pettit in Chapter 9 use restorative justice to argue that the categories of normative theory will be more powerful if they are informed by explanatory theory and vice versa. Bentham's utilitarianism is the leading example of a powerful marriage of explanatory and normative theory. Pettit and Braithwaite argue that freedom as non-domination, the key concept in republican normative theory, has an explanatory power that also commends restorative justice institutions.

Lode Walgrave in Chapter 10 works through the republican normative ideal of dominion (freedom as non-domination) in a new way in relation to restorative justice. Walgrave thinks the criminal justice system should limit its ambitions to restoring dominion rather than promoting it (in the way advocated by Pettit and Braithwaite).

In Chapter 11 Mark Findlay draws on experience with restorative justice in the Pacific to illuminate the risks of colonisation through restorative justice. Methodologically Findlay advocates comparative contextual analysis and programmatically he explores the idea of collaborative justice in cultural contexts as an alternative to restorative justice which may involve restoration to an unjust status quo.

In Chapter 12 John Braithwaite and Heather Strang analyse the preceding chapters to draw some more general lessons about the relationships between emerging restorative justice philosophies and practices. They conclude that until there is some settlement of principles of restorative justice, troubling cases like *Clotworthy* will continue to perplex courts. An attempt is made to define some significant areas of consensus among the contesting restorative perspectives on punishment within the volume and to define some critical research questions for resolving points of dissensus.

All in all the collection manifests the considerable ferment and innovation around attempts to crystallise a restorative philosophy. It also manifests a distinctive history of philosophy being shaped by practices that ordinary citizens find remarkably appealing. As a consequence the philosophy now struggles to keep up with the pace of bottom-up innovation.

Heather Strang
John Braithwaite

Canberra

1 Restorative Justice: Courts and Civil Society

THE HON. SIR ANTHONY MASON AC KBE

This collection of essays begins with the assumption that restorative justice meets a community need, that it is beneficial to the community and that it is here to stay. Hence a question is whether it is to be controlled by any particular agency of the state or whether it is to be controlled by the institutions of civil society as distinct from the agencies of the state.

The answers to this and other questions depend upon many considerations, including aspects of social and political theory. The major question concerns the extent of the contribution that can be made by restorative justice to the problems that confront us. The extent of that contribution partly depends upon the inadequacies in our existing justice system.

Those inadequacies, including the cost to government, are well known. The proponents of restorative justice tend, quite rightly, to focus upon failures of the existing system for they present the sharpest contrast with restorative justice. Those failures are, for different reasons, most serious in relation to juvenile, young and indigenous offenders. These are areas in which restorative justice can make a substantial contribution, to judge from the New Zealand, Canadian and the English experience in policing, particularly. That experience offers the possibility that the concept may be able to play an even wider role in the justice system.

The shortcomings of the current system are so great that we should be looking to and exploring alternative systems. That is why restorative justice is seen by some, not merely as an approach which can be slotted in as an add-on to the existing system administered by a particular court, say a police court or a juvenile court, but also as a viable alternative. Likewise, it is suggested that we should no longer be thinking of applying restorative justice to a particular group of offenders (say indigenous people or juveniles) or even to particular classes of offences (say offences involving family violence). Rather we should be thinking of restorative justice as having a general application.

Here, of course, we are confronted with the facts of history. It is said that restorative justice has been the dominant model of criminal justice in the period of recorded history and that it still is the dominant

1

model in surviving indigenous systems in Asia, Africa, Central and South America and Australia. I question the accuracy of that view. It is not always easy to distinguish between restorative and retributive justice, as several contributors to this volume observe. There is an overlap between the two and that overlap may lead some to ignore or under-estimate the part that retributive justice has played. Be that as it may, much of our modern experience of restorative justice is concerned with its operation in indigenous systems, or as applied to indigenous peoples, in countries such as Canada, New Zealand and South Africa.

There is a debate as to just how effective restorative justice is in the modern world. At this conference we pursued the question whether restorative justice is effective in reducing the crime rate. My own belief is that, in modern society, we cannot expect too much from a system of one-off conferencing and that we should be looking to anchor the concept as an element in a more extensive culture shift. That approach would accord with the Thames Valley police experience in England.

There are significant objections to the adoption of restorative justice, particularly objections made by judges and lawyers. On the other hand, we need to be aware that lawyers are renowned for their opposition to changing the status quo, especially a status quo with which they are familiar and in which they have an interest. We have seen how reluctant many professional lawyers have been to embrace mediation and how long it has taken to break down that reluctance, a reluctance that was initially shared by judges who, I think, now accept that mediation has an important part to play, even if some of them are not wildly enthusiastic about it.

One objection is that restorative justice may be regarded as discriminatory if its availability is confined to particular racial, ethnic, religious or community groups: I will return to this topic in a moment in connection with the *Gladue* case, a landmark decision of the Supreme Court of Canada. In order to meet that objection, it may be desirable, though I do not think it is necessary, to ensure that all admitted offenders have access to restorative justice, even if it appears that indigenous people and youthful offenders are more likely to resort to it, or more likely to benefit from it. The special characteristics or circumstances of these groups may well warrant differential treatment.

Equality of treatment is a central objective of our existing system of criminal justice. The equality principle demands similar treatment *in like cases*. The potentiality of the existing system, when coupled with the restorative justice approach, so that they can operate side by side to produce different outcomes in particular cases, will offend that principle, unless the principles of the existing system are expressed in such a way as to make it clear that, for good reason, certain categories of case are to be dealt with in accordance with the standards of restorative justice. Even then, the fact that a higher percentage of cases involving a particular group, say indigenous people, is dealt with by way of restorative justice may be seen by some opponents or critics as breaching the equality principle. I hasten to add that it is not my view.

Perhaps a stronger objection to restorative justice is the discretionary element inherent in a decision to send a defendant down the restorative justice route rather than deal with the defendant as a matter of routine sentencing, if one route is an alternative to the other. The strength of the objection may be reduced if the concept of restorative justice is integrated in the general sentencing principles applied by the courts. That, it seems to me, is the challenge for the future and it appears that the courts in Canada and New Zealand are beginning to take up that challenge. The decision to send a defendant down the conferencing route might take the form of a judicial discretion to be exercised by the judge or magistrate who has the sentencing responsibility. An exercise of the discretion could be initiated either by the prosecution or those representing the defendant. There is an obvious advantage in spelling out the criteria or considerations to be taken into account in the exercise of the discretion. The procedures should call for consultation between the prosecution and the defendant's representatives so that the suitability of the case for restorative justice is fully explored. In this way, the exercise of the judicial discretion would ordinarily appear as a principled and reasoned determination.

What I have said would involve attaching restorative justice to existing court procedures and treating it as complementary to those procedures. It seems to me that there is little prospect of any other approach being accepted, at least for the time being. By placing restorative justice in the context of the existing court system, we reduce the force of the objections and generate a public expectation that the jurisdiction will be exercised responsibly and cautiously. In that way, it may achieve solid public acceptance and pave the way for a more wide-ranging use of the concept when the detriments of the existing system, especially its cost, become more widely appreciated.

I note that in Germany, it is suggested that administrators are being converted to the view that the public does not believe strongly in punitive sentencing. My apprehension is that the public does believe in punitive sentencing in Australia. Certainly politicians credit the public with that belief. Hence the emphasis on "get tough with crime" political campaigns. As things presently stand, there is a risk for restorative justice if it is identified in the public mind as being "soft" on serious crime. That has been the principal popular complaint, whether justified or not, that has been voiced against the existing system and it is a complaint which politicians take up in their "get tough with crime" campaigns.

The punitive sentencing culture in nations like Australia may explain the lack of judicial support for restorative justice compared with the support to be found in some other jurisdictions. It is possible that this lack of support stems from an over-sensitive concern about judicial participation in politically controversial discussion. Be that as it may, reform and development of the criminal process and dealing with offenders would profit from greater judicial involvement in the examination of the problems.

The New Zealand proposal, unfortunately aborted in 1998, for a pilot scheme to be trialed in four District Courts would have been a valuable experiment. New Zealand has a much better documented experience than we have had in Australia of the interaction between a sentencing judge and the restorative conference. Helen Bowen and Jim Consedine's (1999) *Restorative Justice* sets out five instructive judgments in that area. Sir Michael Hardie Boys, now Governor-General, formerly a well-known Judge of the New Zealand Court of Appeal, has written an enthusiastic foreword to the book. The aborted proposal was all the more important in that administrators were to be appointed at each court to procure facilitation services from the community. The New Zealand experience and thinking may be valuable in showing us that there can be effective community participation in and control of restorative justice procedures, a matter of which I remain to be convinced. Community participation, in the wide sense of "community" seems to me to be fundamental, if we are to avoid the criticism that it is not enough simply to look at the interests of victim and offender. That criticism has real force.

A related problem is how the courts will manage to handle the potential for the inherent conflict that exists between restorative justice and the existing system, particularly on appeal. The source of that conflict is to be found in the fact that the central theme of the existing system is punishment of the offender, not restorative justice. The potentiality for conflict arises directly and immediately from the sentencing tariff administered by the judges. The tariff is designed to promote equality and consistency of treatment. That tariff reflects elements of retribution and deterrence. Prescription by statute of the jurisdiction, criteria, relevant considerations and procedures to be applied by a sentencing judge will assist in overcoming that problem.

The *Clotworthy* Case

The *Clotworthy* case illustrates the difficulties. Mr Clotworthy was convicted on pleas of guilty to two counts, wounding with intent to cause grievous bodily harm, robbery being the motive, and assaulting a police constable, with intent to obstruct him in the execution of his duty. The incident took place in a street in Auckland when the offender demanded money from a passer-by, slashed him in the face and stabbed him in the chest with a knife, severely injuring him. Indeed, he was lucky to survive. The victim had emergency surgery to repair a collapsed lung and diaphragm. He required blood transfusions and was in intensive care for some days. The attack brought on a resurgence of the victim's epilepsy, as a result of which he could no longer drive a vehicle. The offender was aged 27 and had been drinking. The sentencing judge thought that the starting point for sentencing was a sentence in the order of 3-4 years.

Conferencing had been organised by Justice Alternatives, a restorative justice facilitator, with the victim, the offender and their support persons. The victim was understanding and did not demand heavy punishment but was interested in reparation. The offender, who was otherwise a person of good character, was anxious to redeem himself.

In the result, a suspended sentence of 2 years imprisonment was imposed. Reparation was ordered in the sum of $15,000 of which $5,000 was to be an immediate down payment. The purpose of this reparation was to fund plastic surgery for the wounds suffered. In addition, Mr Clotworthy was required to undertake 200 hours' community service.

The Crown appealed on the ground that a suspended sentence for 2 years was inadequate. The Court of Appeal heard submissions from the victim who urged that imprisonment would achieve nothing for the offender or himself.

The Court of Appeal made the point that the public interest in sentencing cannot be confined to victim and offender, stating

> the public interest in consistency, integrity and the criminal justice system and deterrence of others are factors of major importance

The Court considered that the sentencing Judge's starting point for this crime of violence was too low - it should have been 5-6 years, not 3-4 years. The offer of reparation did not justify suspension of the sentence and the serving of a term of imprisonment meant that the offender could not afford reparation at the level ordered. So reparation was limited to $5000, the amount which had actually been paid. The sentence imposed was a term of 3 years imprisonment, that being a reduction from the norm of 5-6 years.

The Court concluded by saying -

We would not wish this judgment to be seen as expressing any general opposition to the concept of restorative justice (essentially the policies behind ss11 and 12 of the Criminal Justice Act). Those policies must, however, be balanced against other sentencing policies, particularly in this case those inherent in s5, dealing with cases of serious violence. Which aspect should predominate will depend on an assessment of where the balance should lie in the individual case. Even if the balance is found, as in this case, to lie in favour of s5 policies, the restorative aspects can have, as here, a significant impact on the length of the term of imprisonment which the Court is directed to impose. They find their place in the ultimate outcome in that way.

In short, as the Crown has argued, this case is too serious for the approach which commended itself to the Judge, but the factors which weighed with him should be and are fully reflected in the sentence which we propose to substitute.

For my part, I am in general agreement with the approach taken by the Court of Appeal under the law as it stands. I do not think that it was defensible, under our existing system of criminal justice, to uphold the orders of the sentencing judge in a case involving such a serious offence involving gross violence. Indeed, in my view, the case was not an ideal vehicle for the restorative justice approach.

The Court of Appeal did, however, give very considerable weight to the conferencing solutions. There was a significant reduction in the term of imprisonment which otherwise would have been awarded. The flaw in the conferencing solution and in the sentencing judge's judgment was a failure to sufficiently recognise the public interest element, an element which is embedded in the existing law.

The *Gladue* Case [1999] 1 SCR 688

An equally important decision was that of the Supreme Court of Canada in *R v Gladue*. The accused, an aboriginal woman, was sentenced to three years imprisonment on a plea of guilty to a charge of manslaughter, arising out of the killing of her common law husband. The accused chased and stabbed him after a party. The accused, affected by drinking alcohol, believed he had been engaged in sexual activity with her sister. He had also angered her by making insulting and offensive remarks to her. She suffered from a hyperthyroid condition which caused her to over-react in emotional situations. She was a young mother and, apart from driving offences, had no criminal record. While on bail, she received alcohol abuse counselling and upgraded her education.

The trial judge considered that, in the light of the gravity of the crime, a suspended sentence would be inappropriate. He noted that the accused and the victim were living in an urban area, off-reserve and not "within the aboriginal community as such". There were, in his view, no special circumstances arising from the aboriginal status of the accused and the victim which should be taken into consideration.

An appeal against sentence was dismissed by the Court of Appeal and the Supreme Court. Part XXIII of the Canadian Criminal Code codifies the fundamental purpose and principles of sentencing and the relevant factors to be taken into account. Section 718(2)(e) requires sentencing judges to consider all available sanctions other than imprisonment and to pay particular attention to the circumstances of aboriginal offenders. The trial judge's notion that a non-sentencing approach was limited to aboriginals living in aboriginal communities was specifically rejected. The Court pointed out that the provision is remedial and is designed to ameliorate the serious over-representation of aboriginal people in prisons and to encourage judges to take a restorative approach to sentencing. In this respect, Part XXIII has placed a new emphasis upon the decreasing use of incarceration.

In discussing the application of Part XXIII to aboriginal offenders, the Court noted that the term of imprisonment imposed on an aboriginal offender might, in some circumstances, be less than the term imposed upon a non-aboriginal offender for the same offence, but went on to state that Part XXIII is not a means of automatically reducing the prison sentence of aboriginal offenders and that it should not be assumed that an offender is receiving a more lenient sentence because incarceration is not imposed. The Court took account of the fact that the accused was granted, subject to certain conditions, day parole after she had served six months in a correctional centre and was later granted full parole on the same conditions.

The Court's judgment has been criticised on the ground that the Court's emphasis was given to restorative justice in its application to indigenous persons, to the extent of ignoring restorative justice in its application to non-indigenous persons. The criticism fails to take account of an ultimate appellate's practice of confining its consideration to the circumstances of the case in hand, not least in sentencing cases, where it has the benefit of the examination of the relevant problems by the courts below. Ultimate appellate courts are generally reluctant to embark upon a dissertation on the law which is not essential to the issue for determination.

Part XXIII of the Code, particularly s 718(2)(e), is an interesting provision. It provides an entry point for restorative justice in the sentencing process, which extends to non-indigenous people. It remains to be seen what the Canadian courts make of it in that context. It is a provision which could be introduced in other jurisdictions.

There are three aspects of the public interest element in judicial sentencing which I should mention specifically. First, crime, especially serious crime, is a matter in which the State and the community have a vital interest. It is not a matter which can be left entirely to negotiation between victim, offender and their respective support groups. There is no reason why the State or the community should necessarily accept the outcome reached in such a negotiation. For one thing, the victim will often favour reparation over punishment and the offender, particularly when he can afford it, will often take the same view. For another thing, the reparation option may be more readily available to those who can afford it.

Secondly, there is the fortuitous element which arises when the offender is fortunate enough to encounter a sympathetic victim or a victim fortunate to encounter an offender wealthy enough to afford substantial reparation. Should such an offender fare better than the offender who encounters an antagonistic victim? The answer to that question may depend upon whether our primary goal is punishment of the offender or restorative justice and which is given priority by the relevant legislation.

Finally, there is the matter of consistency in outcomes. The importance of consistency in criminal punishments has been emphasised from the writings of Aristotle onwards. Nothing is more likely to bring a system of justice into disrepute more quickly than inconsistency in punishment. It is said that the existing criminal justice system is by no means free from fault on this score. That may well be true. But that comment is not a justification for concluding that consistency in punishment is of little relevance. Nor does the comment provide a basis for the conclusion that restorative justice will do better or even as well as the existing system on this score. The prospect is that a system of ad hoc conferencing which has no in-built requirement to ensure consistency in outcomes will generate more inconsistency than the existing system which *now* devotes much more attention to the goal of consistency.

The issues are fundamental. Restorative justice offers real promise for the future and it is imperative that the problems are thought through. That is why I have mentioned some objections and why the generation of a culture shift from a focus on punishment, with its attendant problems, to restorative justice is important. This collection of essays will contribute to the resolution of the problems.

Reference

Bowen, Helen and Consedine, Jim (eds) (1999), *Restorative Justice: Contemporary Themes and Practice*, Ploughshares Publications, Lyttleton, New Zealand.

2 Reforming Criminal Justice: The Potential of Restorative Justice

ALLISON MORRIS AND WARREN YOUNG

Introduction

Over the last 15 years or so, penal practices in many Western countries have been characterised by two quite contrasting, even contradictory, trends. On the one hand, most jurisdictions continue to rely on and even expand the use of formal court processes and have dramatically increased the number of offenders subject to sanctions such as imprisonment and supervision in the community: in other words, they continue to rely on conventional processes and practices which are firmly grounded in what many would regard as the failures of the past. On the other hand, some jurisdictions have begun to use very different ways of responding to offending which involve meaningful participation by victims and offenders in the decisionmaking process, and often produce very different types of sanctions: in other words, they have begun to use restorative processes and practices which many would regard as providing promise for the future if not for the present.[1]

We can illustrate some of the differences between these two trends by reference to a case which recently came before the New Zealand Court of Appeal (*R v Clotworthy* (1998) 15 CRNZ 651). This case involved a very serious offence - the offender held a knife to the victim's throat, demanded money and then, following a scuffle, stabbed him six times. As a result, the victim suffered a number of serious wounds, including a life-threatening one, and an ugly 27 cm long scar across his back. The sentencing judge referred the case to two barristers in Auckland who, at that time, arranged conferences for restorative justice purposes under the name of Justice Alternatives. They convened a meeting between the offender and the victim; two support persons accompanied the victim.

At that meeting, the victim had the opportunity to explain to the offender the physical and emotional effects of the offence upon him. The offender, for his part, expressed considerable remorse, indicated that the offence had been committed after excessive alcohol consumption and maintained that since the offence he had not had a drop to drink. The victim told the offender that he had been to prison, that 'it did not do him much good', and that, rather than the offender going to prison, he would prefer that the offender cover the costs of cosmetic surgery. The victim accepted the offender's apology, and the parties agreed that the offender would pay the victim a total of $25,000 (primarily by way of a bank loan on the security of the home belonging to the offender and his partner) in order to meet the costs of the cosmetic surgery.

When the results of the conference were reported to the sentencing judge, he ordered reparation of $15,000 (the maximum he thought was realistic in the circumstances) and imposed 200 hours community service and a two-year prison sentence suspended for two years: a sentence which could be described as restorative since it met the victim's express wishes. The Crown appealed, on the basis that the sentence was manifestly inadequate. The Court of Appeal subsequently quashed this sentence and imposed a three-year prison sentence with the reparation order being reduced from $15,000 to $5000 in view of the fact that the offender had only $5000 available at that time: a sentence which manifestly did not meet the victim's express wishes.

In reaching this conclusion, the Court of Appeal, while stating that it did not wish to be seen as expressing any general opposition to the concept of restorative justice, clearly regarded the public interest in denunciation and general deterrence as its priority:

> We would not want this judgement to be seen as expressing any general opposition to the concept of restorative justice (essentially the policies behind ss11 and 12 of the Criminal Justice Act).[2] Those policies must, however, be balanced against other sentencing policies, particularly in this case those inherent in s 5, dealing with cases of serious violence.[3] Which aspect should predominate will depend on an assessment of where the balance should lie in individual cases. Even if the balance is found, as in this case, to lie in favour of s 5 policies, the restorative aspects can have, as here, a significant impact on the length of the term of imprisonment which the Court is directed to impose. They find their place in the ultimate outcome in that way.

This statement is generally seen as supportive of restorative justice (McElrea, 1998; Boyack, 1999). We take issue with this. First, the Court of Appeal seemed to view restorative justice in very narrow terms as amounting to little more than reparation. Equally, if not more, important for restorative processes and practices is the involvement of victims, offenders and their "communities of interest" in making the decision how best to deal with the offending. In *Clotworthy*, the victim and offender had already agreed on an outcome which they saw as "right"; the Court of Appeal rejected this. Second, arguably there were "special circumstances" in the *Clotworthy* case if one looked through a restorative rather than a conventional lens. The Court of Appeal's sentencing outcome was clearly against the express wishes of the victim and did not meet those objectives identified as important by him. Current legislation requires the courts to look only to the offence and the offender in assessing "special circumstances", which means that only those factors conventionally used in mitigation - such as youth, a previous good record or strong rehabilitative prospects - are generally considered relevant.[4] Third, the Court of Appeal seemed to see the potential impact of restorative justice primarily operating as further mitigation on the "usual" sentence. Restorative justice, however, does not place a high value on those "rules" which determine "usual" sentences. Rather it seeks to subvert these and substitute others. At the heart of this case, then, are two parallel justice processes and practices which barely interconnected and which involved a fundamental clash of values and interests.

In this paper, we set the scene for a challenge to conventional justice and for advancing restorative justice by contrasting (and perhaps inevitably over-simplifying) the characteristics and values of the two and the ways in which these impact on their respective processes and outcomes. Since penal values and cultural values are inextricably linked, the basic question we are raising is whether it is conventional or restorative justice which embodies the kind of cultural values that we would like to see in the penological future.

Contrasting Values

In brief, the conventional criminal justice system emphasises the centrality of State authority and gives primacy to the abstract interests of the State. Thus offending is seen primarily (and often even exclusively) as a violation of the interests of the State - or perhaps more accurately of the interests of the collective community represented by the State. This State interest, however, is usually presented, or disguised, as the "public interest". Thus Ashworth (1992: 3 cited in Cavadino and Dignan, 1996: 237) sees the criminal law as setting out 'to penalise those forms of wrongdoing which ... touch public rather than *merely private* interests' (our emphasis).[5]

Having assumed this authority, the State then demonstrates it through a process of detached and impersonal decisionmaking by professionals representing the State. Thus it subjects itself to, and gains its legitimacy from, strict adherence to the 'rule of law' and the trappings that accompany that. Conventional justice is also based on an ethic of individualism and individual culpability at both the conviction and sentencing stage; it places a priority on legal rights (thereby promoting equality before the law and consistency of practices); and it focuses primarily on the symbolic and expressive functions of punishment. It also signifies that the State has only a limited role in the care of its citizens (a signification which is softened to some degree by the establishment of rehabilitative programs within the context of the implementation of sanctions). And, in all these respects, conventional justice is distinctly monocultural. For example, the courtroom rituals and sanctions employed in former British colonies during the colonial era were simply adaptations of English justice and, even since then, penal developments have largely reflected trends in England. Indigenous processes and indigenous forms of sanction were essentially excluded, at least at a formal level (for a discussion of the effects of this in New Zealand, see Jackson, 1988; Pratt, 1992).

In contrast, restorative justice returns the conflict[6] to those most affected - victims, offenders and their "communities of interests" - and gives primacy to their interests. By "community of interest" we do not mean elected, appointed or self-appointed community representatives but rather the collection of people with shared concerns about the offender, the victim, the offence and its consequences, and with the ability to contribute towards a solution to the problem which the crime presents or represents.[7] These people can support and negotiate with victims and offenders about appropriate outcomes through restorative processes and are arguably in a better place than judges and other professionals to identify what might prevent future crime. Thus the State no longer has a monopoly over decisionmaking; the principal decisionmakers are the parties themselves. Restorative justice endorses a collective ethos and collective responsibility. Thus it emphasises the existence of shared values which can be used to address the offending and its consequences (for victims, offenders and communities) and to reintegrate victims and offenders at the local community level. It is premised on the belief that the reasons behind the offending, and hence the solutions to it, lie in the community.

Restorative justice also emphasises human rights and the need to recognise the impact of social or substantive injustice and in small ways address these rather than simply provide offenders with legal or formal justice and victims with no justice at all. Thus it seeks to restore the victim's security, self respect, dignity and, most importantly, sense of control. And it seeks to restore responsibility to offenders for their offending and its consequences, to restore a sense of control to them to make amends for what they have done and to restore a belief in them that the process and outcomes were fair and just. And, finally, restorative justice encourages cultural relativity and sensitivity rather than cultural dominance. Processes and outcomes can be shaped by the parties themselves to take account of cultural difference. In essence, the social values underlying restorative justice rely on connections - connections between offenders, victims and communities - rather than on exclusion.

Contrasting Processes

Conventional justice processes take the form of a public ritual and the language, rules and procedures are formal and complex (Carlen, 1976, Ericson and Baranek, 1982). They are designed to eliminate emotion from the process and to retain an atmosphere of detachment and impartiality. The professionals representing the State - judges, lawyers, police officers and court staff - are the principal players in that ritual. Lawyers are responsible for most, if not all, of the dialogue; and judges make the decisions. All of this ritual, of course, does have a purpose and meaning. It signifies how society regards crime and criminals, but it also expresses and signifies the authority of the State. Even the structural and spatial arrangements of the courtroom, and the positioning of the parties involved in the proceedings, indicate who has the real power and who the real participants are. Courtroom practices also make perfectly clear whose cultural values underpin the law (Tauri and Morris, 1997).

In contrast, in a restorative process, the parties with a stake in a particular offence - victims, offenders and their 'communities of interest' - come together and, with the aid of a facilitator, resolve how to deal with the offence, its consequences and its implications for the future. Generally, restorative justice offers a more informal and private process over which the parties most directly affected by the offence have more control. This does not mean that there are no rules[8] which must be adhered to or that there are no rights[9] which must be protected, but rather that, within a particular framework, there is the potential for greater flexibility, including cultural flexibility. Thus the procedures followed, who is present and the venue used are often chosen by the parties themselves.[10] Overall, the intention - or the hope - is to create an environment in which participants feel comfortable and able to speak for themselves and in which the hearts and minds of offenders and victims might be touched, perhaps changed.

Contrasting Outcomes

Conventional justice does not generally impose sanctions for the primary purpose of reducing reoffending, whatever political rhetoric and the strategic plans of official agencies might say to the contrary.[11] Rather, sanctions are imposed by the State for the benefit of the wider community: to reassert the particular values, cultural meanings and symbols underpinning the criminal law and the punishment system, to assert the authority of the State to uphold these, to educate the public about them and to deter individual offenders and others. Because of this, outcomes tend to be abstract in nature and pursued through punitive means. In other words, sanctions are primarily symbolic and expressive.

The aims of restorative justice meetings, on the other hand, are primarily to hold offenders accountable for their offending in meaningful ways and to make amends to victims certainly in a symbolic sense and, where possible, in a real sense too. Restorative outcomes are sometimes viewed as focusing on apologies, reparation or community work, as ways of restoring the property stolen or compensating the victim for the injuries endured and of signifying 'recognition, recompense and reassurance' in Braithwaite and Pettit's (1990) terms. These are certainly key restorative outcomes. But, in fact, *any* outcome - including a prison sentence - can be restorative if it is an outcome agreed to and considered appropriate by the key parties. For example, it might be agreed that a prison sentence is required in a particular situation to protect society, to signify the gravity of the offending or to make amends to victims. Neither protecting society nor signifying the gravity of the offending are excluded within a restorative justice system; rather they are secondary objectives. Moreover, discussion of the consequences of offences is seen as a more powerful way of communicating their gravity to offenders than simply imprisoning them.

One of the hopes of restorative justice is that reconciliation between the offender and victim will occur. This is not always possible - victims may remain angry or bitter; offenders may remain unmoved and untouched.   However, there is no doubt that reconciliation can on occasions take place between victims and offenders - the case of *Clotworthy* referred to earlier demonstrates that.   Other examples observed at family group conferences include invitations by a victim to the offender and his family to join the victim's family for a meal, hugs and handshakes all round at the end of the meeting, and victims deciding to attend court to speak on the offender's behalf.

Contrasting Victims' Experiences

In the conventional justice system, where there is a 'guilty' plea, the effects of offences on victims are communicated to the court, if at all, through a victim impact statement presented by the prosecutor in written form. Even when they do attend court, they are merely witnesses for the prosecution or observers; they are not able to participate meaningfully in the process, as the following comment from the family of a murder victim shows (Maxwell and Shepherd, 1998): *'you have to sit and listen to lies and have no say'.* Consequently, victims, particularly of serious offences, frequently feel alienated from the process; they receive little to aid their healing; and they end up with a sense of grievance.

Victims' presence is central to restorative justice processes. Generally speaking, research shows that many victims want to meet their offender - in Maxwell and Morris's (1993) research, only 6% of all the victims interviewed said that they did not wish to meet the offender. In this way, victims can have a voice - they can say to the offender how they feel about his or her actions and what the consequences of these actions have been for them. Thus a victim at a family group conference was able to tell the offender who had trashed her house as part of a burglary what it felt like to vacuum from the floor the spilled ashes of her dead parent. Another victim was able to speak of her sadness at the theft of tapes which included a farewell from a dying sister.

Being able to participate in restorative meetings means that some of the victims' emotional needs may be met; for example, they may be provided with the opportunity for some healing, for some understanding of what happened and why, and for some closure. Restorative processes put victims at the heart of what happens and, indeed, many victims say that they find the experience positive. About 60% of the victims interviewed in Maxwell and Morris's (1993) research described the conference they attended in these terms: it had provided them with a voice in determining the outcome[12] and, in meeting the offender and the offender's family face-to-face, they could assess their attitude, understand more why the offence had occurred and assess the likelihood of its recurring. In the words of one victim: *'to know what is happening is to be involved'.*

Contrasting Offenders' Experiences

By and large, offenders have the same experience of conventional justice as victims. Pre-trial and trial procedures do not engage them; they rarely participate directly; they are generally expected to communicate with the court through their lawyer; and they are discouraged from any direct dialogue with the victim. They thus can feel alienated from the process and frequently have only a vague idea of what has happened to them. Overall, they remain fundamentally untouched by both processes and outcomes. As one offender put it: *'I don't really know what happened today. I didn't understand the court...'* (Maxwell et al., 1994).

Restorative justice processes require more than the presence of the offender: they require their inclusion. They are expected to directly participate in the process, to speak about their offending and matters associated with it, to interact with the victim, to express their remorse about what has occurred, to apologise for what they have done, and to contribute to decisions about the eventual outcome. From all this, offenders are expected to have a better understanding of their offending and its consequences, to become accountable for the offending in ways which they understand and to contribute to making amends to the victim. The presence of victims also means that offenders' justifications for their offending - 'she could afford it', 'he is insured', and so on - can be challenged. Indeed, restorative conferences are typically emotionally powerful occasions far removed from the typical courtroom scene and from which few offenders can remain immune - signs of distress or embarrassment, even tears, are not uncommon. Overall, about a half of the young offenders interviewed in Maxwell and Morris's (1993) research said that they had felt involved in the conferencing process at least in some way. They were able to say what they wanted to and to speak without pressure: *'It was...quite good...you get to talk openly'.* They also acknowledged the power of meeting victims: *'I didn't want to see the victims but it did have an impact'.*

Contrasting Effectiveness

Almost any criminal justice system is bound to have some effect in terms of one or more of the objectives it is pursuing. The important question is whether or not it is giving emphasis to the right purposes and values and, if so, whether or not it is more or less successful than alternative approaches in achieving these purposes and expressing these values. This said, the effectiveness of conventional and restorative justice cannot readily be contrasted on the same terms since their primary objectives are so different. But even in terms of the objectives to which conventional justice gives priority (but which restorative justice makes secondary) it seems that restorative justice does no worse and, on some dimensions, may actually do better.

    For example, there is little evidence that the ritualistic nature of conventional justice and the abstract nature of most of the sanctions it imposes are any more likely to express society's abhorrence of offending or to operate as a deterrent to offenders or potential offenders than restorative outcomes, provided they incorporate meaningful accountability and are viewed as "right" by the parties, including their "communities of interest". Being confronted by one's victim, for example, is not the "soft option" often portrayed with respect to restorative justice.[13]

    Furthermore, although the rhetoric of conventional justice places emphasis on the protection of the public, and in particular on the use of imprisonment for that purpose, it in fact pursues that objective in a haphazard and often completely misconceived way. A good example of this is the legislative reforms which have occurred in many countries over the last 10 years and which increased both the use and the length of prison terms for certain categories of violent and sexual offenders as a means of protecting the public, despite the fact that there is convincing research evidence that the offenders targeted in such legislation are no more likely to commit another serious offence than property or other offenders (Brown and Cameron, 1995; Brown, 1998). The conventional justice system does, of course, provide some protection for the public, but there is no reason to believe that restorative justice, which does not preclude the option of imprisonment, is incapable of doing so at least as well.

Reducing reoffending is not the primary objective of conventional justice, but in this respect it also seems to do fairly poorly. Reconviction rates for those imprisoned are high[14] and are not much better for those sentenced to community-based sanctions (see, for example, Lloyd et al., 1994; New Zealand Department of Corrections, 1997). And while there is some evidence that rehabilitative programs can make some difference to reoffending rates, they are very difficult to implement within the confines of conventional justice and at best have a limited impact (McGuire, 1995).

On the other hand, there are some encouraging data on reconviction with respect to restorative justice. Maxwell and Morris (1999), for example, tracked a sample of young offenders who took part in family group conferences in 1990-91. About three quarters of these young people were not reconvicted within a year and more than two fifths (43%) had not been reconvicted at all or had been reconvicted only once within six years. Of course, this sample is not comparable to the adults mentioned earlier - these data are indicative only - but, importantly, Maxwell and Morris (1999) also suggest that the probability of reconviction is *reduced* when certain aspects of restorative justice are achieved.

Regression analysis on the limited data Morris and Maxwell (1995) had collected in 1990-91 suggested that those offenders who apologised to victims were three times less likely to be reconvicted four years later than those who had not apologised and that those offenders who participated in conferences with victims were more than four times less likely to be reconvicted four years later than those where no victims had been present.

In their later research, using interview data collected some six years after the original family group conference, they (Maxwell and Morris, 1999) found that young people who attended family group conferences and who felt remorse[15] were significantly less likely to be reconvicted six years after the conference, whereas those young people who felt that they had been shamed[16] by the process were significantly more likely to be persistently reconvicted six years later. Significantly, this suggests that the shaming techniques which are employed in different ways in the conventional justice system and in some restorative justice systems do not themselves produce a positive response from offenders.

What is much more important is reintegration or a sense of belonging. Offenders in Maxwell and Morris's (1999) sample who had the opportunity of taking educational or other training courses, offenders who got jobs, offenders who became partnered, offenders given a sense of self respect and offenders who saw themselves as having a future all featured in the group who were subsequently not reconvicted. It is this combination of factors - believing that what they did was wrong, gaining a sense of belonging and having something of value to lose - which are key influences in the decision to stop offending. In our view, restorative justice is much more likely to produce these than conventional justice because of the reintegrative values and processes discussed above.

One final point in this section: so far, we have contrasted conventional and restorative justice on the basis of the objectives of conventional justice. From what we have said already, however, it is also clear that conventional justice is very ineffective at addressing in meaningful ways either offenders' accountability or victims' needs - the objectives stressed by restorative justice. It is clear that, in restorative justice, offenders can be held accountable, victims can be heard, victims may feel better as a result of the process, and outcomes which more fully address victims' and offenders needs or interests can be reached. Importantly, many of the negative findings in research on current examples of restorative justice relate to bad practice rather than to fundamental flaws in its underlying principles.

In addition, there are advantages in restorative justice to the State. Family group conferencing in the New Zealand youth justice system, for example, has resulted in fewer court appearances - a reduction by almost two thirds between 1987 and 1996 - and fewer custodial sentences - a reduction by more than 50% between 1987 and 1996 (Spier, 1997). And, contrary to public and media perceptions, juvenile crime is not escalating out of control. Though it has increased, the rate of increase over the last ten years is smaller than for adults. The fastest growing crime population has been the over 30s: an increase of 155% compared with an increase of 24% in juvenile crime (Maxwell and Morris, 1997)!

Addressing the Critique of Restorative Justice

Implicit in much of what has been said already is a critique of the processes and practices of conventional justice. However, a number of criticisms have been made about restorative justice and we need to try to address some of these.

The Lack of Proportionality and Consistency

First, it is argued that the sanctions agreed to within a restorative justice framework may not be proportionate to the severity of the offence and are unlikely to be consistent: offenders involved in similar offending may end up with different sanctions (Warner, 1994). For example, Ashworth and von Hirsch (1998: 303) complain about the 'absence of safeguards against excessive penalties'. As desert theorists, they affirm the need for proportionality as a limit on sentences and see restorative justice as having substituted 'the wishes of the individual victim' (Ashworth, 1992, 8, cited in Cavadino and Dignan, 1996: 237) or 'the victim's disposition' (Ashworth and von Hirsch, 1998: 332-3).

Such criticisms can be responded to in a number of ways. Judges do not always deal with like cases alike. However, that is hardly an adequate response. What is more important are the reasons for the inconsistencies. Inconsistencies on the basis of gender, ethnicity or socio-economic status per se - which is what research on the conventional justice system (Hood, 1992; Hedderman and Gelsthorpe, 1997) points to - can never be right.[17] Inconsistencies between outcomes which are the result of genuine and uncoerced agreement between the key parties, including victims, may be.

Furthermore, restorative justice is premised on consensual decision-making. It requires all the key parties - the victims, offenders and their communities of interest - to agree on the appropriate outcome. The State continues to remain a party to decision-making through its representatives - for example, the police or the judiciary depending on the place of the restorative processes in the criminal justice system. But what is different is that these representatives are not the "primary" decision-makers.

Finally, consistency and proportionality are constructs which serve abstract notions of justice. Ashworth and von Hirsch (1998: 334) refer to desert theory providing 'principled and fair guidance'. But there are a number of criticisms which can be made of this: for example, the over-simplification of the gradation of offences.[18] There are some writers on restorative justice who refer in similar terms to 'uniformity', 'fairness' and 'equity' as means of ensuring that outcomes for offenders are not disproportionate to their culpability (see, for example, Van Ness, 1993; Bazemore and Umbreit, 1995). But uniformity or consistency of approach (as opposed to uniformity or consistency in outcomes) is, in our view, what is required and this is achieved by always taking into account the needs and wishes of those most directly affected by the offence: victims, offenders and their communities of interest. Specifically from a restorative perspective, desert theory does not provide outcomes which are meaningful to them. Indeed, desert theory is silent on why equal justice for offenders should be a higher value than equal justice (or, indeed, any kind of justice) for victims.

Failing to Deter

Second, restorative justice is often assumed to be a "soft option" and, as such, may fail to deter offenders. We have already questioned this: on the one hand, the research evidence suggests that penalties have little more than a marginal deterrent effect (von Hirsch et al., 1999) and, on the other hand, being confronted by one's victim in a restorative conference is no "soft option".

Using Victims to Benefit Offenders

Third, it is sometimes argued that victims may be "used" to benefit the offender - for example, by getting the victim to agree to a non-custodial penalty. It is obviously important to ensure that victims are not further victimised through providing good information and support and managing meetings well to ensure that the victim does agree with the proposed outcome (Morris et al., 1996; Umbreit and Greenwood, 1997). It is worth stressing too that, in most restorative justice systems, victims have a veto over the acceptability of the proposed sanction. Criticisms about restorative justice "using" victims also ignores the fact that conventional justice uses victims for its own (the State's) interests without offering any corresponding benefits.

Perpetuating Power Imbalances

Fourth, power imbalances between the parties in the outside world - for example, between a violent man and his female partner - are thought likely to be replicated in restorative justice processes. But processes can be devised whereby power imbalances are minimised or negated through, for example, providing support to the female partner and none to the violent man, or using a shuttle approach instead of face to face meetings (Braithwaite and Daly, 1994). Also, this criticism ignores the fact that most women in violent situations do not rely on criminal justice processes at all. A mere 11% of the women in the New Zealand Women's Safety Survey (Morris, 1997) who said they had experienced violence from their partners had called the police. This is a common finding. Women want the violence to stop; but they do not necessarily want their partner to be criminalised or penalised. A restorative justice framework could increase the options available to them (Carbonatto, 1995; Hudson, 1998).[19]

Infringing Legal Rights

Fifth, legal rights are also thought likely to be infringed in restorative justice processes (Warner, 1994). This can be responded to in two main ways. First, individual or legal rights may be protected by offering offenders legal advice, if this is desired, before they admit responsibility for the offence and before the outcome is ratified, though lawyers might not be entitled to be present at the meeting itself.[20] Second, lawyers could be allowed to attend restorative justice meetings. But this would require an understanding of the difference in emphasis between restorative and conventional justice processes and hence in the role they would play. In criminal justice processes, lawyers advocate: they speak for the offender. And lawyers discourage the offender from talking directly with the victim. In restorative justice processes, it is crucial for offenders to speak for themselves and for dialogue to take place between offenders and victims. Some clarification and re-definition of lawyers' roles would, therefore, have to occur (Morris et al., 1997). The lawyer's primary purpose should be to protect the offender's basic rights, and not to minimise the offender's responsibility or to get the most lenient sanction possible.

Vigilantism

Sixth, restorative justice is sometimes equated with community or popular justice which is equated with vigilantism.[21] It is true that community justice can be repressive, retributive, hierarchical and patriarchal. But these values are fundamentally at odds with the defining values of restorative justice and cannot, therefore, be part of it. Indeed, these are the very reasons why we believe that the "community of interest" should be defined quite narrowly and to exclude the attendance at restorative meetings of "representative" members of geographical or social communities, except where it would be culturally appropriate to do so, as in North American healing circle practices. We would also note that, if there are concerns about communities taking over this process for non restorative purposes, checks could be introduced - for example, courts could provide some oversight of restorative justice outcomes for the purposes of ensuring that the outcomes are in accordance with restorative justice values.

Leaving the "Hard Core" Untouched

Seventh, it is claimed that restorative justice leaves untouched a "hard core" of unrepentant offenders. This is undoubtedly true. All systems have their failures, and conventional justice systems have a large number of them. The real issue is whether or not restorative justice processes offer more potential than conventional justice processes to touch the hearts and minds of offenders and to effect change. Maxwell and Morris's (1999) research on reoffending seems to point to that potential.

Cost

And, finally, it is argued that restorative justice is costly. Certainly, it is time-consuming for victims, offenders and other participants, and if it is used for minor offences where the impact upon the victim has been slight, then the costs might outweigh the potential benefits. It is precisely for this reason that we argue that restorative justice should be used in serious cases — in those cases in which the needs of the parties are most poorly served by conventional justice. However, we would not exclude the use of restorative processes for *any* offences where the parties wished to use them: victim support agencies have long rejected outsiders' descriptions of the impact of any offending as minor. We also see a place for restorative processes in policing and prosecution outcomes as well as in sentencing. Restorative values should be embedded within and throughout *all* our responses to offenders and victims.

Conclusion

There are risks attached to the current commitment by governments to conventional justice: penal populations will continue to grow at no increase in community safety, at considerable cost and with little likelihood of reducing reoffending. In the meantime, restorative justice is continuing to grow rapidly in a piecemeal way. There is undoubtedly popular and community support for it.[22] What we need now is a commitment by governments to make restorative justice a central part of their justice systems. If we can engage governments, we might then be able to reverse these trends and, in particular, we might be able to impact more effectively on reoffending, although we would not wish to argue for restorative justice solely or mainly on this ground.

In promoting restorative processes and outcomes, we are not suggesting that jurisdictions should abandon the use of courts or prisons. Restorative justice does not deal with issues of guilt or innocence; this will remain a task where judges and jurors have irreplaceable advantages. Nor does it remove prisons from available sanctions when parties to the restorative justice process agree to them. And, of course, courts and prisons will have to be used when offenders fail to agree to the outcomes arrived at through restorative processes and when the key participants decide they are appropriate and necessary.[23]

A constant theme in the sociology of punishment is that changes in the forms and processes of punishment are driven more by the wider social fabric than by rational choices about the purposes and means of punishment (Spierenburg, 1984; Garland, 1990; Pratt, 1992; Young and Brown, 1993). In other words, punishment processes and practices both reflect and reinforce a range of social meanings. They tell us about the sort of society we are and want to be; the values we regard as important; the nature of social relations; the nature of and limits to the authority of the State; and the way in which that authority gains and maintains its legitimacy. Restorative justice offers us a new set of values and priorities: values and priorities which we could take with us into the new millennium. The potential of restorative justice to address the failures of conventional justice and to hold offenders accountable in meaningful ways, to hear victims' voices and to address more fully victims' and offenders needs or interests is no longer simply a matter of speculation. The success of restorative processes and practices in New Zealand and elsewhere shows that changes can occur.

Notes

1   The main examples of restorative processes and practices are the various forms of conferencing now found in New Zealand (Maxwell and Morris, 1993), Australia (Alder and Wundersitz, 1994; Bargen, 1995; Palk et al., 1998; Hayes and Prenzler, 1998; Sherman et al., 1998; Daly et al., 1998 and Daly, 1999) and elsewhere (McCold and Wachtel, 1998; Jackson, 1998; Young, 1998; Pollard, 1999 and Branken and Batley, 1998), particularly for young offenders, but there are also several examples of conferencing in the adult arena following similar principles, both by way of diversion and as a process used by judges prior to sentence (Bowen and Consedine, 1999 and Tuhiwai Smith and Cram, 1998). In addition, in the United States and England, victim-offender mediation programs can be seen as reflecting restorative processes and practices (Marshall and Merry, 1990; Umbreit and Stacey, 1996, Umbreit et al., 1997 and Umbreit and Greenwood, 1998).

2   Section 11 of the Criminal Justice Act 1985 requires the court to make a reparation order unless it would be 'clearly inappropriate to do so'. Section 12 requires the court to take into account any offer of compensation made by the defendant and permits the court to take into account the extent to which 'the offer has been accepted by the victim as expiating or mitigating the wrong'.

3   Section 5 of the Criminal Justice Act 1985 requires the court to sentence serious violent offenders to a period of imprisonment unless there are 'special circumstances'.

4   Restorative conferencing is not concerned with producing "lenient" or "rehabilitative" sentences for offenders though some of the cases described in Bowen and Consedine (1999) seem to indicate that this was the result (if not the objective) rather than, for example, making amends to the victim.

5   This is not the place to fully engage with this statement. Suffice to say that, without the holder of the private interests (the victim) reporting the offence, no supposedly public interest can arise. And, without the victim being willing to provide information and give evidence, again the public interest would inevitably falter. Thus "public interest" depends on the actions of the holder of the private interests.

6   Christie (1977), in an important early article on restorative justice (though that term is not used by him), refers to the conflict being 'stolen' by the State. Though we use Christie's term here to acknowledge his contribution, it does not fully capture what is involved in most offending. Thus when A steals B's car, there is no conflict unless A believes the car to be really his. The word "conflict", therefore, can blur the offender's responsibility as in "conflict of interest" and so we will from now on use the word "offence".

7   The role of the community in restorative justice is still being debated. See Crawford, (1997) for a discussion of the various meanings and roles of communities in criminal justice areas.

8   In most jurisdictions, facilitators will follow guidelines or practice manuals. In some, there are statutory guidelines or regulations to follow.

9   Again, these will be reflected in practice manuals or in statutory guidelines or regulations. Some jurisdictions offer legal advice before or after the restorative justice meeting, but others allow lawyers to attend to safeguard the offenders' interests.

10   For example, in New Zealand, family group conferences may be held in a community hall, in the offender's home, on a marae (meeting house) or wherever the parties prefer. Conferences may be attended by a large number of people (basically whoever the offender, victim and their communities of interest invite); they may last for many hours; they may begin with prayers; and they may end with the serving of food. They may be facilitated by kaumatua (Maori elders) and they may follow Maori kawa (protocol).

11   The Department of Corrections in New Zealand, however, has adopted 'the reduction in reoffending' as its overriding strategic goal in the implementation of custodial and community-based sanctions. Its success in achieving this, as we note later, is likely to be limited.

12   Cavadino and Dignan (1996) argue that victims should only have a say in reparative outcomes and not in deterrent, incapacitatory, denunciatory or retributive outcomes. We would not limit the victims' voice in this way. In family group conferences in New Zealand, for example, victims and the other participants are free to take deterrence, incapacitation, denunciation or retribution

into account. The crucial factor is that they all agree about the appropriate sanction.

13   For an analysis of recent research on deterrence, see von Hirsch et al. (1999). Generally, they did not find a correlation between sentence severity and crime rates, but no studies have yet been conducted which considered the deterrent effects of different processes.

14   Over three-quarters of prisoners in New Zealand are reconvicted within $2^{1/2}$ years of their release and over 60% are reimprisoned within five years (New Zealand Department of Corrections, 1997).

15   "Remorse" was a composite variable made up of the offender remembering the family group conference, completing the tasks agreed to at the conference, feeling sorry about the offending and showing it and feeling s/he had repaired the damage resulting from the offence. This construct may be similar to what Braithwaite (1988) meant when he referred to reintegrative shaming.

16   The question asked was 'did the process make you feel a bad person' and so what is being referred to here is similar to what Braithwaite (1988) called disintegrative rather than reintegrative shaming.

17   We acknowledge that desert theorists would not support such inconsistencies either, but we prefer to deal with these criticisms on the basis of how sentencing "is" empirically rather than how it "ought" to be ideally.

18   For a summary, see Tonry (1994).

19   This is a controversial viewpoint and there are many examples of family violence being excluded from restorative justice processes. See Martin (1996) for a summary of this position.

20   South Australia, for example, offers legal advice before and after family conferences in the youth justice system about such matters as whether or not the offender should admit the offence or should agree to the proposed outcome.

21   Von Hirsch and Ashworth (1998, 303) certainly justify conventional justice practices on the grounds that they displace vigilantism and prevent people from taking the law into their own hands.

22   For example, a Listener/Heylen poll in New Zealand in 1994 found that 55% of respondents agreed or strongly agreed that offenders should meet with their victims and where possible try to put things right. Only a quarter disagreed with this. And, in 1995, the Ministry of Justice in New Zealand published a discussion document of restorative justice and invited submissions on it. It recently (1998) published its analysis of these submissions. Briefly, the majority of the 113 submissions made were supportive of restorative justice; only 9 were strongly opposed to it.

23   Some jurisdictions also refer offenders to courts when victims are unwilling to participate in restorative justice processes. We would not preclude the possibility of restorative processes without victims being present though fully accept this changes their character. However, victims' views can still be communicated and victims' needs can still be addressed.

References

Ashworth, A. and von Hirsch, A. (1998), 'Desert and the Three Rs', in A. von Hirsch and A. Ashworth (eds), *Principled Sentencing: Readings on Theory and Policy*, Hart Publishing, Oxford.

Alder, C. and Wundersitz, J. (eds) (1994), *Family Conferencing and Juvenile Justice*, Australian Institute of Criminology, Canberra.

Bargen, J. (1995), 'A Critical View of Conferencing', *The Australian and New Zealand Journal of Criminology*, Special Supplementary Issue, pp. 100-3.

Bazemore, G. and Umbreit, M. (1995), 'Rethinking the Sanctioning Function in Juvenile Court', *Crime and Delinquency*, vol. 41, pp. 296-316.

Bowen. H. and Consedine, J. (1999), *Restorative Justice: Contemporary Themes and Practice,* Ploughshares Publications, Lyttleton.

Boyack, J. (1999), 'How Sayest the Court of Appeal?', in H. Bowen and J. Consedine (eds), *Restorative Justice: Contemporary Themes and Practice,* Ploughshares Publications, Lyttleton.

Braithwaite, J. (1988), *Crime, Shame and Reintegration*, Cambridge University Press, Cambridge.

Braithwaite, J. and Daly, K. (1994), 'Masculinities and Communitarian Control', in T. Newburn and E. Stanko (eds), *Just Boys Doing Business*, Routledge, London.

Braithwaite, J. and Pettit, P. (1990), *Not Just Deserts: A Republican Theory of Criminal Justice*, Oxford University Press, Oxford.

Branken, N. and Batley, M. (1998), *Family Group Conferences: Putting the Wrong Right*, Report of the Family Group Conference Pilot Project of the Inter-Ministerial Committee on Young People At Risk.

Brown, M. and Cameron, N. (1995), 'The Problem of Violent Offending', *New Zealand Law Journal*, pp. 419-24.

Brown, M. (1998), 'Serious Violence and the Dilemmas of Sentencing: A Comparison of Three Incapacitation Policies', in *Criminal Law Review*, pp. 710-22.

Carbonatto, H. (1995), *Expanding Intervention Options for Spousal Abuse: The Use of Restorative Justice*, Institute of Criminology, Victoria University of Wellington, Occasional Papers in Criminology New Series: No. 4.

Carlen, P. (1976), *Magistrates' Justice,* Martin Robertson, London.

Cavadino, M. and Dignan, J. (1996), 'Reparation, Retribution and Rights', *International Review of Victimology*, vol. 4, pp. 233-53.

Christie, N. (1977), 'Conflicts as Property', *British Journal of Criminology*, vol. 17, pp. 1-15.

Crawford, A. (1997), *The Local Governance of Crime: Appeals to Community and Partnership*, Clarendon Press, Oxford.

Daly, K., Venables, M., McKenna, M., Mumford. L. and Christie-Johnston, J. (1998), *South Australia Juvenile Justice (SAJJ) Research on Conferencing, Technical Report, No.1: Research Instruments and Background Notes*, School of Criminology and Criminal Justice, Griffith University, Queensland.

Daly, K. and Kitchner, J. (1999), 'The (R)evolution of Restorative Justice through Research-practitioner Partnerships', in A. Morris and G. Maxwell (eds), *Youth*

Justice in Focus. Conference Proceedings, Institute of Criminology, Victoria University of Wellington.

Ericson, R. and Baranek, P. (1982), *The Orderings of Justice: A Study of Accused Persons as Dependants in the Criminal Process*, University of Toronto Press, Toronto.

Garland, D. (1990), *Punishment and Modern Society: A Study in Social Theory*, Oxford University Press, Oxford.

Hayes, H. and Prenzler, T. (1998), *Making Amends: Final Evaluation of the Queensland Community Conferencing Pilot*, Centre for Crime Policy and Public Safety, Griffith University, Brisbane.

Hedderman, C. and Gelsthorpe, L. (1997), *Understanding the Sentencing of Women*, Home Office Research Study No. 170, HMSO, London.

Hood, R. (1992), *Race and Sentencing*, Clarendon Press, Oxford.

Hudson, B. (1998), 'Restorative Justice: The Challenge of Sexual and Racial Violence', *Journal of Law and Society*, vol. 25, pp. 237-56.

Jackson, M. (1988), *The Maori in the Criminal Justice System*, Department of Justice, Wellington.

Jackson, S. (1998), *Family Justice?*, University of Southampton, Southampton.

Lloyd, C., Mair, G. and Hough, M. (1994), *Explaining Reconviction Rates: A Critical Analysis*, Home Office Research Study No. 136, HMSO, London.

McGuire, J. (ed.) (1995), *What Works: Reducing Reoffending*, John Wiley, Chichester.

Marshall, T. and Merry, S. (1990), *Crime and Accountability: Victim/Offender Mediation in Practice*, HMSO, London.

Martin, P. (1996), 'Restorative Justice - a Family Violence Perspective', *Social Policy Journal*, vol. 6, pp. 56-68.

Maxwell, G. M. and Morris, A. (1993), *Families, Victims and Culture: Youth Justice in New Zealand*, Social Policy Agency and Institute of Criminology, Victoria University of Wellington, Wellington.

Maxwell, G., Robertson, J. and Morris, A. (1994), *First Line of Defence: The Work of the Duty Solicitor*, Institute of Criminology, Victoria University of Wellington, Wellington.

Maxwell, G. and Shepherd, P. (1998), *Evaluation of the Counselling for Families of Murder Victims Scheme*, Department of the Prime Minister and Cabinet Crime Prevention Unit and Institute of Criminology, Wellington.

Maxwell, G. and Morris, A. (1997), 'What do we Know about Youth Crime?', in A. Morris and G. Maxwell (eds), *Youth Justice: The Vision*, Institute of Criminology, Wellington.

Maxwell, G. and Morris, A. (1999), *Understanding Re-offending*, Institute of Criminology, Wellington.

McCold, P. and Wachtel, B. (1998), *Restorative Policing Experiment*, Community Service Foundation, Pipersville.

McElrea, F. (1998), 'The Roles of Community and Government', unpublished paper presented at the Second International Conference on Restorative Justice for Juveniles, Fort Lauderdale, Florida.

Ministry of Justice (1995), *Restorative Justice: A Discussion Document*, Ministry of Justice, Wellington.

Ministry of Justice (1998), *Restorative Justice: the Public Submissions*, Ministry of Justice, Wellington.

Morris, A. (1997), *Women's Safety Survey 1996*, Ministry of Justice, Wellington.

Morris, A., Maxwell, G., Hudson, J. and Galaway, B. (1996), 'Concluding Thoughts', in J. Hudson, A. Morris, G. Maxwell and B. Galaway (eds), *Family Group Conferences: Perspectives on Policy and Practice*, Federation Press, Annandale.

Morris, A., Maxwell, G. and Shepherd, P. (1997), *Being a Youth Advocate: An Analysis of their Role and Responsibilities*, Institute of Criminology, Victoria University of Wellington, Wellington.

Morris, A. and Maxwell, G. (1995), 'Recidivism Revisited', *Criminology Aotearoa/ New Zealand*, a newsletter of the Institute of Criminology, Victoria University of Wellington, No. 5.

New Zealand Department of Corrections (1997), *Strategic Business Plan 1997-1999*, Department of Corrections, Wellington.

Palk, G., Pollard, G. and Johnson, L. (1998), 'Community Conferencing in Queensland', unpublished paper presented at the Australian and New Zealand Society of Criminology Annual Conference, Gold Coast.

Pratt, J. (1992), *Punishment in a Perfect Society*, Victoria University Press, Wellington.

Pollard, C. (1999), '"If your only Tool is a Hammer, all your Problems will Look like Nails"', unpublished paper presented to the conference on 'Restorative Justice and Civil Society', Canberra.

Sherman, L., Strang, H., Barnes, G., Braithwaite, J., Inkpen, N. and Teh, M. (1998), *Experiments in Restorative Policing: A Progress Report to the National Police Research Unit on the Canberra Reintegrative Shaming Experiment*, Australian National University, Canberra.

Spier, P. (1997), *Conviction and Sentencing of Offenders in New Zealand 1987 to 1996*, Ministry of Justice, Wellington.

Spierenburg, P. (1984), 'The Sociogenesis of Confinement and its Development in Early Modern Europe', in P. Spierenburg (ed.), *The Emergence of Carceral Institutions*, Erasmus University, Rotterdam.

Tauri, J. and Morris, A. (1997), 'Re-forming Justice: The Potential of Maori Processes', *Australian and New Zealand Journal of Criminology*, vol. 30, pp. 149-67.

Tonry, M. (1994), 'Proportionality, Parsimony and Interchangeability', in A. Duff, S. Marshall, R. E. Dobash and R. P. Dobash (eds), *Penal Theory and Practice*, Manchester University Press, Manchester.

Tuhiwai Smith, L. and Cram, F. (1998), An Evaluation of the Community Panel Diversion Pilot Project, Auckland Uniservices Ltd, Auckland.

Umbreit, M., Coates, R. and Warner Roberts, A. (1997), *Impact of Victim-Offender Mediation in Canada, England and the United States*, The Crime Victims Report, Civic Research Institute Inc, Kingston.

Umbreit, M. and Greenwood, J. (1997), *Criteria for Victim-Sensitive Mediation and Dialogue with Offenders*, Center for Restorative Justice and Mediation, St. Paul.

Umbreit, M. and Greenwood, J. (1998), *National Survey of Victim Offender Mediation Programs in the US*, Center for Restorative Justice and Mediation, St. Paul.

Umbreit, M. and Stacey, S. (1996), 'Family Group Conferencing comes to the US: A Comparison with Victim-offender Mediation', *Juvenile and Family Court Journal*, pp. 29-38.

Van Ness, D. (1993), 'New Wine and Old Wineskins: Four Challenges of Restorative Justice', *Criminal Law Forum*, vol. 4, pp. 251-76.

Von Hirsch, A., Bottoms, A. E., Burney, E. and Wikstrom, P. O. (1999), *Criminal Deterrence and Sentencing Severity*, Hart Publishing, Oxford.

Warner, K. (1994), 'The Rights of Young People in Family Group Conferences', in C. Alder and J. Wundersitz (eds), *Family Group Conferencing and Juvenile Justice*, Australian Institute of Criminology, Canberra.

Young, R. (1998), 'Integrating a Multi Victim Perspective into Police Cautioning: Some Data from the Thames Valley', Paper presented at an international conference on 'Integrating a Victim Perspective with Criminal Justice', York.

Young, W. and Brown, M. (1993), 'Cross-National Comparisons of Imprisonment', in Tonry, M. (ed.), *Crime and Justice: an Annual Review of Research*, pp. 1-49.

3 Revisiting the Relationship between Retributive and Restorative Justice

KATHLEEN DALY

In this essay, I raise a complex and contentious question: what is the role of punishment in a restorative justice process? I raise the question to invite discussion and debate in the field, not to assert a clear and unequivocal answer. The term "punishment" evokes strong images and feelings in people; it has no singular meaning. This is especially the case when it is linked to a restorative justice process, that is, an informal legal process that includes lay and legal actors, which is partly, but not entirely state punishment. I have not worked out many technical features of the argument,[1] but I am convinced that those interested in the idea of restorative justice need to grapple with the idea of punishment.[2]

I start with several caveats and definitions. I am working within the terms of what Cohen (1985: 251) calls 'the liberal consensus'. This means that I assume that there is individual autonomy (or personal responsibility) in committing crime and a moral legitimacy of criminal law. These assumptions can be easily challenged by critical legal scholars, who call attention to the injustices of criminal law and justice system practices as they are applied in unequal societies. For pragmatic reasons, however, we need to think about what is possible and workable today, even as a more radical critique reminds us of the limits of liberal law and legal reform.

I shall be using the terms "victim" and "offender" in a straightforward, unproblematic way. But, as Cretney and Davis (1995: 160) remind us, drawing from their analysis of violent crime, 'ideal victims' ('vulnerable, respectable, not contributing to their own victimisation') and 'ideal offenders' ('powerful, bad, stranger to the victim') are 'in short supply'.

Finally, when I discuss "restorative justice" processes, I have in mind a particular application: what are variously termed "family conferences" and "diversionary conferences" as practised in the response to youth crime in Australia and New Zealand.[3] From time to time, I'll draw from my knowledge of observing conferences and interviewing participants.[4]

My argument addresses these points:

1. We should stop comparing "retributive justice" and "restorative justice" in oppositional terms. Such a strong, oppositional contrast cannot be sustained empirically. Moreover, seemingly contrary justice practices - that is, of punishment and reparation - can be accommodated in philosophical arguments.
2. There are some key differences between "restorative justice" and other "traditional" modes of justice.
3. We should embrace (not eliminate) the concept of "punishment" as the main activity of the state's response to crime. Using Duff's (1992) terms, restorative justice processes and sanctions should be seen as 'alternative punishments' rather than 'alternatives to punishment'.
4. Philosophical argument and empirical study suggest a complex meshing of censure, symbolic reparation, and restorative or reparative processes and outcomes for victims, offenders, and their supporters. Empirical work suggests that citizens draw from a large justice vernacular, which includes ideas of punishing offenders, deterring them from future offending, and helping them to reform.
5. Some argue that the role of a criminal justice process should be to censure the offence only (von Hirsch, 1993), whereas others say that more should be elicited from a wrongdoer such as 'acknowledged shame' (Braithwaite, 1989; Retzinger and Scheff, 1996) or a 'repentant understanding' (Duff, 1992) for committing a wrongful act. It is believed that without such expression (or a "sign" of such expression), complete reparation is not possible. An ethical question arises in the practice of restorative justice: should symbolic reparation be coerced or would this be considered contrary to the tenets of a restorative justice process?

Point 1:   The Retributive-Restorative Justice Oppositional Contrast is Wrong

The oppositional contrast between retributive and restorative justice has become a permanent fixture in the field: it is made not only by restorative justice scholars, but increasingly, one finds it canonised in criminology and juvenile justice text books. During the first phase of work in the field (i.e., 1970s to mid 1990s), this contrast may have served a useful purpose, but now that we have moved into a second phase of consolidation and reflection, it stymies us. The retributive-restorative contrast builds on the retributive-rehabilitative contrast, which preceded it (see Zehr, 1990; Bazemore and Umbreit, 1995; Walgrave, 1995) and which is associated with these elements:

Table 3.1: Retributive and Rehabilitative Justice

Retributive	Rehabilitative
focuses on the offence	focuses on the offender
focuses on blame for past behaviour	focuses on changing future behaviour
aim: to punish the offence	aim: to treat the offender

Restorative justice advocates have proposed that restorative justice be viewed as a 'third way' (Bazemore and Walgrave, forthcoming), as representing a break from the elements associated with retributive and rehabilitative justice. In my view, restorative justice is best characterised as a practice that flexibly incorporates "both ways" - that is, it contains elements of retributive and rehabilitative justice - but at the same time, it contains several new elements that give it a unique restorative stamp. Specifically, restorative justice practices do focus on the offence *and* the offender; they are concerned with censuring past behaviour *and* with changing future behaviour; they are concerned with sanctions or outcomes that are proportionate *and* that also "make things right" in individual cases.

Restorative justice practices assume mentally competent and hence morally culpable actors, who are expected to take responsibility for their actions, not only to the parties directly injured, but perhaps also to a wider community.[5] As such, restorative justice practices embrace retributive justice assumptions of individual culpability *and* they also include a wider notion of community (or, at times, familial) responsibility for those acts. Ideas of 'reintegrating' offenders (Braithwaite, 1989) by members of relevant communities of care tap into a stronger vision of rehabilitation, in which broader networks of people associated with a lawbreaker, not just state actors, get involved and have a role. Thus, restorative justice should not be viewed in opposition to retributive or rehabilitative justice. Instead, this recent justice practice[6] borrows and blends many elements from traditional practices of retributive and rehabilitative justice in the past century, and it introduces some new terms.

Point 2:   **There are Key Differences in Traditional and Restorative Justice**

There *are* differences, some more apparent than real, between traditional and restorative justice practices, and these are shown in Table 3.2. In restorative justice, victims are to take a more central role in the process; the emphasis is on repairing the harm between an offender and victim; community members or organisations take a more active role in the justice process, working with state organisations; and the process involves dialogue and negotiation among the major parties with a stake in the dispute. These distinctive features of *what* should occur in a restorative justice process stem from differences in the *scope* and associated *decision-making processes* of traditional and restorative justice, together with their *stated aims*.

Table 3.2: Traditional and Restorative Justice

Traditional Justice (retributive and rehabilitative)	Restorative Justice
victims are peripheral to the process	victims are central to the process
the focus is on punishing *or* on treating an offender	the focus is on repairing the harm between an offender and victim, and perhaps also an offender and a wider community
the community is represented by the state	community members or organisations take a more active role
the process is characterised by adversarial relationships among the parties	the process is characterised by dialogue and negotiation among the parties

For *scope*, traditional justice practices cover a wider array of decision-making possibilities than restorative justice practices have covered, at least to date. Whereas traditional justice practices address the fact-finding and penalty phases for guilty (or admitted) offenders, restorative justice practices generally focus on the penalty phase alone.

These differences in scope bear importantly on the decision-making processes that are associated with each justice form.

In traditional justice practices, fact-finding is determined by an adversarial process in which the state assumes the role of a wronged individual, and the penalty is decided by a judicial authority after hearing arguments by prosecution and defence. In almost all restorative justice practices to date, there is no fact-finding phase; consequently, the need for an adversarial process is diminished. Therefore, one apparent difference between traditional and restorative justice - adversarial versus negotiated justice - is an artefact of their differences in scope. The two differ, however, in how offenders learn of the consequences of their actions and how a penalty is fashioned. Taking the conferencing process as an example, there is a larger, more direct role for a crime victim, who communicates the impact of an offence to a wrongdoer. Lay and legal actors, including the victim and offender (and their supporters), are to decide on a sanction in an informal, consensually-based decision-making process.

With respect to *stated aims*, those of traditional justice (that is, both retributive and rehabilitative) are many and varied, including punishing and reforming lawbreakers; and emerging in the 1960s, providing restitution to victims. By comparison, the stated aim of restorative justice is to repair the harm or the injuries caused by a crime to the person victimised, and perhaps also, to a broader community. If we narrow the comparison to retributive and restorative justice, we find that scholars disagree on the relationship between them (for review, see Daly and Immarigeon, 1998). To simplify, some see a sharp disjuncture in the two justice modes, and others do not. Differences turn on (1) the meanings of repairing the harm and retribution and (2) how the idea of punishment fits into justice practices.

For (1), some suggest that the idea of repairing the harm or the injuries caused by crime is amorphous and vague. It moves imprecisely between criminal and civil liability, it seems to ignore the state's public censuring role in responding to crime, and it overlooks the importance of serious crimes that are attempted but not completed (see Ashworth, 1993: 282-86, in response to van Ness, 1993). For "retribution", some use the term to describe a "justification" for punishment (i.e., intended to be in proportion to the harm caused), whereas others use it to describe a *form* of punishment (i.e., intended to be of a type that is harsh or painful).[7] Key differences are apparent among restorative justice advocates on the place of retributivism and proportionality in the response to crime: whereas some (e.g., Braithwaite and Pettit, 1990) eschew retributivism as a justification for punishment, favouring instead a free-ranging consequentialist justification and highly individualised responses, others wish to limit restorative justice responses to a desert-based, proportionate criteria (Walgrave and Aertsen, 1996; van Ness, 1993).

For (2) and the concept of "punishment", in the past three decades, there has been a blurring of boundaries between civil and criminal liability, as compensation to victims and punishment of offenders have increasingly been used, alone and together, in sentencing (Ashworth, 1986). It is unclear how restorative justice practices will relate to this already modified criminal sanctioning picture, in which compensation to victims is already part of sentencing. Moreover, in light of this modified picture, we may ask, how (if at all) is restorative justice distinctive? Restorative justice advocates would likely say that in a restorative justice framework, reparation to the victim (or to the community) are the *primary* aims, and punishment is minimised. Thus, a key difference in the stated aims of retributive and restorative justice turns on the meaning and purpose of punishment.

Point 3:   Restorative Justice Processes and Outcomes are Alternative Punishments, not Alternatives to Punishment

Restorative justice advocates typically set themselves against the idea of punishment, that what they are doing is punishing an offender. Even the term itself may be unspeakable to some. Why might this be the case? I shall not endeavour to answer the question fully, but I suspect that it is part of a broader development in the history of punishment, in which justice elites have increasingly come to imagine and announce that what they *intend* to do in responding to crime is *not* to punish, but rather to *guide, correct, educate,* or *instruct* offenders. These elites - the normative theorists and practitioners - want to exercise their power in a different, more humane way.[8] Such intentions are fine, but they need to be mindful of the empirical world. Do those who are not justice elites or who are on the receiving end of this new penal imagination see it in the same way? Does their experience matter to the justice elites? More generally and of utmost significance: what *is* and *should be* the place of punishment in restorative justice practices? As an interim step between the familiar world of retributive justice (or traditional justice, more generally) and the ideal world of restorative justice, I propose that punishment remain part of restorative justice (in addition to Garvey, 1999, see Barton, 1999 on this point). My proposal will meet some opposition, and one major point of contention will turn on a key question: what is meant by punishment? Related points of contention are whether *any* sanction imposed in a criminal legal process[9] should, by definition, be considered punitive, and whether one can argue that there are non-punitive criminal sanctions.

Some say that punishment practices are the 'intentional' or 'deliberate imposition of pain' on offenders, by which they would include incarceration and fines, but not rehabilitative or reparative measures. This is the position taken by Wright (1991: 15), who wishes to distinguish the *intentions* of legal authorities: he argues that whereas punishment is an intended deprivation, non-punishment is intended to be constructive. As an empirical matter, I am not convinced by the distinction he makes in that it overlooks decades of critique of the rehabilitative ideal, with its associated treatment-oriented intervention. Wright equates punishment with being punitive and non-punishment with being non-punitive. His argument exemplifies how elites may delude themselves into thinking that what they *intend* to do (that is, *not* to punish) is in fact experienced that way by those at the receiving end.

Cavadino and Dignan (1997: 307) make similar assumptions. They suggest that 'reparative measures [could be seen to be the] normal response to offending, with punitive measures being very much the exception'. Further they say, 'it is possible to envisage a perfectly workable future criminal justice system which made minimal use of imprisonment'. Here we find that reparative sanctions are contrasted with those considered to be punitive, and that punitive measures are equated solely with prison. While prison would surely be experienced as punitive, can we assume that non-custodial sentences are not experienced as punitive or as punishment?

Another way to define punishment practices is anything that is unpleasant, a burden, or an imposition of some sort on an offender. Thus, compensation is a punishment, as is having to attend a counselling program, paying a fine, or having to report to a probation officer on a regular basis (see, more generally, Duff, 1992, 1996; Davis, 1992). This is, in my view, a better way to define punishment. If this more inclusive definition were used, it would be impossible to eliminate the idea of punishment from a restorative response to crime, even when a meaningful nexus is drawn between an offence and the ways that an offender can "make amends" to a victim.[10]

Now, of course, punishment as a social institution is considerably more than the array of sanctions or penalties imposed for crime. Garland (1990: 17) suggests that 'punishment is a legal process ... where violators are condemned and sanctioned in accordance with specified legal categories ... The process is ... complex and differentiated, ... involv[ing] discursive frameworks of authority and condemnation; ritual procedures ...; a repertoire of penal sanctions, institutions, and agencies ...; and a rhetoric of symbols, figures, and images by ... which the penal process is represented to its various audiences'. The variety of sites and practices of punishment lead Garland to conclude that punishment has 'a whole range of possible referents' and 'is likely to exhibit internal conflicts and ambiguities'. Using Garland's definition, we could all agree that restorative justice is one practice in a broader conceptualisation of punishment as a social institution.

But if we shift from Garland's broad conceptualisation of punishment to the more narrow one of a 'repertoire of penal sanctions', we may wonder, why does punishment have negative connotations in people's minds? Perhaps it is associated with humiliating, harming, or degrading people? Surely, we know this is true historically and today. There is no reason to assume, however, that this must be the case, unless one argues that any sanction imposed by a legal authority on a convicted (or admitted) offender is, by definition, harmful or unjust because the criminal justice system is unjust. Restrictions and prohibitions for a range of penalties (including those associated with restorative justice) can be identified that address their potentially 'degrading or intrusive character' (von Hirsch and Narayan, 1993: 80-87).

There are other reasons why punishment has come to have negative connotations. Drawing from British penal history, Duff (1992: 56) suggests one historical strand: the pre-statutory emergence of probation in the 19th century. The 'early police court missions, from which statutory probation then grew, sought to save offenders from imprisonment by offering to supervise' them, offering a 'merciful second chance'. In its pre-statutory form, probation was considered an alternative to punishment, more precisely an alternative to *imprisonment*. Duff suggests that the view of probation as an 'essentially non-punitive measure' was reinforced by 'the growth of the "treatment model" that dominated the probation service's self-conception after 1945'.[11] As such, whereas '"punishment" [was] conceived as bare retribution or deterrence, probation was seen as a mode of non-punitive treatment ... [and thus] ... the coercive elements of probation [e.g., reporting to a probation officer] [were] not seen ... as punishment ...'. (p. 57).

Duff (1992: 71) suggests that reparative justice[12] should be seen as containing *alternative punishments* rather than as *an alternative to punishment*. Here, he is concerned to address the penal abolitionist stance that punishment should be rejected, by proposing instead that we distinguish 'the very concept of punishment itself' from 'certain conceptions of punishment'. Put another way, Duff wants to retain the *concept* of punishment and to see the development of alternative conceptions and modes of punishment. I find Duff's argument persuasive in characterising the *current* meaning and place of punishment in the response to crime, including responses that are termed restorative.

For restorative justice advocates, a key question is this: what is to be gained by saying that restorative justice is an alternative to punishment? In raising this question, I am concerned specifically with the sanction itself (e.g., compensation, community service, apology), not the process of deciding that sanction, which as I suggested in Point 2, can differ from traditional justice practices and in that way could modify the meaning of punishment to an offender and victim. Following the lead of some philosophers (like Duff) and several socio-legal scholars (e.g., Ashworth, 1986, 1993; Campbell, 1984; Davis, 1992; Zedner, 1994), I find it difficult to see how one can distinguish what is punishment and non-punishment in traditional or restorative justice practices, and even more so *from the point of view of those who receive those sanctions.* From the perspective of lawbreakers, the distinction will seem no different from (and just as disingenuous as) that between punishment and treatment. From the point of view of victims, it denies legitimate emotions of anger and resentment toward a lawbreaker and some sign of expiation. And from the point of view of the community, certain harms may appear to be condoned, not censured as wrong, if they are not punished.[13] The weight of philosophical and legal argument and empirical inquiry suggests to me that punishment, broadly defined to include retributive censure, should form part of what occurs in a restorative justice process. I hasten to add that I am not arguing that justice and punishment are the same or that justice is done when punishment is delivered. My point is more subtle and in a subjective sense, more complex than that. It is to say that the ability of victims to be generous and forgiving and for offenders to "make amends" to victims - elements that are desirable objectives in a restorative justice process - can only come about during or after a process when punishment, broadly defined, occurs.

Point 4:   **Philosophical Argument and Empirical Evidence Suggest a Complex Meshing of Censure, Symbolic Reparation, Restorative Processes, and "Just-ness"**

For philosophical argument, I draw from Duff's (1992, 1996) work on punishment as communication and the relationship between punishment and reparative justice. There are a variety of positions on the relationship between punishment and reparative/restorative justice, and I would place Duff on the continuum between a mainly desert-based view of censure (von Hirsch, 1993; Narayan, 1993) and a highly consequentialist view (Braithwaite and Pettit, 1990), although he is closer to a desert-based position.

Duff (1992: 53-54) suggests that ideally punishment should be

- *communicative*, not merely 'expressive' because it should be a two-way communication, not a one-way directive aimed at a passive wrongdoer and
- *retributive* in that it aims to impose on the offender 'the suffering (the pain of condemnation and of recognised guilt; the burden of reparation), which s/he deserves for his/her crime'.[14]

Precisely because punishment is retribution for a past offence, Duff argues that it is

- *forward-looking* in that it aims to 'induce and manifest that process of repentance, reform, and reparation which will restore the offender's moral standing in the community' (Duff, 1992: 54).[15]

For Duff, punishment ideally is 'a penance ... that is, something which a wrongdoer imposes on [themselves], as a painful burden to which [they] subject [themselves] because [they have] done wrong' (p. 52). Duff imagines that an offender would be involved in the determination of their own punishment, in discussion with legal authorities and, where appropriate, a victim. Although he does not have the conferencing model specifically in mind in his 1992 publication,[16] his scenario of 'communicative punishment' is what ideally is supposed to occur in the conference process.

The relationship between censure, as retributive and backward-looking, is connected to its forward-looking capacity in a key passage in Duff (1996). Just before this passage, he signals agreement with Braithwaite (1989) and Braithwaite and Pettit (1990) that censure ought not be exclusionary or stigmatising, and that 'our condemnation or blame must ... be such as to allow and assist the process' of 'enabl[ing] [an offender] to repair [their] relationship with a victim and ... community'. He continues:

That is, "don't you see what you have done" which is the central message of blame should not be our final word, the *end* of our engagement with the wrongdoer; it should, rather, be the *beginning* of a process whose final aspiration is to reconcile [the wrongdoer] with those whom [s/he] has wronged. So too with communicative punishments. ... They aim ... to induce the pain of accepted censure and recognised guilt. But the point of doing this is precisely to work toward the goals of repentance, reparation, reconciliation, and rehabilitation. Such goals are not distinct from "punishment"; rather, they are the proper goals of punishment itself, and goals that ... can be properly achieved only through a punitive, communicative process (Duff, 1996: 82-83; emphasis in original).

What this means is that before it is possible to consider 'repairing the damage caused by crime', the offender must give some "sign" to a group that s/he has wronged another. If that does not happen, then initial movement toward reparation[17] may not be possible. In plain language, we might ask, did an offender "show remorse" (more precisely "genuine remorse")[18] for their wrongdoing?

Empirical studies of conferencing can show how this works in practice. Braithwaite and Mugford (1994) give examples of interactions among participants in conferences they observed in Wagga, Wagga (New South Wales, Australia) and in Auckland (New Zealand) in the early 1990s. The authors agree that wrongdoing should be censured ('denounced') in a conference, and they emphasise that the act, not the actor should be denounced. In depicting the effectiveness of a victim to describe the impact of a crime to an offender, Braithwaite and Mugford (1994: 144) consider an offender who has 'developed a capacity to cut themselves off from the shame [of] exploiting other human beings':

[These offenders] deploy a variety of barriers against feeling responsibility. But what does not affect the offender directly may affect those who have come to support [the offender]. *The shaft of shame fired by the victim* in the direction of the offender might go right over the offender's head, yet *it might pierce like a spear through the heart of the offender's mother.* ... So while the display of the victim's suffering may fail to hit its intended mark, the anguish of the offender's mother ... may succeed in bringing home to the offender the need to confront rather than deny an act of irresponsibility (emphasis added).

There is such dramatic emotional imagery here, with 'shafts of shame' and 'spears' flying about in the conference process! These emotional elements can be present in conferences, although not uniformly in such a heightened dramatic form. Such imagery gives us an idea of what should happen in a conference: offenders should feel a vicarious sense of punishment via seeing the anguish of their mothers receiving a 'shame of shame'. I think it unfortunate that conferences are termed reintegration ceremonies because the term does not reflect the fact they contain both a 'shaming phase' (as illustrated above) and a 'reintegration phase' (Braithwaite and Mugford, 1994: 146). The latter depends on the former, and indeed, is meaningless without it.

While censure and denunciation are terms used by both Duff and Braithwaite, they use different words to describe the *result* of that action: for Duff, it is the 'pain of accepted censure' and for Braithwaite, a 'shaft of shame' or 'acknowledged shame'.   Whereas Duff wishes to separate shame and guilt, Braithwaite focuses on shame alone, perhaps assuming that it is an emotion state that incorporates guilt.[19]   Retzinger and Scheff's research on the role of shame in conferences brings out more of the emotional elements involved.

Retzinger and Scheff (1996: 316-17) suggest that while material reparation (e.g., compensation or community service) may result from a conference, 'symbolic reparation' is the 'more ambiguous' though 'vital element' that needs to occur if the conference is to be successful at all.[20]   Two steps in the 'core sequence' are required, they say, to achieve symbolic reparation.   In the first, the offender 'clearly expresses genuine shame and remorse over his or her actions'.   And next, 'in response, the victim takes at least a first step towards forgiving the offender for the trespass'.   The authors suggest that this core sequence generates repair and restoration of the bond between victim and offender; it may be quite brief, 'perhaps only a few seconds', but they propose, it is 'the key to reconciliation, victim satisfaction, a decreasing recidivism' (p. 316).[21]   The core sequence also affects the ability to reach an amicable settlement.   Without it, they suggest that 'the path toward settlement is strewn with impediments'.   Indeed, they found that for a total of nine conferences they had observed, the core sequence did not occur in any of them during the formal part of the conference, although it did in three cases, after the formal end of the conference.

Therefore, Retzinger and Scheff propose that if an offender can 'shar[e] and communicat[e] shame, instead of hiding or denying it', then it may be possible to repair the damage to 'the bond' between an offender and victim (and perhaps others, as well).   Retzinger and Scheff's 'shame' is similar to Duff's concept of an offender's coming to have a 'repentant understanding of what s/he did' and making 'some apologetic expression of remorse for the harm caused to the victims' (Duff, 1992: 49).   The authors do not assume that shame or repentant understanding will in fact occur in mediated victim-offender encounters.   However, and this point is key to the legal philosopher of punishment and the social-psychologists of emotions: it is crucial that an offender show signs of remorse or shame when admitting responsibility for a crime, and that this is a prerequisite for any subsequent reparatively (or restoratively) oriented communications between a victim and offender (and no doubt other participants such as the supporters of victims and offenders).[22]

For some time, I have pointed out that however much restorative justice advocates may wish to draw a strong contrast between retributive and restorative justice, this contrast is not borne out empirically in restorative justice practices (Daly and Immarigeon, 1998). Having observed many conferences, I find that elements of censure, paying back the victim, and helping the offender can all feature in a conference discussion. Retributive, restorative, and rehabilitative principles and terms are intermingled, or they may shift in emphasis, depending on the conference phase. When I noted this empirical finding at a session at the 1998 American Society of Criminology meetings, Lode Walgrave responded with, 'Yes, this is a problem'. But, I wonder, what is the problem? Is there something wrong with the idea of censure or retribution? Or is it that both retributive and restorative ideas are brought into one discussion? As Duff, Retzinger, and Scheff point out, censuring activity and subsequent (or simultaneous) signs of remorse may be a precondition for any movement between victims and offenders. In short, one cannot begin a restorative justice process by announcing "let's reconcile", "let's negotiate", or "let's reintegrate".

I would like to put the case more strongly. At present, most people have a limited range of ideas about the response to crime; among them are punishing wrongdoers, stopping them from doing it again, keeping them away from the community, teaching them a lesson, and helping them to help themselves. These are commonsense understandings of a just response to crime (or to individual offenders), and restorative justice scholars would be wise to *work with* them (or perhaps to *re-work* them) in building interest in the idea. Any putatively new justice idea - however radical - will contain residual bits of the old. For many critics, restorative justice already sounds like a repackaging of rehabilitation in that it seems to give wrongdoers a second chance or appears to be a soft option. When we talk about a just or an appropriate response to crime (whether toward one person or in the aggregate), we are not talking about a singular thing. As a political and policy matter, it may be mistaken to excise the idea of punishment from a restorative justice process. It may not be strategic politically nor comprehensible culturally. People's ideas and feelings about punishment cannot be censored or willed away even if restorative justice advocates may wish otherwise.

One feature of conferences is that they permit *time* to discuss things that matter to people: time for anger and forgiveness, and time for several justice principles - not just one - to be expressed. As reported by Strang et al. (1999: 62-65) from the RISE project, punishment is aired as a principle in deciding outcomes in youth justice conference cases *as often or more often than in court cases* (see also Sherman et al., 1998: 87-99). Although principles of repaying the victim and community were expressed more often in conferences than in court, the most frequently aired principle in both settings was preventing future offences, not restoration or punishment.   What explains these findings?   In part, they suggest that conference participants want to talk about multiple justice principles, not just one, and in part, there is time to do so.

Compared to courtroom interactions, there is greater potential for an offender at a conference to explain what happened, for an offender's parent or supporter to say how the offence affected them, and for a victim to speak directly to an offender about the impact of the offence and any lingering fears.   Some critics may be concerned that this wide latitude of discussion is too open-ended, and they would want to curtail it.   For example, they would argue that a legal authority should not be permitted to coerce an offender into accepting an outcome, and participants should not engage in "stigmatising shaming" that puts down any person.   Such problems are easily addressed.   But what if it is an offender's *parent* who puts down their child?   And what if, in witnessing this, the victim begins to feel more sympathetic to the young person's situation?   These interactions occur in conferences, not infrequently, and they set up the possibility for alliances to form between victims (or their supporters) and young people.

The restorative justice *process*, involving as it does mediation, direct exchanges between victims, offenders, and their supporters, permits the potential for honesty and humanity to emerge in ways foreclosed in a courtroom process (or one dominated by formal legality).   It is the *process*, not the sanctions *per se* that most distinguishes informal (and restorative justice) from formal (and retributive or rehabilitative) justice. It is *within this process* where the meaning and purpose of a restorative sanction can be forged, agreed upon, and taken on by an offender for a victim (or, where relevant, others).   It is the understanding between an offender and victim (and often others present) of *how* a sanction connects meaningfully with a harm that can make a process and outcome in part "restorative", at least ideally.[23]

Point 5:   Ethical Problems in the Practice of Restorative Justice

Duff terms his 'communicative account of punishment' an 'ambitious' one, which is a good way to distinguish it from that of von Hirsch (1993). (For an exchange of views, see von Hirsch, 1993, Ch. 8; Duff, 1996: 53-67).[24]   While working with a desert-based notion of censure, von Hirsch wants to limit the 'censure conveyed through punishment ... [to the] person externally' (von Hirsch, 1993: 72), and not attempt to 'elicit certain internal states' from the actor, 'whether those be shame, repentance or whatever'.   Should these behaviours occur spontaneously, that is all right in von Hirsch's view; his concern is that state censure should not attempt to elicit them. Rather, state censure should adopt the role of 'judges' not 'abbots'.

Although it may be appropriate for a monk's superior to impose a penance and not simply to censure a monk's wrongdoing, von Hirsch asks, 'why should the state be entitled to use its coercive powers to seek to induce moral sentiments of repentance?' Not surprisingly, von Hirsch is also concerned with the effect that 'personalised penances' would have on proportionality; ultimately, though, his concern is that 'it should not be the business of the state to try to engineer [an appropriate moral response]' (von Hirsch, 1993: 77).

Several points can be offered. In defence of von Hirsch's position, we should be concerned that conference participants will look for signs or clues that an offender is genuinely remorseful for their actions. If the desired signs are not seen, then for how long will conference participants continue to try to elicit them? Or if the desired signs are not seen, does the sanction become more severe? Of greater concern is a misreading of the signs themselves. Some offenders may show external states of "hardness", but are deeply distressed internally.[25] Others may withdraw from the conference process because it is a "shame job" that they, as a minority group person, cannot accept.

Upon reflection, we can see that signs of an offender's guilt and remorse have been a longstanding element in the ways in which legal officials and lay actors respond to wrongdoing. When police officers say an adolescent has an "attitude problem", they are referring, in part, to an "unrepentant" attitude. When judges discuss the role of a defendant's demeanour in court, they are referring, in part, to the degree of "respect for the law" that the defendant appears to display. A good deal of a formal-legal reaction to crime is bound up, then, in eliciting internal states of remorse.[26]

If we apply von Hirsch's critique to the conference context, there are other things to consider. Because the sanction in a conference is decided by (ideally) the victim, offender, and their supporters, there is no clear judicial role as such. Apart from a conference coordinator and police officer, the conference participants are not members of particular legal or religious communities. They have other kinds of affiliations with offenders and victims, most frequently via familial, marital, household, friendship, or community ties. These personal relationships may convey a moralising influence that is closer to the role of an abbot than a judge; but the better relational metaphor may be parent or teacher or respected community authority.

Whereas for von Hirsch the idea of eliciting particular emotional states (like remorse or contrition) should not be the aim of a sanctioning process, for others, this is the raison d'être of reparative or restorative justice. Davis (1992: 205) encapsulates the idea well when he says that the harm from crime is 'not just material [but involves] damage to a social and moral relationship'. Thus, if reparation 'is to be complete, [it] must make some attempt to make amends for the victim's loss of the presumption of security ... [for example] by some effort to reassure the victim that his or her rights are now respected'. Davis suggests that while it is straightforward to see the retributive (desert-based) logic to material reparation, 'one component in reparation cannot be coerced' by a court order, and that is the victim's 'trust that the appropriate moral standards are shared by the offender'. For a victim to be reassured, 's/he must believe that the attitude in question is *freely expressed* ... [which] can only be achieved by the victim and offender themselves' (Davis, 1992: 205, emphasis added). Again we see that commentators are concerned that offenders come to recognise the moral wrong of crime, not just its material harm.

Here then is problem of process, which is also an ethical problem, for restorative justice. Commentators suggest that for a restorative/reparative process to work effectively, there needs to be a genuine admission of responsibility, remorse, or guilt for a wrong. Unless that symbolic reparation occurs, the rest will not follow easily, and as Retzinger and Scheff suggest, there will be many impediments to settlement. To date, restorative justice processes have been used mainly in cases where an offender admits or has "not denied" the offence to a police officer (and at times, to a magistrate). But that does not tell us what an offender (and their supporters) may say in a conference when they meet "their" victim and others associated with an offence. An interrelated set of ethical questions arises. Should an apology (or other reparative-like gesture or movement) be coerced, if only gently from an offender? What if a victim cannot "hear" or "see" an offender's remorse and offer of apology, but other participants can? What should be the role of laypersons and legal officials in coaxing or persuading the symbolic reparation elements of the restorative justice process?

The symbolic reparation sequence is at the heart of a restorative justice process. It may be induced by (or occur simultaneously with) retributive-based censure or denunciation of the act. Signs of remorse, contrition, or shame may be difficult to read, and that may pose a problem for the ethical practice of restorative justice. Although it may seem paradoxical to some restorative justice advocates, the conclusion I draw is that punishment, defined broadly to include retributive censure, should not be excised from a restorative justice process. Rather, punishment can be seen to make restorative justice possible.

Notes

1   I am grateful to John Braithwaite, Antony Duff, and Lode Walgrave for their comments on an early version of this paper in February 1999. They raised many key questions about the meaning of punishment and its relationship to restorative justice, which I only partly address here.

2   In revising the paper since the February 1999 conference, I have become aware of a similar argument made by Stephen Garvey (1999). He too proposes that punishment (as "penance" and as "atonement") is required for restorativism, and I shall note the similarities in our positions, together with clarifications he offers. While his argument draws from a wider reading of the legal and philosophical literature than mine does, I draw selectively from this literature and from empirical research.

3   I have observed over 50 such conferences since coming to Australia in 1995; and as part of my research project on conferencing in South Australia, members of my research team and I have observed 89 youth justice conferences and interviewed over 170 young people and victims associated with those conferences, both in 1998 and in 1999. See Daly et al. (1998) for the project design and rationale.

4   There is great variety in conference practices and their organisational placement in Australia and New Zealand. In Australia, conferencing is now routinely used in statutory-based schemes in four jurisdictions (South Australia, Western Australia, Queensland, and New South Wales). Statutory-based schemes were legislated in Tasmania in 1997 (although not resourced and thus not implemented as of 1999), and in the Northern Territory in 1999 (although used only in selected cases). Australian conferencing began in the early 1990s with non-statutory schemes trialed by police departments and with police officers running the conferences; today there are two jurisdictions (the ACT and Victoria) without a statutory basis for conferencing. ACT conferencing is police-facilitated and based in police departments; Victorian conferencing is used only as a pre-sentencing option and for a relatively small number of cases. Throughout Australia, conferencing is used mainly for admitted offenders in youth justice cases (it is also legislatively established and used in care and protection matters in South Australia). In New Zealand, conferencing is legislatively established for the entire country, and it is used in both juvenile cases and care and protection matters. In the ACT, conferences were used in handling adult drink driving cases from 1995-97, and conferences continue to be used, in selected instances, in disposing adults.

   While there is jurisdictional variation in the expected composition of conference participants and their conference roles, the general idea is that an offender, their supporters, the victim, and their supporters meet to discuss the offence and its impact; they jointly discuss the sanction, with at least one legal actor (a police officer) present. In most jurisdictions, conferences are a diversion from a juvenile court disposition (and potential court conviction), although they are also used as a pre-sentencing option in New South Wales, Queensland, and Victoria. Conferences normally last from one to two hours. For overviews of jurisdictional variation, see Bargen (1996, 2000), Daly (2000), Daly and Kitcher (1999), and Hudson et al. (1996). In Australia, restorative justice practices, using the conference model, have also been applied to disputes in schools and workplace organisations.

5   I use the term "community" here and elsewhere with great reservation; it is deployed by so many to mean so many things (Crawford, 1997; Lacey, 1996; Pavlich, 1999); it is more likely to be discursively present when it is empirically absent (Lacey and Zedner, 1995).

6   Some advocates like to chronicle a 2000-year history of restorative justice, but such presentist and ethnocentric histories gloss over an extraordinarily diverse and complex story of justice practices around the world; and worse, such histories wrongly attempt to authenticate a modern western justice practice by citing its origins in pre-modern indigenous societies (for elaboration, see Blagg, 1997). I use the term to refer to a modern, post World War II conception of justice, largely emerging in first-world industrialised societies, but also having resonance for nation-building in some countries (such as South Africa).

7   Drawing from Cottingham's (1979) summary of the many meanings of retribution, it is likely that restorative justice advocates use retributivism to mean "repayment" (to which they add a punitive kick) whereas desert theorists, such as von Hirsch, use retributivism to mean "deserved" and would argue for decoupling retribution from punitiveness.

8   One can see this development as part of the "civilising" process of modern penal practices, which included new ways for elites to talk about punishment (see Pratt, 1998).

9   This may include sanctions that are not fashioned or imposed solely by a state authority, as is the case for conferencing in the Antipodes and circle sentencing in Canada.

10   Garvey (1999) argues this point in a different and more convincing way than I do. Drawing on Hampton's (1992) distinction of crime as both a 'material harm' and a 'moral wrong', Garvey proposes that the harm (or material loss) may be addressed through reparative measures, but that the wrong ('the morally false message ... of disrespect' to a victim) is addressed by punishment (p. 1821). He suggests that restorative justice 'promise[s] ... atonement without punishment, ... but can't really deliver on that promise' (p. 1830). 'Restorativism - gentle and inspiring as it may be - is ultimately self-defeating.   [It] cannot achieve the victim's restoration if it refuses to vindicate the victim's worth through punishment ... nor can it restore the offender, who can only atone for his wrong if he willingly submits to punishment' (p. 1844).

11   One would want to add to this history the emergence of the juvenile court in the late 19th and early 20th centuries, with its emphasis on helping and reforming youthful lawbreakers. This institutional innovation played importantly into punishment ideologies, which were subsequently applied to adult offenders.

12   Duff and other British commentators tend to use the term reparative justice whereas USA and Australian commentators more often use restorative justice.

13   Thus, by retaining the concept of punishment and by not equating restorative justice with a non-punitive response, there may in fact be no dilemma in applying a restorative justice response to cases of rape and racial harassment (see Hudson, 1998).

14   I interpret Duff to define punishment as censure for wrongdoing, which may also include an added sanction (e.g., community service), but need not.

15   Garvey (1999: 1806) terms his (and Duff's) understanding of punishment as a 'fused' theory, neither purely teleological nor purely deontological, but containing elements of both.

16 When he wrote the article, conferencing had just begun in New Zealand, and it was only being used in one town in New South Wales (Wagga Wagga).

17 I am less inclined to assume that victim-offender reconciliation is possible or desirable unless the offender is doing most of the emotional work. A good deal depends on the precise content and context of an offence, including victim-offender relations. Garvey (1999: 1804) suggests that 'reconciliation lies not with the wrongdoer, ... [but] instead with the victim, since reconciliation requires the victim's forgiveness'. Such forgiveness is dependent, however, on the offender's having completed the four steps 'leading to expiation ... repentance, apology, reparation, and penance' (pp. 1804-5).

18 The remorse versus genuine remorse distinction is made by laypersons and legal authorities alike to refer, respectively, to offenders who *were sorry that they were caught* and those who *really were sorry for what they did*.

19 They emphasise different things in the censuring process. Duff seems to be saying that after (or simultaneously with) censuring an act, the offender expresses the 'pain of accepted censure'. Braithwaite seems to assume that shame will occur after the offender's act is denounced, and he gives more attention to modes of reintegration. Whereas Duff highlights the censuring of an act and the associated 'pain' (but is less precise about what happens next), Braithwaite passes over censure, but highlights 'shame' and 'reintegration'. As we shall see in the discussion of Retzinger and Scheff (1996), their emphasis is closer to Braithwaite's in that they pass over censure and move directly to the 'core sequence'.

20 Retzinger and Scheff's identification of 'material' and 'symbolic reparation' is analogous to Garvey's identification of the methods of addressing the 'harm' and 'wrong' of crime (see note 10), although Garvey would argue that victim movement toward forgiveness can only be expected to occur after the offender has completed the steps toward expiation, among them secular penance (or punishment).

21 This is a major claim, which they do not support with empirical evidence. Recent work by Maxwell (1999: 200) suggests that the following conference-based measures were 'significant predictors of persistent reconviction' for young people in New Zealand: 'not agreeing with the conference outcome; not remembering the conference, not completing tasks, not feeling sorry and showing it, and not feeling they had repaired the damage; and shame [which was defined as] being made to feel a bad person'. Thus, there appears to be a variety of indicators of 'persistent reconviction' of which stigmatising shame and unacknowledged shame are a part (Braithwaite, 1989).

22 There are, of course, many ways to achieve movement between a victim and offender; many sequences are possible, not one. Moreover, a conference process may engage the potential for movement, which may only come after an offender completes an undertaking (such as community service). Thus, a restorative justice process (or outcome) is not limited to what occurs in a conference alone, but could take some time.

23 If later in time, an offender fails to fulfil the agreed upon outcome, then for the victim, there is little or no restorative justice.

24 I cannot do justice to the many important points raised in Duff (1996). Among the most relevant to the comparison of his ambitious account and von Hirsch's

more restricted one is whether one has a communitarian or liberal theory of society (p. 88).

25   This may be a good example of what Retzinger and Scheff (1996: 318) refer to as 'being ashamed of being ashamed'. Emotions are kept in check and offenders appear 'not to be sorry', but after they leave the conference, they 'uncheck' the emotions.

26   Whether legal authorities *should be* eliciting such internal states is, of course, another matter. It would be difficult to imagine enforcing prescriptions against the behaviour, although it is possible to announce what is legal and illegal in questioning witnesses, suspects, defendants, or those under state supervision or custody.

References

Ashworth, A. (1986), 'Punishment and Compensation: Victims, Offenders and the State', *Oxford Journal of Legal Studies*, vol. 6, pp. 86-122.

Ashworth, A. (1993), 'Some Doubts about Restorative Justice', *Criminal Law Forum*, vol. 4, pp. 277-99.

Bargen, J. (1996), 'Kids, Cops, Courts, Conferencing and Children's Rights: A Note on Perspectives', *Australian Journal of Human Rights*, vol. 2, pp. 209-28.

Bargen, J. (2000), 'Kids, Cops, Courts, Conferencing and Children's Rights: A Note on Perspectives and Update for 1996-98', in W. Jones and L. Marks (eds), *Children on the Agenda: The Rights of Australia's Children*, Prospect Press, Sydney (in press).

Barton, C. (1999), *Getting Even: Revenge as a Form of Justice*, Open Court Publishing Company, Chicago.

Bazemore, G. and Umbreit, M. (1995), 'Rethinking the Sanctioning Function in Juvenile Court: Retributive or Restorative Responses to Youth Crime', *Crime and Delinquency*, vol. 41, pp. 296-316.

Braithwaite, J. (1989), *Crime, Shame and Reintegration*, Cambridge University Press, Cambridge.

Braithwaite, J. and Mugford, S. (1994), 'Conditions of Successful Reintegration Ceremonies', *British Journal of Criminology*, vol. 4, pp. 139-71.

Braithwaite, J. and Pettit, P. (1990), *Not Just Deserts: A Republican Theory of Justice*, Oxford University Press, New York.

Campbell, T. (1984), 'Compensation as Punishment', *University of New South Wales Law Journal*, vol. 7, pp. 338-61.

Cavadino, M. and Dignan, J. (1997), *The Penal System, An Introduction*, second edition, Sage, London.

Cohen, S. (1985), *Visions of Social Control: Crime, Punishment and Classification*, Cambridge University Press, Cambridge.

Cottingham, J. (1979), 'Varieties of Retribution', *Philosophical Quarterly*, vol. 29, pp. 238-46.

Crawford, A. (1997), *The Local Governance of Crime: Appeals to Community and Partnerships*, Clarendon Press, Oxford.

Cretney, A. and Davis, G. (1995), *Punishing Violence*, Routledge, London.

Daly, K. (2000), 'Restorative Justice in Diverse and Unequal Societies', *Law in Context*, (in press).

Daly, K. and Immarigeon, R. (1998), 'The Past, Present, and Future of Restorative Justice: Some Critical Reflections', *Contemporary Justice Review*, vol. 1, pp. 21-45.

Daly, K. and Kitcher, J. (1999), 'The (R)evolution of Restorative Justice through Researcher-Practitioner Partnerships', *Ethics and Justice*, vol. 2, online at www.ethics-justice.org/v2n1.

Daly, K., Venables, M., McKenna, M., Mumford L. and Christie-Johnston J. (1998) *South Australia Juvenile Justice (SAJJ) Research on Conferencing, Technical Report No. 1: Project Overview and Research Instruments*, School of Criminology and Criminal Justice, Griffith University, Brisbane, Queensland, online at www.aic.gov.au/rjustice.

Davis, G. (1992), *Making Amends: Mediation and Reparation in Criminal Justice*, Routledge, London.

Duff, R. A. (1992), 'Alternatives to Punishment - or Alternative Punishments?', in W. Cragg, (ed.), *Retributivism and Its Critics*, Franz Steiner, Stuttgart, pp. 44-68.

Duff, R. A. (1996), 'Penal Communications: Recent Work in the Philosophy of Punishment', in M. Tonry (ed.), *Crime and Justice: A Review of Research*, University of Chicago Press, Chicago, pp. 1-97.

Garland, D. (1990), *Punishment and Modern Society*, University of Chicago Press, Chicago.

Garvey, S. (1999), 'Punishment as Atonement', *UCLA Law Review*, vol. 46, pp. 1801-58.

Hampton, J. (1992), 'Correcting Harms versus Righting Wrongs: The Goal of Retribution', *UCLA Law Review*, vol. 39, pp. 1659-1702.

Hudson, B. (1998), 'Restorative Justice: The Challenge of Sexual and Racial Violence', *Journal of Law and Society*, vol. 25, pp. 237-56.

Hudson, J., Morris, A., Maxwell, G. and Galaway, B. (eds) (1996), *Family Group Conferences: Perspectives on Policy and Practice*, Criminal Justice Press, Monsey, New York.

Lacey, N. (1996), 'Community in Legal Theory: Idea, Ideal or Ideology?', *Studies in Law, Politics and Society*, vol. 15, JAI Press, Westport, Connecticut, pp. 105-46.

Lacey, N. and Zedner, L. (1995), 'Discourses of Community in Criminal Justice', *Journal of Law and Society*, vol. 23, pp. 301-25.

Maxwell, G. (1999), 'Researching Re-Offending', in A. Morris, and G. Maxwell (eds), *Youth Justice in Focus: Proceedings of an Australasian Conference held 27-30 October 1998 at the Michael Fowler Centre, Wellington*, Institute of Criminology, Victoria University of Wellington, Wellington.

Narayan, U. (1993), 'Appropriate Responses and Preventative Benefits: Justifying Censure and Hard Treatment in Legal Punishment', *Oxford Journal of Legal Studies*, vol. 13, pp. 166-82.

Pavlich, G. (1999), 'The Force of Community', Paper presented to Restorative Justice and Civil Society conference, Australian National University, February.

Pratt, J. (1998), 'Towards the "Decivilizing" of Punishment?', *Social and Legal Studies*, vol. 7, pp. 487-515.

Retzinger, S. and Scheff, T. (1996), 'Strategy for Community Conferences: Emotions and Social Bonds', in B. Galaway and J. Hudson (eds), *Restorative Justice: International Perspectives*, Criminal Justice Press, Monsey, New York, pp. 315-36.

Sherman, L. W., Strang, H., Barnes, G. C., Braithwaite, J., Inkpen N. and Teh, M-M. (1998), *Experiments in Restorative Policing: A Progress Report to the National Police Research Unit on the Canberra Reintegrative Shaming Experiments (RISE)*, Australian National University, Canberra, online at http://www.aic.gov.au.

Strang, H., Barnes, G. C., Braithwaite, J. and Sherman L. (1999), *Experiments in Restorative Policing: A Progress Report to the National Police Research Unit on the Canberra Reintegrative Shaming Experiments (RISE)*, Australian National University, Canberra, online at http://www.aic.gov.au.

Van Ness, D. (1993), 'New Wine and Old Wineskins: Four Challenges of Restorative Justice' and 'A Reply to Andrew Ashworth', *Criminal Law Forum*, vol. 4, pp. 251-76, 301-6.

Von Hirsch, A. (1993), *Censure and Sanctions*, Oxford University Press, New York.

Von Hirsch, A. and Narayan, U. (1993), 'Degradingness and Intrusiveness', in A. von Hirsch (1993), *Censure and Sanctions*, Oxford University Press, New York, Ch. 9, pp. 80-87.

Walgrave, L. (1995), 'Restorative Justice for Juveniles: Just a Technique or a Fully Fledged Alternative?', *The Howard Journal*, vol. 34, pp. 228-49.

Walgrave, L. and Aertsen, I. (1996), 'Reintegrative Shaming and Restorative Justice: Interchangeable, Complementary or Different?', *European Journal on Criminal Policy and Research*, vol. 4, pp. 67-85.

Wright, M. (1991), *Justice for Victims and Offenders*, Open University Press, Philadelphia.

Zedner, L. (1994), 'Reparation and Retribution: Are they Reconcilable?', *Modern Law Review*, vol. 57, pp. 228-50.

Zehr, H. (1990), *Changes Lenses*, Herald Press, Scottdale, Pennsylvania.

4 Empowerment and Retribution in Criminal Justice

CHARLES BARTON

Restorative justice critiques of the status quo in criminal justice often miss their mark because of the mistaken belief that current practice in criminal justice is essentially, or predominantly, retributive. What is being overlooked is that restorative justice responses often contain retributive and punitive elements themselves – and sometimes, such as in serious cases, necessarily so. Therefore, blaming retribution, or even punitiveness, for the ills of the criminal justice system is largely beside the point. Punishment and retribution cannot be ruled out by any system of justice. By implication, a more plausible critique of the status quo is needed.

That critique, I argue, is that the status quo in criminal justice silences, marginalises, and disempowers the primary stakeholders in the criminal justice dispute. These are the victim, the offender, and their primary circles/communities of influence and care – typically, their respective families, friends, peers, and colleagues. Their disempowerment is the single most significant reason why the criminal justice system so often fails to achieve justice for those on the receiving end of the criminal justice response, including victims and the general community, who continue to suffer the consequences of the system's inability to prevent reoffending and crime.

It is my contention that the chief weakness of the status quo is the greatest strength of restorative justice interventions. Contrary to the implied suggestion in many restorative justice critiques, the strength of restorative justice responses does not lie in their rejection of punitiveness and retribution, but in the empowerment of communities who are the best placed to address *both* the causes *and* the consequences of the unacceptable behaviour in question.

The arguments of this paper proceed as follows. I start by identifying the basic elements of the received view in the restorative justice movement, as to what is wrong with the status quo in criminal justice. This is followed by a disambiguation and critique of the claim that the problem with the criminal justice system is that it is retributive. I show that this view, as well as the view that restorative and retributive justice are incompatible, are both mistaken. To provide restorative justice critiques of the status quo with more bite, next I propose a shifting of the focus from punitiveness and retribution to critical questions of *empowerment and disempowerment*. Finally, I show how such a shift in focus allows healthy critiques of restorative justice interventions themselves in the development and evolution of best practice in this relatively new area.

The Received View, and Why it is Inadequate

Restorative justice critiques of the status quo in criminal justice are characterised by two main beliefs. The first is that the criminal justice system is a failure because traditional, court-based responses to crime are retributive, in that the system is only interested in retaliation and punishment, or at best, in retributive justice. The other main element of the received view is that punishment, retribution, and retributive justice are incompatible with restoration and restorative justice.[1]   It is my contention that restorative justice critiques of the status quo are unsustainable on both these points. I shall take them in turn.

To be sure, I do not wish to take issue with the claim that the status quo is not particularly interested in restorative justice. What I do question, rather, is the claim that the problem with the criminal justice system is that it is retributive. This, I believe, is an inaccurate diagnosis, but showing it to be so requires a disambiguation of the claim, which can be interpreted, and is often meant, in at least two ways. These interpretations are derived from the two senses in which the term "retribution" and its derivative "retributive" are being used in the literature. These terms have a standard, proper sense and a corrupted, queer sense.

In their proper sense, as indicated in dictionary definitions, these terms refer to the idea that punishment is imposed on a wrongdoer as a matter of just deserts, that they are being punished because they deserve to be punished for their wrongful behaviour. This means that the "just deserts" conception of retribution is defined by reference to a specific type of reason or rationale that is behind the imposition of the punishment, namely the offender's ill-desert, and which is satisfied, in a manner of speaking, through some sort of negative repayment, or pay-back, which is punishment.

By contrast, in their queer and corrupted sense, "retribution" and "retributive" are being used to mean nothing more than "punishment" and "punitive", respectively. This is a corrupted sense for several reasons. First, it ignores the etymology of the word "retribution", which is the Latin *"retribuo"* = "I pay you back".

Second, it flies in the face of current dictionary definitions, which are all in terms of the "just deserts" conception already explained. Third, it ignores the vast body of literature on retribution and punishment, which makes a meaningful and important distinction between those two concepts.

The problem with this indiscriminate use of the "retributive" label is that it creates conceptual muddle and linguistic imprecision in an already difficult area. This alone is reason enough to respect and follow established convention – a brief explanation of which may help those unfamiliar with it appreciate the point. In the area of punishment justification, *punishment* is a much wider notion than *retribution*, as punishment includes not only desert-based punishment, (which is the only one properly called retribution), but also punishment imposed on people with instrumental (utilitarian and consequentialist) reasons in mind, such as, for instance, deterrence, correction, and the rehabilitation of the offender. In the proper sense of the word, such punishment is not retributive, but instrumental, as it is not imposed with the offender's negative moral deserts in mind, but the desirable consequences the punishment is believed, or hoped, to have.

The difference between the two types of reasons for punishment is thought to be significant. That difference, in fact, forms the basis of the longstanding debate over the moral acceptability of retributivist *versus* consequentialist justifications of punishment.[2] Therefore, from the point of view of the many scholars already working in this area, it is misleading to characterise just any kind, or form, of punishment as "retribution" or "retributive", regardless of the reasons that underlie its imposition. "Punishment" and "punitive" are not synonymous, respectively, with "retribution" and "retributive", and the distinction between retributive and instrumental punishment should not be blurred in critiques of the criminal justice system, faulting the status quo for being retributive.

I turn now to evaluate that diagnosis under the two interpretations made possible by the distinction I have just drawn between retribution and punishment. Under the "just deserts" interpretation, (a) the problem with the criminal justice system is alleged to be that it is only interested in giving wrongdoers their just deserts. Under the punishment interpretation, (b) the problem with the criminal justice system is claimed to be that it is punitive, and punishment, it is alleged, doesn't work. I examine these claims in turn.

(a)   The Problem with the Status Quo is that it is Only Interested in Giving Wrongdoers their Just Deserts

There are two major difficulties with this claim. First, even a cursory glance will reveal that the language of criminal legislation is largely instrumental, rather than retributive. Laws are predominantly couched in utilitarian, consequentialist language where deterrence, public safety, the protection of people's rights, and the correction of offenders are the primary reasons and justifications for punishment. The second problem for the above claim is closely related to the first. Sentencing judges rarely justify their sentences with reference to the idea that offenders need to be given their just deserts. Their foremost considerations are the public interest in safety and deterrence, rehabilitation and correction of offenders, the integrity of the criminal justice system in terms of consistency with established precedents, and the general principle that, insofar as it is possible, like cases should be treated alike. Retribution in the "just deserts" sense rarely rates mention as a consideration by sentencing judges, and even when it does, it is hardly the dominant reason for the imposition of the penalty in question.

Perhaps the most telling example of instrumental reasoning being dominant in our courts is provided by *The Queen v Clotworthy 1998*. This is a fascinating case in which the New Zealand Court of Appeal sent an offender to gaol against the wishes of the primary victim. After discussing the matter with the offender in a restorative justice meeting, the victim considered imprisonment a wasteful and inappropriate way to resolve the matter. Instead, the offender undertook to pay the victim's medical bills by remaining employed. With some modifications, the District Court approved the agreement and the matter was settled to everyone's satisfaction, except the Crown's, who subsequently succeeded in overturning the agreement in the Court of Appeal.[3] The following excerpt contains the main elements of the Justices' reasoning in their decision.

> We record that Mr Cowan [the victim] was present at the hearing. We gave him the opportunity to address us. He reiterated his previous stance, emphasising his wish to obtain funds for the necessary cosmetic surgery and his view that imprisonment would achieve nothing either for Mr Clotworthy or for himself. We can understand Mr Cowan's stance. He is to be commended for having forgiven Mr Clotworthy and for the sympathetic way he has approached the matter. It must be said, however, that a wider dimension must come into the sentencing exercise than simply the position as between victim and offender. The public interest in consistency, integrity

of the criminal justice system and deterrence of others are factors of major importance (The Queen v Clotworthy 1998: 12).

The instrumental nature of the reasoning behind this judgement is clear. There is no mention of the offender having to "pay" for his wrongful action through a harsher punishment, or of the offender's "just deserts" anywhere in the summary of arguments, or in the justification of the decision to impose a three year custodial sentence. On the contrary, there is much weight given to the need to maintain sentencing consistency in the interests of the public and of the criminal justice system, and the importance of deterring others from committing similar crimes. Interestingly, arguments that Mr Clotworthy was not in danger of reoffending and that he presented no risk to the public by staying out of gaol were accepted by the prosecution and by the Court. Notwithstanding, the Court concurred with the prosecution that 'This was more than moderately serious offending, and the need to deter others for public safety reasons is too important' (The Queen v Clotworthy, 1998: 14). In view of such consequentialist reasoning by sentencing judges, it is simply not credible to blame retribution for the ills of the court system. To be sure, there are many things wrong with the wisdom of the Justices in the above decision and I shall return to them later. Retribution, however, is not one of them.

In light of these considerations, the criticism that the criminal justice system is only interested in giving offenders their just deserts is dubious and can be easily rejected by defenders of the status quo by pointing out that they are doing what they are doing, not for retribution, but for the greater good of society.

(b)   The Problem with the Criminal Justice System is that it is Punitive and Punishment doesn't Work

This claim also has two main difficulties with it. One is that many people remain convinced that punishment is, or can be, an appropriate response to criminal wrongdoing, especially where serious wrongdoing is concerned. This comes through unambiguously in Umbreit's surveys of crime victims.

> Without question, nearly all citizens at large and crime victims specifically want criminals to be held accountable through some form of punishment. '... Oftentimes, the need for punishment was expressed in terms of accountability'. 'Justice to me requires some punishment'. 'It doesn't have to be severe but has to be something that causes them to know they did something wrong and they have to pay for that' (Umbreit, 1989: 52, 54).

The second difficulty with the implicit rejection of punishment in the above claim is that it is far more probable than not that, overall, punishment and its threat play a major role in order maintenance. To be sure, this was the main reason why the prosecution took the Clotworthy case to the Court of Appeal, and seemed to be one of the main reasons why the appeal was upheld. One need not agree with the particular judgment reached in that case – I certainly do not – to appreciate the sense in the reasoning behind it. Even if Mr Clotworthy himself was not in danger of reoffending if given a non-custodial sentence, the need for deterring others from committing similar offences was considered a weighty enough reason to justify a custodial sentence.

More generally, even if the threat of punishment is no longer a deterrent to a relatively small number of repeat offenders, that does not mean that the prospect of punishment, such as imprisonment, for instance, is not a deterrent to the majority of people who otherwise might be more tempted to break the law and violate the rights of others in pursuit of their own goals and interests. At best, the evidence on this point is inconclusive, but the phenomenon of sharp increases in mindless vandalism, looting, and violence by otherwise law abiding citizens when they feel that they can get away with it, should cause us to re-think the wisdom of rejecting punishment altogether.

Also, at a conceptual level, it is far from clear that a criminal justice system is even conceivable (without logical contradiction, as in the idea of a married bachelor), if punishment is ruled out as a possible response to criminal offending. A system that manages, controls and responds to crime without resorting to any form of punitiveness may well prove preferable to current practice, but it would be a misnomer to refer to it as a criminal *justice* system. It would be more appropriate to call it a crime *management* system, or a crime *control* system. Where criminal justice is concerned, the concept of justice seems to presuppose the idea of a punitive response, if not that of retribution in its proper, "just deserts" sense.

Such conceptual points, of course, concern the meaning of key terms and of proper language use. While they do indicate the essential nature of the relevant subject or practice, they will not settle substantive, pragmatic and moral questions, such as whether punishment is a wise or appropriate response to criminal wrongdoing.

To settle such questions conclusively, we would need empirical data of the kind we do not possess. What we do have, however, are established practices, social conventions, and traditions that determine, guide, or regulate our responses to criminal wrongdoing on both pragmatic and moral grounds. The acceptability of punitive responses, and indeed the insistence on such responses where the crime is especially abhorrent and great, is a reflection of a deeply entrenched tradition that regards punishment as a fitting, and often necessary, response to serious forms of anti-social behaviour. What makes such responses appropriate is the *retrospective* responsibility mature (and intellectually unimpaired) members of society bear for their behaviour.[4] (Barton, 1999: Ch. 8).

This tradition, and the ongoing popular belief that punishment is an appropriate, and sometimes necessary, response to serious wrongdoing, are reflected in our laws; and indeed in the laws of virtually all known societies and cultures, from the despotic to the democratic – so far so that it is hard for us to even imagine a social order where punitiveness was ruled out as an appropriate response to serious wrongdoing. Therefore, it should come as no surprise that restorative justice practices do not reject punitive measures, but include and use them in constructive ways, and mostly to maximum effect, for the benefit of everyone involved. This brings me to the second main point against restorative justice critiques of the status quo, namely that it is a mistake to think of restorative justice as being the opposite of punishment or even of retribution. These are compatible and, therefore, the former does not require a rejection of the latter.

Restorative and Retributive Justice are Compatible

In practice, restorative justice responses incorporate punitive and retributive measures and elements in what appear to be optimum doses and degrees. Typically, they are mixed in with other measures such as increased social and community support to eliminate the underlying causes of the offending, and where indicated, further education and treatment. Indeed, it is difficult to see how restorative justice processes could become a widely accepted, let alone the preferred, response to crime, unless they were either complemented by punitive responses through other fora, such as the courts, or allowed direct incorporation of punitive elements in restorative justice outcomes and resolutions, as in fact they do. This has been recognised by Judge McElrea, a prominent supporter of restorative justice interventions in response to crime. In connection with conferencing rape cases, he makes the telling point that conference outcomes 'might still include imprisonment as part of a sentencing package. Punishment can still play a part in restorative justice without it being the dominating influence it is today' (McElrea, 1996: 7).

This point should be well taken, especially by advocates of restorative justice. It is vitally important because, unless punitive outcomes are allowed to be part of agreements, the use of alternative dispute resolution processes will never be an accepted practice in criminal justice. This is especially true of those areas where restorative justice responses are needed most: the more serious offence categories where the harm, and the potential for further and ongoing harm, are the greatest (Barton, 1999: Ch. 9). This point also comes through with startling clarity in the documented restorative justice conference between the parents and friends of a murdered young man and his killers (Dee Cameron, 'Facing the Demons: An Inside Story', Australian Broadcasting Corporation, Sydney, 1 June 1999.)

Once again, it is a mistake to think that punitive elements of an agreement automatically undermine or weaken its restorative potential. Quite the contrary. Some appropriate level and form of punitiveness will enhance the effectiveness of the restorative justice response, and will often have to form part of agreements to be acceptable to the relevant parties. That wrongdoing deserves punishment is a fundamental aspect of our reality, even if that reality is, in part, socially constructed. Our liability to punishment is an ineliminable part of what defines us as mature and responsible members of the moral community. As a result, in many cases of serious victimisation, no amount of therapy, or indeed conference discussion, may replace a victim's and the community's need to know that wrongdoing is punished, that justice, including justice in the retributive, "just deserts" sense, is done.

The incorporation of punitive and retributive elements in restorative justice processes, resolutions and outcomes should not cause alarm. The notion that punitiveness and retribution are incompatible with restoration is a myth, and is shown to be so by both history and current practice. Current restorative justice practices have been inspired by, and in many respects modelled on, traditional community-based systems of conflict resolution, which have been well known for their retributive character. A traditional Maori meeting that dealt with a rapist murderer, for example, could easily see the man being executed by his own family as "utu" (repayment), for what he had done, and the retributive character of the Australian Aboriginal practice of spearing the offender as "pay-back" is equally obvious. Claims to the contrary, that such indigenous practices are not really retributive, are but pious misinterpretations of indigenous practices and traditions in matters of wrongdoing and punishment – a point I have argued in more detail elsewhere (Barton, 1996, 1999), and shall take up again further below.

Far from having to reject punishment and retribution from the available range of responses, what needs to happen in restorative justice interventions is that any punitive response to wrongdoing is complemented with genuine caring, acceptance and reintegration of the person, as opposed to stigmatising, rejecting or crushing them – provided, that is, that they appreciate the moral gravity of their behaviour and are intent on making amends. This way, far from defeating restorative justice, a well pitched punitive measure will form part of, and will enhance restoration for everybody involved. Unfortunately, offenders who are otherwise whole-minded but refuse to respect the rights of others, and choose not to abide by the reasonable norms and laws of civil society, or who, in the context of a restorative justice meeting treat the victim and other participants with defiance and contempt, leave little or no alternatives to punishment and incapacitation.[5]

By failing to recognise and appreciate this point, advocates of restorative justice are hindering their own cause. But they are also creating confusion. Especially because of the mistaken belief that punishment and retribution are incompatible with restoration, some advocates of restorative justice contradict themselves. For example, Morris and Young assert that retributive justice is 'fundamentally at odds with the defining values of restorative justice and cannot, therefore, be part of it', while also believing that 'restorative justice ... [does not] remove prisons from available sanctions when parties to the restorative justice process agree to them' (Morris and Young, 1999, in the sections Vigilantism and Conclusion, respectively).

Worse, other advocates of restorative justice tend to give severely distorted interpretations of traditional revenge practices of indigenous people – which, as I have argued elsewhere, are essentially retributive in character in the proper sense of that word (Barton, 1996, 1999). In the face of overwhelming evidence to the contrary, the retributive character of these practices tends to be disguised, played down, or outright denied in the restorative justice literature. For instance, Wundersitz and Hetzel describe and identify as 'appropriate reparation by the "offender"' the Australian Aboriginal practice of "pay-back" which, as they admit, 'could include some physical "reprisal" such as ritual spearing' (Wundersitz and Hetzel, 1996: 136). Consedine goes even further when he explicitly denies the retributive nature of "pay-back" in Aboriginal Australia.

> In all cases we have outlined, while there is so much verbal emphasis on revenge, it is plausible to infer that underlying this is a general aim of achieving order and balance. An injury is done, the status quo is upset, retaliation provides a means by which this may be restored. ... [This] is essentially a restorative process, not a retributive one (Consedine, 1995: 113).

These are confused and misleading interpretations of what, clearly, are retributive practices, and the 'conceptual gerrymandering' involved in such reinterpretations of traditional revenge practices has been rejected elsewhere (Barton, 1999: Ch. 10). The process of "pay-back" is indeed highly ritualised and is closely monitored and controlled by the community. It is important, however, that the word "ritual" does not mislead the reader. Such "ritual spearing" signifies real spearing, and sometimes multiple spearing of the wrongdoer – often resulting in very serious injuries, and sometimes death. More to the point, while such "pay-back" is restorative in the sense that it restores social peace between the conflicting parties and between the wrongdoer and the rest of their community, and while to aboriginal people it might be less punitive than imprisonment, it is neither credible, nor helpful to describe it as 'reparation by the "offender"', or worse, to assert that the practice is 'not a retributive one'. The Aboriginal Australians themselves call it "pay-back" and their justification for it is deontological, rather than instrumental in the way Consedine's reinterpretation suggests. Their customary laws, which they refer to as "The Law", require that wrongs *must be* punished through "pay-back". This is a sacred duty and it is accepted and insisted on by all members of the community, wrongdoers and victims included, as being right on account of "The Law". And, while it is true that the restoration of social order and social peace are unthinkable without fulfilling the requirements of "The Law" in terms of "pay-back", the inevitable restorative function of "pay-back" is no ground for a redescription of its basic character as if it were a non-retributive, consequentialist practice.

It is a justified conclusion in light of the above, that restorative justice is quite compatible with retributive justice. The particular degree, form, and mix of retributive and punitive elements in a restorative justice response will, of course, depend on a number of different factors, such as culture, tradition, and circumstance. Positive results from restorative justice programs[6] indicate that concerned communities of care are the best placed to get this mix right. They are not obtained through a supposed rejection of punishment and retribution by restorative justice programs and interventions.

A Summary of the Arguments so far

Anti-retributivist critiques of the status quo are like toothless tigers. They make much noise, and may even impress the naive, but ultimately they have no bite. They miss the mark on two counts. On the first count, the diagnosis that the problem with the criminal justice system is that it is retributive cannot be sustained in either the proper, "just deserts", or the corrupted, "punishment", sense of the word. In the former sense, it is simply not true that the system is only interested in giving offenders their just deserts. The language of legislation and the obvious instrumental reasoning in judicial sentencing both contra-indicate such a diagnosis. As to the latter sense, the claim that the problem with the system is that it is punitive is equally dubious. Established practice and the authority of tradition lend strong support to the view that punishment and its threat play an important role in order maintenance. This is further supported by the popular view, according to which punishment is an appropriate, and often necessary, response to serious wrongdoing, as without some appropriate level and form of punishment, justice, including restorative justice, is simply impossible. Finally, the evidently false assumption that punishment and retributive justice are incompatible with restorative justice, in that the former cannot figure in restorative responses to crime, make this particular line of attack on the status quo doubly beside the point.

The diagnosed failure implicit in that last point, namely the failure to recognise evidently punitive and retributive elements in restorative justice interventions and outcomes, indicates, not only a failure to identify the chief problem with the criminal justice system, but an even more disconcerting lack of understanding of the nature of restorative processes and restorative justice itself. If this is right, two further conclusions follow. First, an alternative diagnosis to the ills of the justice system must be found. Second, for such a diagnosis to be adequate, it must give a plausible account, not only of what is wrong with the status quo in criminal justice, but also of what makes restorative justice responses preferable – because, as we have seen, simple rejections of punitiveness and retribution fail this test. This is the task of the next section.

Disempowerment in Criminal Justice

The problem with the status quo is that it disempowers the primary stakeholders in the criminal justice dispute, namely, the victim, the offender, and their respective social circles of support and care, which, typically, consist of their respective families, close friends, peers and colleagues.[7] These people are the primary stakeholders in the sense that they have the most to gain or lose by a criminal justice intervention and its outcome. Their empowerment in terms of meeting, discussing and resolving criminal justice matters should be sought, not only because they have the most to gain or lose from the success or failure of the intervention, but also because, typically, they happen to have the best chance of achieving the following three important objectives that should be pursued in any criminal justice response:

- Prevent reoffending by eliminating the underlying causes of the unacceptable behaviour in question.
- Reduce and, as far as possible, repair the harmful consequences of the criminal wrongdoing in question, especially the harm caused to the victim.
- Achieve a maximally satisfying resolution or agreement that will meet both the material and the emotional needs of the principal parties concerned (Retzinger and Scheff, 1996). The ultimate aim should be to help the parties achieve closure in terms of emotional conciliation and a feeling that the matter has been dealt with fairly, that justice has been done.

A feeling of satisfaction that justice has been done is difficult to achieve for the primary stakeholders, unless they are empowered to have their say in terms of what they consider to be right or wrong, fair or unfair, and express keenly felt but legitimate emotions of hurt, disappointment, and anger in socially acceptable ways. As shown by victim accounts of their experiences of the traditional court system, unless these things can happen, the parties will not feel that they have been heard, or that they and their feelings and views matter in the decision-making process (Giuliano, 1998). Also, unless important stakeholders are actively involved in formulating an agreement or resolution, they will be less likely to feel ownership over it, will be less likely to be committed to honouring it, and will be less likely to feel satisfied with it (Barton, 1999). Finally, by comparison to third parties, such as legal and other professionals, primary stakeholders are more likely to know the finer details of the circumstances and the needs of the offender and the victim, and therefore are better able to foresee whether some proposed resolution is going to achieve the above mentioned objectives, and indeed whether the proposed agreement is viable or is more likely than not to set the participants up for further disappointment and failure.

In light of these considerations, and assuming that the primary function of criminal justice interventions is indeed to promote peace and social harmony by means of ensuring justice for the parties concerned, the suggested diagnosis of the ills of the status quo should be uncontroversial. The criminal justice system, which is epitomised by the traditional court process, is anything but empowering to the primary stakeholders. In their purported mission to protect the innocent and punish the guilty, contemporary criminal justice systems marginalise and disempower the very people who have most at stake in particular criminal justice interventions. Most significantly, victims and accused alike are discouraged and denied real opportunities to take an active role in the legal processing and resolution of their cases. In effect, they are reduced to the status of idle bystanders in their own cases in what, after all, is *their* conflict.

A paradigm illustration of what is wrong with the status quo is Sir Anthony Mason's suggestion that the courts could implement restorative justice principles by there being a coming together of the judge, the prosecutor and the defence lawyer to make a decision as to whether some offender should be given a conference or not (see Chapter 1 of this volume). Now, you might ask, what is wrong with that? The simple answer is that it perpetuates the disempowerment of the key stakeholders in a very important decision – a decision that is likely to make a huge difference in terms of how the case is going to be resolved, which, in turn, has serious implications for the primary stakeholders involved. This kind of monopoly by legal professionals over important decisions in the criminal justice process is the hallmark of the status quo. The most serious problem with it is that it unnecessarily silences and disempowers the very people who are the best placed to make the decisions in question. Such a system is likely to result in many inappropriate decisions being made, with the result that those who have the most at stake will unnecessarily miss out on the potential benefits of a face to face meeting. This is because, apart from being quite often poorly informed, disinterested third parties tend to have their own set of priorities in making such decisions – priorities that are priorities only to them, and which are typical of a bureaucratic state apparatus, and which are often contrary to the more basic and immediate needs and interests of the key parties.

In terms of the empowerment paradigm, the alternative to Sir Anthony Mason's suggestion is obvious. It is the victim and the offender, along with their respective families or communities of support, that should be asked whether they would like to meet face to face to discuss and try resolving the matter between them. If they would, let them and give them the required expertise and support to maximise the chances of a successful outcome. If they do not wish to have such a meeting, their wishes must be respected just the same and the case can proceed to court.

In other words, this is where empowerment of the primary stakeholders in criminal justice must start: by giving them the power to choose between alternative ways of resolving the matter. Whether resolution should be attempted by way of court, victim-offender mediation, sentencing circle, or a conference, or indeed by some other method, or some kind of combination of these, should be left to the primary stakeholders to decide. If they cannot reach consensus between them, then the matter can be decided by appropriately qualified professionals, but not before that. Indeed, such general principles of empowerment should be present in all of the major criminal justice agencies: policing, court, and corrections.

Empowerment, of course, must continue to be present throughout a restorative justice process, be it a conference, victim-offender mediation, sentencing circle, or whatever. Essentially, the emphasis must be on primary stakeholders being actively involved at all stages and making all the important decisions. And, as long as their proposals, including their proposals for resolution, are within reason and the limits of law, their decisions must be respected and accepted as final. This is the point on which the justices in the Clotworthy case fell short. Rather than showing respect to the wishes of the primary stakeholders, and especially those of the victim, they presumed to know better how the case should be resolved. Because of this presumption, they set aside a sensible agreement between the offender and the victim and imposed their own sense of right and wrong - a judgment that left the victim, as well as the offender, deeply unhappy, as it caters for a set of priorities that are at odds with their needs and interests. Additionally, the result is that the victim received significantly less compensation than contained in the initial agreement, as Mr Clotworthy lost his job and became unproductive because of the three year custodial sentence. Also, tax payers are forking out $150,000 to keep Mr Clotworthy in gaol, allowing him to learn how to be a more efficient criminal. The predictable result is that he is likely to come out more of a danger to the community than he ever was before. Even with, or rather, especially since, the protection of the community from crime was a consideration in the judges' reasoning for their decision, defenders of the status quo must excuse the ordinary citizen for asking the obvious question: Where is the sense in it? Judgments such as this only succeed in supporting calls for a substantial and urgent transfer of power from the professionals of the legal system to the primary stakeholders (McElrea, 1996, 1999).

To summarise, by comparison to the anti-retributivist line of attack discussed earlier, a more effective critique of the status quo is possible by pointing to the institutionalised and systematic disempowerment of the primary stakeholders by the legal profession – a profession that has placed itself at the centre of the criminal justice process and, by doing so, systematically silences and marginalises the primary stakeholders in the course of criminal justice responses to crime. Most of the ills of the criminal justice system can be traced back to this feature of the system. Therefore, it is not retribution, but the disempowerment of the primary stakeholders that restorative justice critiques of the status quo must focus on. The same holds true when evaluating restorative justice interventions – a point taken up in the remaining section.

Disempowerment in Restorative Justice

It would be naive to think that all restorative justice interventions are positive and wonderfully successful. All too often they are not. Especially when a program is poorly implemented, without proper training in conflict resolution and facilitation techniques, or with an ill-defined vision and poor understanding of how to implement restorative justice principles in practice, many conferences fail and a significant number of them victimise and re-victimise the key participants. My suggestion is that such unhappy experiences for offenders, victims, and their supporters are the result of silencing and disempowerment, or rather the result of conference coordinators failing to empower them in appropriate ways to speak their minds, and stand up for what they, in good faith, believe to be right and fair. For example, victims can experience marginalisation and severe disempowerment when they are not invited to attend their conferences; are given inadequate notice or consideration in setting the time and venue of the meeting; attend ill-prepared in terms of holding realistic expectations, knowledge of the process, awareness of their rights and responsibilities, or attend without a strong group of supporters on whom they can lean if the meeting gets difficult. In the absence of such safeguards, victims are vulnerable and can feel intimidated and re-victimised, especially if the offender or their family prove hard to deal with. The same holds true for offenders and their families who can find the experience overwhelming and humiliating, unless they are similarly prepared and adequately supported during what is for them a very difficult time.

The thesis that disempowerment (including the mere lack of empowerment) leads to unsatisfactory results for the key participants in restorative justice interventions can be demonstrated by reference to family group conferences (FGCs). While there tends to be a lot of focus on the successes of FGCs, the reality is that they can fail to achieve restorative justice for the parties concerned in an alarmingly high number of cases. Not only can FGCs fail in terms of reaching agreement between the parties, but they can make things worse for those who have already been victimised through the initial crime. For example, in the samples studied by Maxwell and Morris:

- Only in 41% of cases did victims attend the FGC – mostly because they were not invited or were given insufficient notice.
- Of those victims that attended, only in 49% of cases did they express *any* degree of satisfaction with the outcome (my emphasis).
- Only about a third of victims went away from the FGC feeling better.
- 25% of the interviewed victims said they felt worse as a result of attending the FGC, and

- 38% of FGCs attended by victims who were interviewed resulted in the victim saying they felt worse (Maxwell and Morris, 1993: 119; 1996).

Similarly, with respect to offenders, Maxwell and Morris found that:

- Only a third of young offenders felt involved and often said little in their FGCs.
- 26% of a sample of 14 – 16 year olds referred to FGCs in 1990-91 had been (re)convicted within 12 months.
- 64% of them had been (re)convicted after just over four years, and
- 24% of them had been persistently reconvicted over the same period (Morris and Maxwell, 1997).

These results are disappointing. In light of the much emphasised potential of community empowerment in dealing with crime, these reoffending rates, for example, clearly fall short of legitimate expectations (Alder and Wundersitz, 1994, 1998; Barton, 1996, 1999; Braithwaite, 1989, 1996; Braithwaite and Mugford, 1994; Maxwell and Morris, 1993, 1996, 1997; and generally the works referred to in Note 1). Also, from a victim justice perspective, some of the above figures ought to be of the gravest concern. Victims of crime have a lot at stake in the way the criminal justice system deals with their cases, and the above rates of revictimisation raise important moral and legal questions about the appropriateness and legitimacy of exposing victims to high risks of further victimisation in criminal justice interventions.

The above statistics also underlie the urgency of acting on Braithwaite's observation, that 'We need quality research on when and why restorative justice fails' (Braithwaite, 1996: 24). Here then is a clear hypothesis that would be well worth testing through research: *Restorative justice fails in cases where one or more of the primary stakeholders is silenced, marginalised and disempowered in processes that are intended to be restorative. Conversely, restorative justice succeeds in cases where the primary stakeholders can speak their minds without intimidation or fear, and are empowered to take an active role in negotiating a resolution that is acceptable and is right for them.* Without such all-round empowerment of the primary stakeholders concerned, restorative justice processes will be restorative only in name. They will not succeed in realising the restorative potential of individual and community empowerment, which, in the final analysis, is the fundamental starting point of restorative justice.

This analysis, of course, is at a relatively high level of generality, whereas the devil tends to be in the detail. Therefore, research must focus on the many ways in which empowerment and disempowerment are engendered and experienced in restorative justice processes. As mentioned above, my personal observations of FGCs in a range of programs on both sides of the Tasman clearly indicate that disempowerment and unsatisfactory outcomes tend to happen when individual stakeholders are not properly prepared, encouraged and supported to speak their minds, participate actively in negotiations and the making of key decisions. All parties must be enabled to negotiate from a position of knowledge, and with confidence that they can deal with this matter and make a positive difference in the outcome.

This, however, requires addressing imbalances of power created by differences in age, gender, culture, social status, institutional affiliation, etc. To give just one more example, unless the conference coordinator is highly skilled in the conduct of multi-party negotiations and conflict resolution, and has a clear understanding of the dynamics of interpersonal conflict escalation and resolution as they relate to the concept of restorative justice in terms of empowerment, they are unlikely to succeed in enabling an already timid or crushed young offender find their voice. Yet, unless this happens, the young person's experience will most likely be one of continued disengagement throughout the process, and of humiliation, victimisation and bullying by adults, who, in their own turn, and understandably, will feel equally frustrated and dissatisfied with the young person and the whole conferencing experience. It is my firm belief, however, that a properly trained and skilled facilitator can prevent such failures in the vast majority of cases. This can be done, for instance, by

- proper preparation of the parties concerned,
- inviting the right mix of supporters in sufficiently large numbers on both sides,
- helping the young person to find their voice by encouraging them to have first say in the conference (unless this is culturally inappropriate) to explain and own up to all aspects of what they did, and to accept responsibility for their behaviour voluntarily. Unless this happens from very early on in the conference, an angry victim or a stern police officer can easily, even if inadvertently, knock the last shred of confidence, and/or moral concern for the victim and the rest of society, out of already frightened, timid, disengaged, angry, or defiant young offenders.[8]

This kind of awareness and practitioner competence in terms of effective techniques of mediation and facilitation are crucial for consistently good, all-round satisfying processes and outcomes in restorative justice terms. Without them, restorative justice interventions can only hope to be the kind of dubious, hit and miss affairs indicated by the above statistics, which brings me to the concluding point of my paper. This is that an effective restorative justice critique of the status quo requires more than a different and more relevant framing of the problem of what is wrong with it. The extra thing needed is results, consistently good results, from the restorative justice programs that have already been established. Without them, no restorative justice critique of the status quo can hope to maintain credibility in the long run, let alone make a difference in the face of bureaucratic priorities, inertia, and the understandable resistance to change by professionals who find it difficult to re-conceptualise and re-define their roles in terms of a different paradigm of justice.

Notes

1   These beliefs are evident, for example, with varying emphases, in Bird, 1998; Braithwaite and Pettit, 1990; Consedine, 1995; Dignan and Cavadino, 1996; Galaway and Hudson, 1996; Jones, 1996; McDonald, Moore, O'Connell and Thorsborne, 1995; Moore, 1993; Morris and Young, 1999; Munn, 1993; Sherman, Strang, Barnes, Braithwaite, Inkpen and Teh, 1998; Umbreit, 1989; Van Ness, 1990, 1996; 1997; Walgrave, 1995; Wright, 1991, 1996; Wundersitz and Hetzel, 1996; Zehr, 1990; also, in Bowen, Boyack, Consedine, Hayden and Henderson, Hickey, and Lapsley, in Consedine and Bowen, 1999, and generally most writers on restorative justice.

2   Walgrave (1995), for instance, has a meaningful and active engagement with retributivist and instrumental conceptualisations of the criminal justice system – even though, as I am arguing in this paper, retributive interpretations of the system and its objectives are far from compelling.

3   For a more detailed description of the case, see Boyack, 1999.

4   They bear this responsibility quite independently of the likely consequences of those responses, even though the likely consequences should, by all means, be taken into account.

5   But see Braithwaite and Mugford (1994), who have put forward compelling arguments, not necessarily incompatible with the view I have just expressed, that we should never give up making attempts to reintegrate an offender into the community of law abiding citizens, no matter how hopeless it may seem at the time.

6   To be fair, empirical data on conferencing success is ambivalent. In terms of participant satisfaction, for example, the results from some programs are nothing short of outstanding, showing near-perfect results (Moore, 1995; Palk et al., 1998; Tuhiwai Smith and Cram, 1998). In other programs, the results are not as good but, arguably, they are still better, all things considered, than court (Sherman, et al., 1998; Maxwell and Morris, 1993, 1996; Maxwell, 1998; Morris

and Maxwell, 1997). There are two likely explanations for the discrepancies between programs. One is that, by comparison, programs with lower satisfaction figures are the ones that tend to take on high risk cases. The other one is that these programs haven't yet addressed some important practice issues, such as adequate and ongoing training for practitioners and quality feedback systems on practice. While currently, there is no credible data that would establish the degree to which these factors impact on participant satisfaction in the various programs, it is a clear implication of my analysis here that disempowerment of key stakeholders through poor practice is heavily implicated in sub-optimal results and low satisfaction figures.

7   In another context Daly points out quite rightly that 'The problem in criminal-court practices is not that the female voice is absent, but that certain [gender] relations are presupposed, maintained, and reproduced' (Daly, 1989: 2).

8   The good sense in giving young offenders first say in conferences has been emphasised by Braithwaite and Mugford as early as 1994 (p. 150), and by others, such as Patrick Power and myself in conversations with conference administrators and practitioners. The point has also been raised at international conferences, but with no discernible impact on practice. The human dimension seems to dictate that, not unlike the legal professionals they so readily criticise, restorative justice administrators and practitioners are as susceptible as anybody else to seek the comfort of the familiar, and to close their minds too quickly to suggestions and opportunities for improving practice. Therefore, it is very important that good systems and practices are implemented from the very start of a restorative justice program. Unless this is done, changes for the better become increasingly difficult and painful. Even relatively small changes will be met with resistance from within the program by well meaning people who almost invariably equate the concept of best practice with whatever they happen to have become familiar and comfortable with.

References

Barton, C. (1996), 'Revenge and Victim Justice', PhD thesis, The Australian National University, Canberra.

Barton, C. (1999), *Getting Even: Revenge as a Form of Justice*, Open Court Publishing, Chicago and La Salle.

Barton, C. and van den Broek, K. (1999), 'Restorative Justice Conferencing and the Ethic of Care', *Ethics and Justice*, vol. 2, pp. 55 – 65.

Bird, S. (1998), *Conference Convenor Training Package*, Department of Juvenile Justice, Sydney.

Boyack, J. (1999), 'How Sayest the Court of Appeal?', in J. Consedine and H. Bowen (eds), *Restorative Justice: Contemporary Themes and Practice*, Ploughshares Publications, Lyttleton, New Zealand.

Braithwaite, J. (1989), *Crime, Shame and Reintegration*, Cambridge University Press, Cambridge.

Braithwaite, J. (1996), *Restorative Justice and a Better Future*, Dorothy J. Killam Memorial Lecture, Dalhousie University, 17 October 1996.

Braithwaite, J. and Mugford, S. (1994), 'Conditions of Successful Reintegration Ceremonies', *British Journal of Criminology*, vol. 34, pp. 139 – 71.

Braithwaite, J. and Pettit, P. (1990), *Not Just Deserts*, Clarendon, Oxford.

Consedine, J. (1995), *Restorative Justice: Healing the Effects of Crime*, Ploughshares Publications, Lyttleton, New Zealand.

Consedine, J. and Bowen, H. (eds) (1999), *Restorative Justice: Contemporary Themes and Practice*, Ploughshares Publications, Lyttleton, New Zealand.

Daly, K. (1989), 'Criminal Justice Ideologies and Practices in Different Voices: Some Feminist Questions about Justice', *International Journal of the Sociology of Law*, vol. 17, pp. 1-18.

Dignan, J. and Cavadino, M. (1996), 'Toward a Framework for Conceptualizing and Evaluating Models of Criminal Justice from a Victim's Perspective', *International Review of Victimology*, vol. 4, pp. 153–82.

Galaway, B. and Hudson, J. (eds) (1996), *Restorative Justice: International Perspectives*, Criminal Justice Press, New York.

Giuliano, B. (ed.) (1998), *Survival and Beyond: An Anthology of Stories by Victims of Crime and a Victims' Resource Guide*, The National Association for Loss and Grief, ACT Inc., Canberra.

Hudson, J., Morris, A., Maxwell, G. and Galaway, B. (eds) (1996), *Family Group Conferences: Perspectives on Policy and Practice*, The Federation Press, Australia.

Jones, K. (1996), 'Restorative Justice: The Theoretical Dream of Idealism', LLB (Hons) Research Paper, Criminal Law and Procedure (LAWS 511), Law Faculty, Victoria University of Wellington, New Zealand.

Maxwell, G. and Morris, A. (1993), *Family, Victims and Culture: Youth Justice in New Zealand*, Social Policy Agency and Institute of Criminology, Victoria University of Wellington, Wellington.

Maxwell, G. and Morris, A. (1996), 'Research on Family Group Conferences with Young Offenders in New Zealand', in J. Hudson, A. Morris, G. Maxwell, and B. Galaway (eds), *Family Group Conferences: Perspectives on Policy and Practice*, The Federation Press, Australia, pp. 88-110.

Maxwell, G. (1998), 'Researching Reoffending: Recent Research on Family Group Conferences', Paper presented to the conference: *Youth Justice in Focus*, Victoria University of Wellington, Wellington, October 1998.

McDonald, J., Moore, D., O'Connell, T., and Thorsborne, M. (1995), 'Coordinating Family Group Conferences', in B. Wachtel and T. Wachtel (eds), *Real Justice Training Manual*, The Piper's Press, Pipersville.

McElrea, F. W. M. (1999), 'Taking Responsibility in Being Accountable', in J. Consedine and H. Bowen (eds), *Restorative Justice: Contemporary Themes and Practice*, Ploughshares Publications, Lyttleton, New Zealand.

McElrea, F. W. M. (1996), *Rape: Ten Years' Progress?*, An address to the Interdisciplinary Conference, Wellington, 29 March 1996.

Moore, D. (1993), 'Shame, Forgiveness, and Juvenile Justice', *Criminal Justice Ethics*, Winter/Spring, pp. 3-25.

Moore, D. (1995), *A New Approach to Juvenile Justice: An Evaluation of Family Conferences in Wagga Wagga – A Report to the Criminology Research Council*, Charles Sturt University, Wagga Wagga.

Morris, A. and Maxwell, G. (1997), 'Family Group Conferences and Convictions', *Occasional Papers in Criminology*, New Series: No. 5, Institute of Criminology, Victoria University of Wellington, Wellington.

Morris, A. and Young, W. (1999), 'Reforming Criminal Justice: The Potential of Restorative Justice', Paper presented to the conference: *Restorative Justice and Civil Society*, The Australian National University, Canberra, February 1999.

Munn, M. (1993), 'Restorative Justice: An Alternative to Vengeance', *American Journal of Criminal Law*, vol. 20, p. 99.

Palk, G., Hayes, H., and Prenzler, T. (1998), 'Restorative Justice and Community Conferencing: Summary of Findings from a Pilot Study', *Current Issues in Criminal Justice*, vol. 10, pp. 138-55.

Retzinger, S. M. and Scheff, T. J. (1996), 'Strategy for Community Conferences: Emotions and Social Bonds', in B. Galaway and J. Hudson (eds), *Restorative Justice: International Perspectives*, Criminal Justice Press, Monsey, NY, pp. 315–36.

RISE Working Papers (1997), Papers #1–#4. *A Series of Reports on Research in Progress on the Reintegrative Shaming Experiment (RISE) for Restorative Community Policing*, Law Program, Research School of Social Sciences, Institute of Advanced Studies, Australian National University, Canberra.

Sherman, L., Strang, H., Barnes, J., Braithwaite, J., Inkpen, N., and The, M. (1998), *Experiments in Restorative Policing: A Progress Report*, Law Program, Research School of Social Sciences, The Australian National University, Canberra.

Strang, H., and Sherman, L. W. (1997), 'The Victim's Perspective', in RISE Working Papers, *A Series of Reports on Research in Progress on the Reintegrative Shaming Experiment (RISE) for Restorative Community Policing*, Law Program, Research School of Social Sciences, Institute of Advanced Studies, Australian National University, Canberra, Paper #2.

The Queen v Clotworthy, (1998), Appeal Court of New Zealand 114/98, Wellington, New Zealand.

Tuhiwai Smith, L. and Cram, F. (1998), *An Evaluation of the Community Panel Diversion Pilot Programme*, Auckland Uniservices Limited, The University of Auckland, Auckland.

Umbreit, M. S. (1989), 'Crime Victims Seeking Fairness, Not Revenge: Towards Restorative Justice', *Federal Probation*, vol. 53, pp. 52–7.

Van Ness, D. W. (1990), 'Restoring the Balance: Tipping the Scales of Justice', *Corrections Today*, vol. 52, pp. 62–6.

Van Ness, D. W. (1996), 'Restorative Justice and International Human Rights', in B. Galaway and J. Hudson (eds), *Restorative Justice: International Perspectives*, Criminal Justice Press, New York.

Van Ness, D. W. (1997), *Restoring Justice*, Anderson, Cincinnati.

Walgrave, L. (1995), 'Restorative Justice for Juveniles: Just a Technique or a Fully Fledged Alternative?', *The Howard Journal*, vol. 34, pp. 228–49.

Wright, M. (1996), *Justice for Victims and Offenders: A Restorative Response to Crime*, second edition, Waterside Press, Winchester.

Wundersitz, J. and Hetzel, S. (1996), 'Family Conferences for Young Offenders: The South Australian Experience', in Hudson, J., Morris, A., Maxwell, G. and Galaway, B. (eds) (1996), *Family Group Conferences: Perspectives on Policy and Practice*, The Federation Press, Australia, Chapter 7.

Zehr, H. (1990), *Changing Lenses*, Herald Press, Scottdale, PA.

5 Restorative Justice: Retribution, Confession and Shame

SEUMAS MILLER AND JOHN BLACKLER

Introduction

The term "restorative justice" has come to mean many different things to different people. So much so that we fear it is beginning to cease to have any clear reference. It is apparently being used to refer to an extraordinarily wide and diverse range of formal and informal interventions, including: (1) victim/offender conferences in criminal justice contexts; (2) discretionary problem solving policing initiatives in disputes between citizens; (3) conflict resolution workshops in organisational contexts; (4) team building sessions in occupational settings; (5) marital advice and counselling sessions; (6) parental guidance and admonishment of their misbehaving children; (7) apologising for offensive or otherwise hurtful remarks in institutional and other settings.

The scope of the term "restorative justice" has widened to the point that it now has within its purview – at least potentially – any and all harmful, conflictual or otherwise morally problematic actions, situations, or relationships. But even the term "justice" – let alone restorative justice – cannot sensibly embrace the totality of what is harmful or otherwise morally problematic. Many moral problems are not principally matters of injustice. A drug addict may well be doing great harm to herself, but she is not necessarily committing, or been in receipt of, any injustices. Interventions of various kinds may be necessary if a child is to undergo appropriate moral development; but such interventions are not necessarily in response to any injustice, and being developmental ex hypothesei they are not restorative or re-educative in any sense. Conflict may arise from a variety of causes other than injustice, including distrust, lack of sympathy, jealousy and ambition. Finally, many acts of wrongdoing are not principally acts of injustice. Murder is profoundly wrong, but it is not essentially wrong by virtue of being unjust. Naturally, many sorts of wrongdoing give rise to questions of justice. For example, it would be unjust for a murderer to go free. But many sorts of wrongdoing are not essentially issues of justice.   Consider again the drug addict or the unreasonably jealous husband.

Sometimes the term "restorative justice" is used not to refer to these conflictual and other moral problems themselves, but rather to their solutions.   But obviously the solutions are as diverse as the problems, and any given solution is not necessarily describable as a state of justice.   Solving conflict amongst co-workers might merely require an independent referee to allow the various parties to have their say, and discharge some pent up emotion.   But the solution is not necessarily a state of justice; the predominant values in question might be trust, or even just good order.   Moreover, there may well be no offender or victim per se, and no injustices may even have taken place.

Perhaps a more plausible way to delimit the notion of restorative justice is to focus not on the problems or the solutions to the problems, but rather on the methodology for solving an admittedly wide array of problems.   But it is by no means clear that there is in fact such a single method, or unified set of methods.   Certainly, it is difficult to see from our above list just what this method or set of methods is.   In some quarters a negative definition is apparently on offer.   Restorative justice, on this view, is defined as any non-punitive method for resolving moral problems or repairing moral relationships.   But there are too many non-punitive methods for this suggestion to be a helpful one.   And in any case, as we will see below – and has been forcefully argued by many philosophers over centuries, including very recently by Charles Barton (Barton, 1999; Hegel, 1942), punishment cannot be eliminated as an element in restoring justice.   Consider in this connection murder.   The person who has suffered the wrong – the deceased victim – cannot be dispensed any restorative justice. Retributive justice is called for.   This is not to say that restorative justice has no part to play in relation to, for example, the victim's family.   For instance, in the case studies below, we discuss Terry O'Connell's filmed conference with a murderer and the victim's family which displays the potential role that a restorative justice mechanism can have in relation to a murderer, and the friends and relatives of the person murdered.   In so doing of course, it does not remove the need for retributive justice. Far from it.

In the light of the above, we have decided to restrict our use of the term "restorative justice" to contexts in which moral rights – as distinct from other sorts of wrongdoing or harm causing - have been, or might potentially be, infringed, and there is a need for redress or repair in relation to these infringements.   Moreover, we are especially concerned with those moral rights that the criminal justice system has been designed (however inadequately) to protect, e.g. rights to protection from force, fraud and theft.   Other kinds of problems, including many conflict situations, are no doubt in various respects similar to cases in which moral rights have been infringed, and no doubt sometimes also susceptible to treatment by similar methods, but we doubt that this is typically or even very often the case. Nor should we be taken as necessarily rejecting the value or efficacy of any or all the methods that are used under the banner of restorative justice. There does seem to be a need in our society to explicitly confront moral problems and to revive a variety of formal and informal mechanisms for exposing and resolving them. At any rate, on pain of losing our grip on the topic of restorative justice, we have opted for our narrow definition.

The general concept of justice is complex and embraces notions of procedural justice (e.g. fair trial) and distributive justice (e.g. fair wages) as well as the notion of justice of greatest interest to us, namely, commutative justice or justice in the sphere of punishment, rehabilitation, reintegration and the like. In relation to punishment, there are an array of theories on offer, including consequentialist and retributive theories. A third category of theory are so-called restorative justice theories (Ten, 1987). Consequentialist accounts punish only to promote good consequences; including deterrence of would-be wrongdoers, rehabilitation, incapacitation and the like. Retributive theories emphasise the deserts of the wrongdoer; those who do wrong deserve to be punished, irrespective of consequentialist considerations of deterrence, prevention of future harm, and so on. Restorative theorists emphasise the moral education of the wrongdoer and his/her reintegration into the community.

We want to stress at the outset that we do not believe that these general accounts are mutually exclusive. Indeed, in our view elements of all three kinds of theory are required if a satisfactory theory of commutative justice is to result. Surely, consequences, including harm reduction are important considerations, and deterrence – based on a credible threat of punishment - does in certain circumstances work. Consider the enforcement of speeding and drink driving laws. On the other hand, the evidence suggests that restorative justice programs in relation to juvenile offenders also work. Consider in this connection the so-called Wagga Wagga model, and its evaluation (Moore, 1995). The success of these practical programs constitutes support for restorative justice as a theory. Moreover, reintegration might itself be a consequence to be aimed at. So restorative justice is not necessarily an alternative to all forms of consequentialism. Finally, some retributivist sui generis principles, such as that the guilty ought to be the ones to be punished or the ones to compensate victims, need to be maintained in many circumstances.[1] Indeed, as we will argue in detail below, retribution ought to be a component element in many restorative justice programs. In short, we are pluralists. Moreover, qua pluralists we do not accept that any unitary theory, be it consequentialist, retributivist or restorative, can adequately accommodate the plurality of moral considerations in play. For example, in our view even sophisticated consequentialists do not in the final analysis succeed in reducing or otherwise accommodating retributivist considerations (Braithwaite, 1990). As pluralists we do not disregard, attempt to explain away or otherwise downplay, moral consequences, the importance of deterrence, or the internal moral dynamics of reintegration, merely because we are also committed to punishment as desert. Nor do we see workable deterrence-based or restorative justice programs as being able to jettison retributivist principles.

In Australia, restorative justice, or at least its applications in criminal justice contexts, has been associated with the likes of John Braithwaite (Braithwaite, 1989) and Terry O'Connell. These and others have developed and implemented institutional mechanisms such as youth conferencing, and in so doing have in effect resurrected the institution of confession and (implicitly) the theoretical moral framework which underpins it. They have, of course, developed other sorts of restorative justice programs that are not predominantly confessional in character. For example, O'Connell's work in the behavioural change program in the NSW Police Service in local area commands seems principally an exercise in resolving workplace conflict and team building. As such it requires voluntary participation, open and frank discussion, agreement on procedures and goals, and presupposes some framework of shared moral principles.

Moreover, confession has been used in a wide variety of situations in which moral principles have been infringed, but not any moral rights. So the device of confession has been used in contexts above and beyond what we have been calling restorative justice contexts. Nevertheless, we believe that confession is a central element in many restorative justice programs, and the exploration of it may assist in the process of providing a philosophical foundation for, and taxonomy of, the varieties of restorative justice programs.

Here it is also important to point out that restorative justice in general, and many of its associated institutional mechanisms, are not something new and exotic. They have been part and parcel of systems of justice for thousands of years, both in western and other cultures. For example, the institutional device of confession is a mechanism of restorative justice. Moreover, confession in one form or another has existed in most societies, including Christian societies, Japanese society and Maori society (Hepworth, 1982).

At any rate, in order to focus our discussion we shall outline three Australian conferencing case studies. We have chosen one example of what we take to be a successful conference, a second example which is a manifestly unsuccessful conference, and as our third example a conference the success or failure of which is somewhat unclear.

Case Studies and Ethical Analysis

Case Study 1: David's Story²

David was 16 years old and lived in a large rural town. He had lived with his retired parents, both of whom were very supportive. He had two sisters, both had left home. One sister, Peta had worked as a police officer in the same town. Up until the age of 15 David was considered a regular young lad, but then began committing (with others) some minor crime. Having experienced the normal police cautions and court appearances, nothing seemed to make a difference. David became involved in more serious crime including motor vehicle theft and house burglary. His final series of offences included theft of the complete contents of a house, including the motor vehicle. This was the second occasion David had broken into this house. He was remanded in custody, then released for assessment prior to being sentenced to 6 months detention in a juvenile remand centre. David's sister Peta negotiated to have a conference conducted just prior to the court (sentence) hearing. The conference was not proposed nor intended to have any bearing on the court outcome.

David's reflection David was interviewed on national radio about the conference process. David said;

> I would not even think of spitting on the footpath. I have learnt so much and now I have got a job, I feel that I will never get into trouble again.

When asked, what was the most important thing to come from the conference David said: 'Just understanding how my behaviour affected so many. It is a great process, but a very hard one'.

David's family Life has been difficult with David continually getting into trouble. Nothing made a difference and his family were frustrated, not knowing what to do. For Peta, being a police officer had its own special problems. It seemed that she was not able to influence David. The conference was at least worth a try.

After 3 hours of strong emotional engagements, David and his family felt a great sense of relief. Finally, it appeared that something had worked. David began to understand that his family, apart from being badly hurt, did actually care for him. David's radio interview, which took place approximately 12 months after the conference, allowed David to reflect on where he had come from – quite some distance.

David's many victims   The sense of loss and violation on the victim's part was all too real. The family who were broken into twice by David had since experienced a separation and divorce. For that victim's family, there were so many unresolved emotional issues that it was not surprising to hear the mother (from that family) say with such feeling:

> If I had a piece of "fourbi-two" (timber) I would smash your head in.

All the victims spoke about their sense of loss and grief, and their feelings of "not-being-safe" were very painfully expressed. Towards the end of the conference, the conference dynamics had changed from anger and disgust to interest and hope. Each victim began to describe David as 'not a bad young bloke (person)'. Some were prepared to help David beyond the conference, offering themselves as contact people if David needed someone to talk with.

Beyond David's conference   David spent 6 months in juvenile detention and then began living with his sister Peta. He now is employed in the area of his choosing. The conference was a significant event in David's life. His family have an increased confidence that David will not reoffend. Relationships have generally improved in David's family, and for the victims, the conference gave them an opportunity to be heard and validated. The conference did bring a sense of closure for many who had experienced isolation and disconnection.

Case Study 2: Drink Driving[3]

An early-twenties single mother had been selected for a conference in respect of a "Drive with Prescribed Concentration of Alcohol" offence (drink driving). She attended with her mother and father with whom she resided. She also brought along her boyfriend. There was conflict between the parents and the boyfriend, but inasmuch as the boyfriend sided with her against her parents, he was the only supportive person the young woman saw she had present.

On the evening of the offence, the young man had been engaged in his usual practice, spending the evening at a club drinking with companions. Intoxicated and fearful of being stopped by police for a random breath-test, he had his girlfriend drive him home in his car. Randomly stopped by the police, she was breath-tested and apprehended.

It emerged during the conference that she had her infant child in the car at the time of the offence - of which her parents had been unaware. The parents remonstrated with her: responding angrily to their reaction, she said, 'I didn't tell you, because I knew you would go on at me'.

The young woman was ostensibly an independent adult, yet as her behaviour attested, obviously still cared for her parents' good opinion. That existing relationship was where the conference's emphasis should have been placed. The opportunity of allowing the young woman to observe the effect of her dangerous behaviour on her elderly parents, was largely disregarded.

The admonitory episode began with a video show, a road-safety horror film. To a kid raised on video splatter-flicks, the effect was minimal. There followed a dressing-down from a uniformed ambulance driver who had no direct connection with the offence and who tried to shame and scare the young woman with stories of dead children pulled in pieces from car wrecks. When there are no actual victims, persons such as ambulance drivers, relatives of drunken drivers' victims and representatives of the community in which the offence occurred are often invited to attend a conference. In this instance these persons upbraided the subject for driving whilst intoxicated, and generally deplored this behaviour for the purpose of shaming the subject. There was no part in this punishing activity, other than as passive witnesses, for the subject's intimate group.

The ambulance driver's diatribe, incoherently delivered in one-liners such as, *'If the cops don't get you, we will'*, failed to elicit any response from the angry-faced and intransigent young woman; but then it wasn't an interactive process - it was something that was being done to her. Then we heard from a man in a dark suit who had been sitting quietly - he was revealed to be an undertaker: his sad tale didn't elicit any response from the girl. Then it was the convenor's turn to deplore her behaviour. The approach taken was intended to pierce her only defence – stubbornness - and was aimed at generating a shame response. It was purposive only of her degradation; its effect could only counterproductively have been destructive of any notion of self-worth.

Appreciation of her limited social skills and low levels of intellectual attainment and self-esteem - experienced as the imperfectly-parented daughter of inept parents - a person, also in a harmful relationship with an uncaring and anti-social man - should have precluded her from conferencing. She was not a suitable subject for a simple conference in a family group setting: not suitable without preparatory and supportive activities, that is.

It was then time to decide what penalty the young woman should pay. What about donating a pint of blood to the blood bank? What about two pints of blood?   The young woman reared back and looked fearfully at the ambulance man, as if expecting him to advance on her and extract the penalty on the spot; she regarded the undertaker narrowly.   A penalty was eventually decided upon, without much reference to the young woman.

The punishment-rite was not concluded with an end to the shaming - it remained open-ended and ongoing, and, in respect of her prior experience, probably cumulative.   The acrimonious relationship that existed prior to the conference still remained as the angrily muttering participants left.

Case Study 3: Murder [4]

This conference was conducted by Sergeant Terry O'Connell at the Central Industrial Prison, Malabar, in 1999.   It related to the 1994 murder of a young man, a gratuitous and unprovoked shooting in the course of the armed robbery of a Pizza Hut.   The arrest, trial and subsequent conviction of the four young male offenders - the legal process that is - left a range of unmet needs amongst the deceased youth's workmates, friends, relatives and parents and also among the convicted offenders.   They expressed a need to be understood to each other in ways that had not been possible within the legal system as it is currently constituted.

Two of the four offenders agreed to participate in the conference conducted by Sergeant O'Connell.   Neither of them had possessed firearms but both acknowledged their participation in the crime and their shared culpability with the offender who fired the fatal shot.   They desired too, to acknowledge the harm and pain they had caused and sought an opportunity to express regret and contrition, and to offer apology to the deceased's intimates and parents.

The offenders would gain nothing in way of parole benefits or remission of sentence from their participation - neither did they sensibly expect forgiveness from the deceased's friends or relatives.   What appeared to have been directing the offenders' participation were the more important and as yet unresolved emotions flowing from a finding of guilt in the trial in the court of their own conscience.

On the part of the deceased's parents there was a desire to gain some insight and find answers to some of their questions regarding the seemingly meaningless death of their son.   And whilst the deceased's parents hoped to move from the hopelessness of their current existence, to some hope for the future, there could be no hope for forgiveness from them.   The mother benchmarked her requirement: she would forgive the offenders anything, but only if her son could be restored to life. The father remained furiously angry - an emotion that appears to have largely powered his creation of a victim pressure group following his son's death.

The circle of victims of course, included two intimates of the offenders; the mother of one expressed sorrow for her son's actions and admitted to emotions of guilt, but the deceased's parents immediately reassured her that she should not feel guilty.

Ethical analysis As mentioned above, in our view the kind of conferencing illustrated in the three above case studies is not only a quasi-institutional embodiment of principles of restorative justice, it is in fact the resurrection, or continuation, of that ancient and widely used paradigm of restorative justice mechanisms, namely, the institution of confession.

Confession ideally consists of: (i) voluntary but painful confrontation of an individual with his or her moral failing; (ii) truthful communication/expression of this moral failing to an/other person(s) such as a person's so-called significant others or the rest of the social group; (iii) feelings of shame in respect of those moral failings; (iv) emotional release from the burden of bottled up guilt; (v) resolve or commitment on part of individual to refrain from wrongdoing and to try to make amends for past wrongdoing. Confession presupposes: (i) the existence of social norms which the individual has voluntarily infringed, but which the individual accepts, or can be persuaded to accept; (ii) the moral worth of an individual is something that the individual believes and feels to be very important to him/herself; and (iii) the moral approval of others is very important to the individual. Finally, confession can result in: (i) behavioural change in the light of this moral watershed; moral reaffirmation by the moral community (and perhaps in some cases reintegration of the wrongdoer back into the moral community to which he or she belongs).

If this is what confession consists of, and presupposes, it is easy to see that David's conference (case study 1) is essentially the deployment, albeit in a contemporary secular setting, of the institutional device of confession. It is also clear that the other two case studies are similarly attempts to deploy this device.

In our view the drink driving conference (case study 2) exemplifies some of the dangers inherent in the use of confessional devices. First, there was an ambiguity in the young woman's wrongdoing. After all, she was cajoled into drink driving by her boyfriend in order to protect him. Second, the process was not such as to get any purchase on her own independent moral judgment in relation to her actions. It was rather a heavy handed, and hamfisted, attempt to mobilise social disapproval in order to shame her into submission and confession. Third, there was in fact no commitment on her part to refrain from wrongdoing in the future, and genuinely to try to make amends for her past actions. Fourth, there was no closure in the sense of a negotiated resolution that all parties could live with.

The murder conference (case study 3) exemplifies not so much the dangers, as the limitations of confessional devices. The wrongdoers are sincere in their expressions of remorse and contrition. Some of the family and friends of the victim appear to want restoration. But there is an insurmountable barrier. The victim is dead. The wrongdoing can never be undone. The substantive moral damage can never be repaired. On the other hand, there was a certain restoration of the moral relationship between the victim's family and friends on the one hand, and the offender's mother on the other. And perhaps some of the offenders and some of the loved ones of the victim found some kind of peace that they did not have before.

We can conclude that confession has proved to be a powerful device for moral transformation and reconciliation with victims in many different times, places and contexts, including criminal justice contexts. However, it is a device which has important limitations and can be misused. Accordingly, even if restorative justice and its associated institutional mechanisms are as successful as their proponents claim, there are some important qualifying and somewhat deflationary points that need to be made concerning confessional devices in particular.

First, confession can be used, and simply deployed as a mechanism for social control by those who happen to be in charge of the processes. Indeed, historically, confession has often failed, been misused and at times served grossly immoral purposes. Consider the Soviet communist show trials of the 1930s or the Chinese Peoples' Courts of the Cultural Revolution. Confession can simply be an exercise in social control for its own sake, and have as its main effect the destruction of the moral autonomy of the individual. Accordingly, the use of confessional devices cannot be given a general endorsement either in non-religious, non-political restorative justice settings or elsewhere.

Second, and relatedly, restorative justice mechanisms should involve moral reflection and moral judgment making – we don't mean judgmentalism – directed to the truth; they ought not simply be the occasions for socially imposed, uncritical triggering of emotions such as shame, emotions that have been unhinged from cognitive states grounded in moral reality, or even moral reflection.

Third, restorative justice mechanisms might have problems in relation to crimes in which the victim does not exist or exists only in a diffuse form. For example, in the case of murder, the victim has ceased to exist; so in what sense can any important moral relationships be restored? Again, in the case of many crimes, such as fraud, the victim is a corporation or government organisation or – in the case of tax fraud and drink driving – the community as a whole. Accordingly, there is no specific human victim who can confront the offender, and no easily identifiable moral relationship that can be restored, other than perhaps tangential relationships, such as those with loved ones.

It might be replied that in the above sorts of cases it is the moral relationship of the offender to the community at large that is at issue, and this can be restored by, for example, having community representatives (in the case of drink driving and tax evasion). Unfortunately, as our second case study illustrates, the presence of such representatives does not seem to generate the requisite moral emotion; and for the good reason that they are only victims in an attenuated sense. On the other hand, in so far as compensation can be paid, and the community is accepting of that as a morally adequate response, then reintegration may well be possible. However, such a process of reintegration is based on paying one's dues – hardly a notion exclusive to restorative justice.

Restorative Justice and Retributive Justice

As has already been mentioned, among the proponents of restorative justice there is a strong tendency to contrast restorative justice and retributivism, and to disparage the latter and strongly recommend the former. This recommendation is often based on the following two claims. First, it is claimed that retributivist, but not restorative conceptions, are punitive. Second, it is claimed that the restorative justice program, unlike the retributivist criminal justice system, emphasises informal processes that place the moral relationship between the victim and the offender at the centre of the stage. By contrast, the retributivist system involves a formal process of applying abstract principles of justice by state functionaries to offenders. The victim has no part to play. Let us first respond to the latter claim by first reminding ourselves of the fundamental role the criminal justice system is at least supposed to have.

The criminal justice system ought to buttress and enforce social norms. Social norms are a society's accepted moral principles. As such, social norms are fundamental to social life. Thus social norms against random killing enable cooperative economic and family institutions. Moreover, social norms are in large part enshrined in the criminal law or its equivalents. Theft, assault, murder, rape, child molestation, fraud, and so on are actions which violate social norms in contemporary societies, and they are also criminal acts. Indeed it is because they are held to be profoundly morally wrong that perpetrators of these acts are held criminally liable. Moreover, some of these actions are regarded as morally worse than others (e.g. murder is morally worse than theft). Accordingly, the punishment meted out for murder is in general greater than for theft. In short, the criminal law is essentially a formalisation, regimentation and attempted objectification of society's most basic moral principles. Individuals can afford to disagree about, and indeed infringe with impunity, many moral principles; but not those moral principles enshrined in the criminal law. In effect, these moral principles are agreed by the society to be objectively valid. Moreover, these moral principles include not only prohibitions against specific forms of behaviour, but also moral principles in relation to moral responsibility and punishment. For example, the principle that moral responsibility consists in part in having an intention to commit a wrong or the principle that only those who are responsible for crimes should be punished and that the wrongdoer should be the one to pay compensation.

So criminal justice systems have developed complex sets of moral principles of the kind described above over long periods of time. Some of these principles are doubtless questionable or imperfectly applied. Moreover, there may well be a need to make greater use of informal processes, and to give victims a greater role in both formal and informal processes. However, the point we want to stress here is that any system of justice – whether based on principles or restorative justice, retributivist justice or some other conception – that has pretensions to substantially replace existing systems would also need to provide its own complex set of principles. Having an array of processes is hardly sufficient. In short, the so-called restorative justice paradigm is in its theoretical and institutional infancy; or at least it is in such infancy if it sees itself as something more than simply a set of ancillary institutional processes to be grafted on to the existing system.

Let us turn to punishment. Restorative justice is often contrasted with retributive justice, on the grounds that the latter is held to be committed to punishment for its own sake, the former to abandoning punishment in favour of shame, reconciliation and forgiveness. We will argue that there is an ineliminable role for principles of retributive justice, including punishment, in the concept of restorative justice. We will further argue that the concept of shame is more closely related to punishment than might have been thought. Consequently, shame and punishment are not alternatives, but go hand in hand within an acceptable restorative justice framework.

Let us first introduce some distinctions. First, there is the suffering in the form of painful feelings of shame experienced by an offender who undergoes a restorative justice process. Secondly, there is the restitution that an offender might be called upon to provide to his victim (e.g. return stolen goods). This is a burden imposed on the offenders; it is not simply restoring the victims' prior circumstances by some third party (e.g. the taxpayer). Third, there is the compensation that might be paid by the offender to the victim to make up for the harm done (e.g. the psychological suffering inflicted by the knowledge that one had had one's goods stolen, or the loss of not being able to use the stolen item for a period). Again this is a burden imposed on the offender, and is a burden above and beyond that comprising the restitution. Fourth, there is the punishment that might be imposed on the offender for his wrongdoing. By punishment it is not here meant simply restitution or compensation. For example, a thief might not only need to pay back the money he/she stole (restitution) and make some further payment for the harm done to the victim (compensation); he/she might also need to be punished for doing wrong.

Armed with this fourfold distinction, let us consider suffering in relation to confession. Confession necessarily involves suffering on the part of the confessor – minimally it involves the painful feelings of shame generated by his own as well as others' knowledge of his wrongdoing. So punishment, at least in the sense of painful feelings, is part and parcel of the restorative justice process, including in the case of confession. Part of the point of confession is to get wrongdoers to confront the fact of their wrongdoing, and that is necessarily a painful process.

Moreover, a wrongdoer accepts the community's principles of justice in relation to restitution, compensation and punishment. Accordingly, a wrongdoer will typically accept the proposition that he or she – rather than some third party, such as the taxpayer – ought to provide restitution and compensation. Accordingly, restorative justice entails the imposition of burdens on the guilty above and beyond the suffering associated with shame. To this extent it embraces a retributivist principle.

But what of punishment, as distinct from the suffering of shame or the burdens of restitution and compensation? If punishment is an accepted moral principle in the community then the wrongdoer will also accept that he or she should be punished. But this still leaves the question of whether punishment should in fact be inflicted. Here there are two questions that need to be kept separate. These are: whether the guilty should suffer and/or be made to redress the results of their wrongdoing?; if the guilty should suffer, who should inflict the suffering? In general suffering is a bad thing to be avoided and not to be inflicted on oneself or others. But we have already seen that the suffering of the guilty is justifiable - indeed mandatory - within a restorative justice framework, to the extent that it is involved in the shaming process and involved in restitution and compensation. But could there be a justification for some further infliction of suffering, namely, punishment for doing wrong? Suppose a man is hell bent on making his wife suffer, say by continually beating her up. For her part she is an innocent victim. A court case ensues and he is found guilty. He is very wealthy and able to pay an amount to her by way of restitution and compensation. The wife's physical health returns, and she is no longer fearful of him since they divorce, go their separate ways and the magistrate's threat to lock him up next time deters him from any further actions. However, he has gone unpunished. For the money he paid to her was of no great consequence to him, given his wealth. Nor does he accept that he has done anything wrong. As far as he is concerned, he would cheerfully do exactly as he did, given the same circumstances. After all, it gave him a certain amount of pleasure to be able to dominate and inflict suffering on his wife. More specifically, if the wife-beater is to be reintegrated into the community, could this be done without some form of punishment? Here, Hegel (1942), Simone Weil (1952), Reinhold Niebuhr (1986), and more recently, Eric Reitan (1996) and Charles Barton (1999) are instructive.

What this kind of case serves to illustrate is what might be called the moral bond between individuals.   After all, morality is predominantly concerned with interpersonal relationships, including relationships to strangers as well as to the members of one's family and immediate community.   Offenders breach these moral bonds.   On a reintegrative theory, some form of punishment is necessary for the purposes of reintegration, and it is necessary for reintegration by virtue of the fact that the punishment (a) 'washes away the stigma of the crime' (Niebuhr, 1986: 29) that is a barrier to restoration of moral bonds, and (b) educates the moral judgment of the criminal so that he conforms to the requisite moral principles. In the case of our example it is hard to see how either of these two goals could be achieved in the absence of any punishment.

An important additional point to be made here, is that, as Niebuhr puts it, the punishment should not belittle or degrade, but rather inspire repentance and reintegration (Niebuhr, 1986: 29).   Accordingly, it should accord with reasonable moral principles that the offender could come to accept as reasonable and just, and ideally actually consent to. This leads to the question as to what precise form such punishment should take. It could certainly be argued that imprisonment is not the best form of punishment for many, if not most, crimes.   But this important issue is beyond the scope of this paper.

Notes

1   This is not a sui generis consequentialist principle though consequentialists might think that they can derive it from their favoured consequentialist principle in conjunction with certain contingent empirical facts.

2   This case study is from Terry O'Connell (1995).

3   This account was written by John Blackler and based upon an actual conference that he attended.

4   The conference was recorded on film by Dee Cameron and presented to the Restorative Justice and Civil Society conference at the Australian National University, Canberra, on February 17th 1999.

References

Barton, C. (1999), *Getting Even: Revenge as a Form of Justice*, Open Court Publishing Company, La Salle, Illinois.

Braithwaite, J. (1986), *Crime, Shame and Reintegration*, Oxford University Press, Melbourne.

Braithwaite, J. and Pettit, P. (1990), *Not Just Deserts: A Republican Theory of Criminal Justice*, Clarendon Press, Oxford.

Hegel, G. W. F., trans. Knox, T. (1942), *The Philosophy of Right*, Oxford University Press, Oxford.

Hepworth, M. and Turner, B. S. (1982), *Confession: Studies in Deviance and Religion*, Routledge and Kegan Paul, London.

Moore, D. (1995), *A New Approach to Juvenile Justice: An Evaluation of Family Conferencing in Wagga Wagga*, Report to the Criminology Research Council, Canberra.

Niebuhr, R. (1986), 'God's Justice and Mercy', in R. M. Brown (ed.), *The Essential Reinhold Niebuhr*, Yale University Press, New Haven.

O'Connell, T. (1997), 'Dawn or Dusk in Sentencing', unpublished paper delivered at CIAJ National Conference in Montreal, Canada.

Reitan, E. (1996), 'Punishment and Community: The Reintegrative Theory of Punishment', *Canadian Journal of Philosophy*, vol. 26, no. 1, pp. 57-82.

Ten, C. L. (1987), *Guilt and Punishment*, Clarendon Press, Oxford.

Weil, S. (1952), 'The Needs of the Soul', in *The Needs for Roots*, Putnam's Sons, New York.

6 Restorative Justice and Reoffending[1]

GABRIELLE MAXWELL AND ALLISON MORRIS

Introduction

There is now a considerable amount of research which has explored the factors linked to reoffending. Many of these are similar to the findings of research on the onset of offending: in particular, the importance of factors relating to early childhood, family and education has been stressed (see, for example, Fergusson et al., 1992 and 1998; Farrington, 1994, Graham and Bowling, 1995; Hawkins et al., 1998; Lipsey and Derzon, 1998). There is also now a considerable amount of research which has explored "what works" in terms of interventions aimed at preventing reoffending (see, for example, Utting, 1996; Loeber and Farrington, 1998; Sherman et al., 1998; Sherman, 1999). And there is some research on the potential effects on reoffending of subsequent life events such as establishing relationships, finding employment, and having a stake in life (see, for example, Farrington, 1994; Moffittat and Harrington, 1996). There has, however, been remarkably little research on the impact of processes on reoffending or the extent to which these may minimise the adverse effects of previous negative factors in the offender's life experience.

The explicit objective of this research, therefore, was to assess whether or not processes can impact on reoffending. In particular, the research aimed at investigating the potential effects of conferencing on reoffending by examining what distinguished the non-convicted from the persistent reconvicted in a sample of New Zealand young people who had experienced a family group conference in 1990/91. Conferencing is now commonly viewed as an example of restorative justice in practice. The critical elements they share are a meeting between all those involved in the offence (victim/s, offender/s, families, friends and significant others), the participation of all those involved in a search for a way of resolving the harm that has been done, acknowledgment by those responsible for the harm caused by their role in the offence, attempts to make amends for the harm done, and attempts to increase the chances of the reintegration of victims and offenders into the community by restoring connectedness (cf. Walgrave, 1998, Van Ness and Strong, 1997 and Zehr, 1990). Therefore, this research offered the opportunity to examine the potential impact of restorative processes on preventing reoffending and encouraging reintegration.

The Model and the Method

We have previously reported (Morris and Maxwell, 1996) on the conviction records of a number of young people who were first contacted in 1991 as part of our research on youth justice in New Zealand (Maxwell and Morris, 1993). This paper relied on the limited data on offending obtainable from police files together with the data on the family group conference process obtained in 1990 and 1991.

The next stage of our research was to contact these young people and their families to see where their lives had got to some six years on and to collect further data from them. We were able to interview 108 of those who had had family group conferences and 98 family members. Overall, we were able to collect information on 72% of the young people in the original sample by interviewing either them or a family member. Throughout the rest of this paper, this group are referred to as "young people" to distinguish them from their parents. However, it is important to remember that they were young adults aged 20-24 at the time that the interviews were carried out.

In developing our interviews we were guided by previous literature on factors associated with offending and reoffending. We organised these variables into a model that is set out in Figure 6.1.

Reconviction Pattern

The above model is organised around four main groups of variables: those that relate to early life experiences, those that relate to youth justice processes, those related to the provision of effective programs, and subsequent life events. Our data throw light on some aspects of three of these factors: early life experiences, youth justice processes, in particular the impact of the family group conference, and subsequent life events. Together we propose that these variables will predict ultimate outcomes that include the probability of life events and the way the young person feels about his or her life.

We were not able to assess the impact of effective programs because of the limited provision of rehabilitative services to the sample but it is important to bear in mind that they too may be a crucial variable affecting the probability of reoffending. Nor were we able to explore the differences between penal and community sanctions because penal sanctions were so rarely imposed in the youth justice system.

In the six and a half years since the family group conference that led to the young people coming into our sample, 29% had not been reconvicted and a similar proportion, 28%, were persistently reconvicted.

Figure 6.1: Proposed Model for Understanding Reoffending

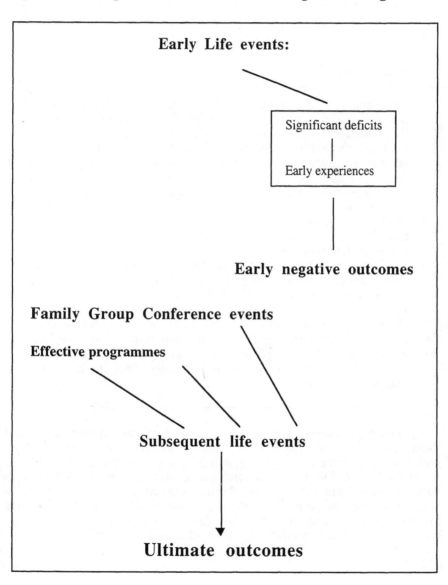

The remaining 43% had been convicted at least once but their offending was less serious, less frequent and less persistent. This latter group were sub-classified into those who offended once only - 'once only reconvicted', those who appeared to be similar in offence pattern, to the persistently reconvicted for the first four years after their family group conference but who had not offended in the last two years - 'improving reconvicted', and the remainder - 'other reconvicted'. The definition of the reconviction categories is set out below.

Definitions of Reconviction Categories:

* *the persistent reconvicted (PR)* were characterised by the frequency and volume of their offending in criminal matters; they were defined as having appeared in court on criminal matters (excluding breaches of orders) on five or more occasions or, where they were eligible to reoffend for less than four years (because of a period of custody) as having appeared on at least three occasions and/or as having been convicted of five or more offences;
* *the improving reconvicted (IR)* had offended persistently for a time but had not been reconvicted in the 12 months prior to our interview with them;
* *the occasional reconvicted (OR)* had appeared in court more than once but had committed less than five offences;
* *the once only reconvicted (OOR)* had appeared in court and been convicted on one occasion only; and
* *the not reconvicted (NR)* included all those for whom no court conviction had been registered, although some may have been dealt with through police warnings, police diversion or appeared in court and been subsequently discharged or had charges withdrawn.

The possibility of unreported reoffending was considered and all those interviewed were asked if they had committed any offences which had not been detected since the family group conference. However, when we looked for possible anomalies in our categorisation that may have resulted from offences not being detected or not resulting in a conviction, we did not find anything sufficiently critical to justify altering the classification. Thus, we can conclude that the reconviction category proved a good indicator of reoffending.

Method of Determining Predictive Factors

The answers to questions asked in the interview that were likely to be predictive of reconviction pattern were identified by examining the differences in the probability of a reply between the three main groups: the persistently reconvicted, the not reconvicted and the remainder. However, there were large numbers of these items and many seemed likely to be correlated. Thus, the next step in the analysis was to identify the clusters of items that were interrelated and to obtain scores on each of these clusters. The strategy used to do this was, after inspecting the results of several different multivariate clustering techniques, to select variables that were statistically and conceptually related. Some items did not go together statistically but were conceptually linked and these were grouped where there was other criminological research to support this (Maxwell and Morris, 1999).

Once the data set was reduced to a manageable number of new variables that appeared to be both conceptually and statistically meaningful, canonical discriminant analyses were carried out (SAS Institute, 1990: Ch. 16). This statistical technique aims to identify variables that discriminate between a number of different groups - in this case the reconviction groups. It also provides information on the relative importance of the variables in discriminating between groups and it describes how many of the sample are successfully reclassified into their original group by using the statistical predictors that have been identified.

Discriminant analyses were performed separately for the variables derived from interviews with young people (84 cases) and for the variables derived from interviews with the parents (88 cases). Finally, an analysis was performed that examined the effect of combining the parent and young person variables for the 71 cases where both sets of data were available.

Results

The results for the parent data set showed that one major statistical factor emerged that explained just under half the variance between the groups. A better fit came from the analysis based on the interviews with the young people. Here two factors emerged that accounted for nearly 70% of the between group variance. When data from both the parent and young persons' replies was combined, 90% of the between group variance could be explained by two factors (Maxwell and Morris, 1999: 54).

A plot of the young persons' data from the canonical correlations demonstrated that the five reconviction categories had been clearly distinguished from one another. The degree of differentiation achieved was surprising given the difficulties of sample size and the reliance we had to place on variables that were often simplified estimates and often confounded with one another.

These findings mean that predicting reconviction is possible. It can be done using data from parents but is more effective when information is obtained from young people and most effective of all when information is obtained from both sources. The important variables that emerge from the analyses are described below.

Early Experiences Predictive of Reconviction

From parents:
- being a problem child: difficult, in trouble, bored, running away;
- the child not having an effective relationship with their father;
- a lack of support for the parent/s while the children were young.

From young people:
- early anti-social behaviour;
- early involvement in drug and substance use;
- having poor relationships with family while growing up;
- early offending and involvement with the law;
- offending being motivated by rebellion;
- a lack of school qualifications;
- not doing well at school;
- truanting, being suspended and expelled from school;
- transience: having many homes and schools;
- psychological problems;
- not being involved in sports and good at them;
- being a victim of bullying.

From both:
- family violence and harsh physical punishment;
- having a poor relationship with parent/s while growing up;
- parental problems: not enough money, crime, alcohol and drugs;
- a lack of parental supervision;
- being bored and hanging around in his/her spare time;
- a lack of cultural pride and knowledge.

Early Childhood Experiences

A number of clusters of variables have been identified around early life experiences. Those clusters that were most predictive of the difference between not being reconvicted and being persistently reconvicted and which seemed to us to be the most interesting are listed below. The descriptions are phrased to indicate the pattern most characteristic of the 'persistently reconvicted' group and least characteristic of those 'not reconvicted'. Some of the factors could be conceptualised as risk factors, for example being a problem child, early anti-social behaviour and family violence. Others can be seen as protective factors such as having effective family relationships, doing well at school and being adequately supervised by parents while growing up. The importance of these factors as predictors of offending and reoffending has previously been demonstrated by other researchers (Farrington, 1994; Moffitt and Harrington, 1996).

The Impact of the Family Group Conference

We asked a number of questions about the family group conference. These included whether or not young people and parents agreed with the decisions and felt involved in the process, whether or not remorse and shame were felt, and whether or not tasks were completed. Significant items are shown below.

Conference Events Predictive of Reconviction

From parents:
• lack of remorse - not feeling your son/daughter was sorry;
• shame: being made to feel a bad parent;
• not a fair outcome and did not agree with it.

From young people:
• not agreeing with the conference outcome;
• lack of remorse: not remembering the conference, not completing tasks, not feeling sorry and showing it and not feeling they had repaired the damage;
• shame: being made to feel a bad person;
• not feeling involved in FGC decision-making.

The findings presented in the above box are consistent with restorative justice theory which emphasises the importance of repairing the harm to victims (Zehr, 1990; Van Ness and Strong, 1997). They are also consistent with Braithwaite's (1989) notion of the importance of reintegration and the potential harm that can result from stigmatic shaming. It could be suggested that our finding of the importance of remorse may provide support for the value of what Braithwaite calls 'reintegrative shaming'. However, we would suggest that further research and debate is necessary to determine whether or not the use of shame in conferencing can ever be regarded as a necessary component in inducing remorse or preventing reoffending.

Perhaps the most exciting result from this study is the evidence that successful family group conferences can have an impact on future offending behaviour. We have identified here the critical variables that make for success, namely that the conference was a memorable event, that it evoked remorse and that it led to the young person attempting to make amends for what he/she had done.

Events after the Family Group Conference

A number of subsequent life experiences also showed a significant relationship with whether the person was classified in the persistently reconvicted category or whether they were not reconvicted. These are listed below. These findings are consistent with theories which emphasise the importance of close relationships and a meaningful role in life as critical to subjective wellbeing (Andrews and Withey, 1976; Campbell, Converse and Rogers, 1976).

Subsequent Events Predictive of Reconviction

From parents:
- a poor relationship with the young person.

From young people:
- not feeling good: things have not gone well, not feeling good about self;
- having criminal associates;
- not being close to other people;
- not having a partner;
- an unstable life style: living in many different places;
- not having training or having got a job;
- not having someone close getting sick or dying.

Conclusion

It would be desirable to carry out more detailed multivariate analyses of recent events together with early life events and family group conference factors. It is important to tease out what happens over time - we would like to be able to make some statements about if *x* happens then *y* is more likely but if *z* occurs, it is less likely. However, there are limits to what can be concluded from a study with a relatively small sample size.

Nevertheless, the analysis so far supports the view that reconviction is not an outcome that is simply determined by early life events. What happens at the family group conference can be critical. And so too are the events that happen after the family group conference.

There are important messages from these findings for the youth justice system. The first is that, as shown in other research, prevention of offending by successful early intervention is likely to be the most effective strategy. The second is that it is unrealistic to expect the youth justice system to be able to prevent all reoffending because both early life events and subsequent life events have a powerful impact. The third is that simply holding a family group conference is not enough - there are a number of critical elements that have to be present if the family group conference is going to make a difference to the probability of offending in the future and these are:

- seeming fair to the parents and involving young people in the process and in the decisions;
- avoiding leaving parents and young people feeling bad about themselves; and, above all,
- achieving a process that increases the chance that the young person will feel truly sorry for what they have done, show their remorse to the victim and make amends for what has happened.

Finally, one other set of potential outcomes of the family group conference may also be critical. This is whether or not measures are put in place to help the young person acquire skills or to remedy deficiencies such as psychological problems, drug and alcohol abuse and learning deficits. Previous research (Utting, 1996; Lipsey and Darzon, 1998; Sherman, 1997; Loeber and Farrington, 1998) has demonstrated that effective programs can reduce reoffending. A number of characteristics of effective programs have already been identified by these studies. For example, Andrews (1999) shows that programs for young people are likely to be effective in reducing offending if the young people are at *risk* as indicated by their involvement in offending; if the programs address *criminogenic needs* such as alcohol and drug use, anger and aggression and so on; if the programs are *responsive* to the particular populations for whom they are offered and are provided in *community* settings rather than custodial institutions (Andrews, 1999).

In conclusion, this study demonstrates that not only do past experiences and post-offence experiences affect the probability of reoffending but so too does the nature of the processes put in place by the criminal justice system. Restorative approaches can make a difference.

Note

1   An earlier version of this paper was presented at the Youth Justice in Focus conference in Wellington, October, 1998 and was published in the proceedings of that conference. For a more detailed statistical analysis of the results discussed here see Maxwell and Morris, 1999.

References

Andrews, D. A. (1999), 'What Works in Young Offender Treatment: A Meta-analysis', Forum on Corrections Research.

Andrews, F. M. and Withey, S. B. (1976), *Social Indicators of Wellbeing*, Plenum, New York.

Braithwaite, J. (1989), *Crime, Shame and Reintegration*, Cambridge University Press, Cambridge.

Campbell, A, Converse, P. E., and Rodgers, W. L. (1976), *The Quality of American Life*, Russell Sage, New York.

Farrington, D. P. (1994), 'Human Development and Criminal Careers', in M. Maguire, R. Morgan and R. Reiner (eds), *Oxford Handbook of Criminology*, Oxford University Press, Oxford.

Fergusson, D. M., Horwood, J. L. and Lynskey, M. T. (1992), 'The Childhoods of Multiple Problem Adolescents: A 15 Year Longitudinal Study', *Journal of Child Psychology and Psychiatry*, vol. 35, pp. 1365-74.

Fergusson, D. (1998), 'The Christchurch Health and Development Study: An Overview and Some Key Findings', *Social Policy Journal of New Zealand*, vol. 10, pp. 154-76.

Graham, J. and Bowling, B. (1995), *Young People and Crime*, Home Office Research Study 145, Home Office, London.

Hawkins, D. et al. (1998), 'A Review of Predictors of Youth Violence', in R. Loeber and D. Farrington (eds), *Serious and Violent Juvenile Offenders: Risk Factors and Successful Interventions*, Sage, London.

Levine, M., Eagle, A., Tuiavi'i, S. and Roseveare, C. (1998), *Creative Youth Justice Practice*, Social Policy Agency and Children, Young Persons and Their Families Service, Wellington.

Lipsey, M. and Derzon, J. (1998), 'Predictors of Violent or Serious Delinquency in Adolescence and Early Adulthood', in R. Loeber and D. Farrington (eds), *Serious and Violent Juvenile Offenders: Risk Factors and Successful Interventions*, Sage, California.

Loeber, R. and Farrington, D. (1998), *Serious and Violent Juvenile Offenders: Risk Factors and Successful Interventions*, Sage, California.

Maxwell, G. M. and Morris, A. (1993), *Families, Victims and Culture: Youth Justice in New Zealand*, Social Policy Agency and Institute of Criminology, Victoria University of Wellington, Wellington.

Maxwell, G. M. and Morris, A. (1999), *Understanding Reoffending: Full Report*, Institute of Criminology, Victoria University of Wellington, Wellington.

Moffitt, T. E. and Harrington, H. L. (1996), 'Delinquency: The Natural History of Antisocial Behaviour', in P. A. Silva and W. R. Stanton (eds), *From Child to Adult: The Dunedin Multidisciplinary Health and Development Study*, Oxford University Press, Wellington.

Morris, A., Maxwell, G. M. and Robertson, J. P. (1993), 'Giving Victims a Voice: A New Zealand Experiment', *The Howard Journal*, vol. 32, pp. 304-21.

Morris, A. and Maxwell, G. M. (1997), 'Family Group Conferences and Convictions', *Occasional Paper No 5*, Institute of Criminology, Victoria University of Wellington, Wellington.

SAS Institute (1990), *SAS/STAT User's Guide, Version 6*, fourth edition: vols 1 and 2, SAS Institute, Cary, NC, USA.

Sherman, L., Gottfredson, D., Mackenzie, D., Eck, J., Reuter, P. and Bushway, S. (1997), *Preventing Crime: What Works, What Doesn't, What's Promising*, Department of Criminology and Criminal Justice, University of Maryland, Baltimore.

Utting, D. (1996), 'Reducing Criminality among Young People: A Sample of Relevant Programmes in the United Kingdom', *Home Office Research Study 161*, Home Office, London.

Walgrave, L. (1998), 'Restorative Justice for Juveniles: Potentialities, Risks and Problems for Research. A Selection of Papers Presented at the International Conference, Leuven, 1997', Leuven University Press, Belgium.

Van Ness, D. and Strong, K. H. (1997), *Restoring Justice*, Anderson Publishing Company, Cincinatti.

Zehr, H. (1990), *Changing Lenses: A New Focus for Crime and Justice*, Herald Press, Scottdale, PA.

7 Young Women Offenders and the Challenge for Restorative Justice

CHRISTINE ALDER

Like many discussions of youth policy and juvenile justice, most of the literature thus far on restorative justice in this area assumes a generic rather than a gendered youth population: young women are virtually invisible. The failure to consider gender implies an assumption that the outcomes and the processes will be the same for boys and girls. At this point there is no research that allows examination of this assumption. Nevertheless, a co-ordinator of family conferencing in South Australia, has noted that, 'conferencing with young women does raise many ethical, political and social considerations which differ from those which may arise when dealing with other ... youths' (Jan Kitcher in Baines, 1996: 43).

Some consideration has been given to the appropriateness of the use of conferencing in cases in which women or girls are victims of violence (Stubbs, 1995, 1997; Hudson, 1998). While some of the issues raised in these discussions are pertinent, the focus of this chapter is identification of issues that need to be considered when young women are in conferences as "offenders" rather than as "victims". In this chapter I draw on research on girls' experiences of juvenile justice more generally to suggest that there are issues that need to be acknowledged and addressed if the promises of restorative justice are to hold true for girls. Conferences, while not the only form of restorative justice, are the most widely implemented form in juvenile justice in Australia and therefore are the focus of much of this discussion.

Although it is hard to establish a definitive set of principles which defines "restorative justice" (Daly, 1998), some of the more frequently stated objectives present potential improvements over current juvenile justice practice for young women offenders. A first potential benefit is the meaningful involvement of young women offenders in the decision-making process. In relation to programs and policies more broadly, the National Council for Research on Women in the United States (Phillips, 1998) recommends that 'girls' collaboration is solicited in authentic and meaningful ways, through involvement in the design and implementation of programs...'. Certainly research with young women in the juvenile justice system in Australia indicates that more meaningful involvement in the making of decisions about their lives is of significant concern to girls (Community Services, Victoria, 1992; Alder and Hunter, 1999; Department of Youth and Community Care, 1999).

An indication that conferencing might constitute such an arena for young women in juvenile justice is provided by the observations of those involved in conferencing in Victoria. Drawing on their experiences, Mark Griffith and Sharon Williams suggest that conferencing can be empowering for girls in that it enables them to contribute in more meaningful ways than court procedure in the sentencing plan (Baines, 1996). In research on young women's juvenile justice experiences in South Australia (Alder and Hunter, 1999), only one of the young women interviewed had been involved in a conference, and she commented:

> Yes my family came to it and all the people that my family are involved in came too, to talk about the stuff that was going to happen and I was able to help decide what was going to happen with me. They didn't just say, well, your going to [detention] for 12 months for property damage. They said "What do you think should happen?" and I told them what I thought should happen and my mum and that said they think that's fair and I thought that was really good. They respected your opinion like what you thought should happened. And what I said happened, which I thought was really good.

Consistent with this comment, in Adelaide, Jan Kitcher (in Baines, 1996) similarly found that co-ordinators uniformly felt that girls were able to express their feelings in conferences, and in fact observed that they were more eloquent than the boys. An indication of this was the observation that girls were more likely to argue about the outcome.

In their recommendations for programs and services for girls the National Council for Research on Women in the United States (Phillips, 1998) notes further that 'Partnerships among family, schools, community programs, and cultural organisations can provide opportunities for girls, and let them know that they are valued community members'. Potentially, conferencing with young women offenders might provide a mechanism for the involvement of a range of community agencies and services, outside of juvenile justice, in the establishment of new opportunities for these young women.

Young women who have committed a criminal offence find themselves particularly stigmatised in a culture in which being "bad" is inconsistent with expectations of femininity in a way that it is not necessarily inconsistent with understandings of masculinity for young male offenders. It is perhaps not surprising therefore, that young women in the juvenile justice system are particularly concerned that they are treated with respect and dignity (Alder and Hunter, 1999). The principles of restorative justice which espouse maintenance of the integrity and dignity of the offender are therefore of interest to those of us concerned about the well being of young women in the juvenile justice system.

While the principles of restorative justice hold some promise for young women offenders, I want to turn in the rest of the chapter to consider research on young women in the juvenile justice system which presents a number of concerns and issues that need to be acknowledged and considered. The first concern has to do with community values, expectations and understandings about girlhood and their implications for decision-making in relation to girls' behaviour. A second set of observations relate to girls' experiences of juvenile justice. Finally, there is a growing body of research on the perceived difficulties of working with girls.

Community Values and Expectations

Traditionally juvenile justice system responses to young women have been significantly influenced by members of the community other than juvenile justice personnel, in particular their family, teachers, social workers, and neighbours (Carrington, 1993; Gelsthorpe, 1986). Consistently, research in the United States, Britain and Australia has shown that decisions in relation to young women taken by all these parties have reflected concerns about girls' sexuality and their independence - their 'passionate and wilful' behaviour (Alder, 1998; Hudson, 1984). As a consequence, research through the 1970s and 1980s showed that young women in juvenile justice were often the subjects of more prolonged and intrusive interventions than boys (Chesney-Lind and Sheldon, 1992).

Although various reforms attempted to address this situation, for example, the deinstitutionalisation of status offenders legislation in the United States, more recent research suggests that in numerous ways the intent of such reforms is being circumvented (see Chesney-Lind and Joe, 1996; Poe-Yamagata and Butts, 1996). It would appear that community expectations in relation to the behaviour of young women and a willingness to use intrusive, coercive forms of control to enforce those expectations, is not easily curbed.

Given the breadth of feminist research documenting the extent to which girls' behaviour is judged, controlled and disciplined informally

(Heidensohn, 1985), we cannot assume that informal processing will necessarily be benign or neutral. Noting the extent of the literature on gender bias in courts and legal practice, Bargen and Stubbs (in Baines, 1996) argue we should be wary of assuming that informal processes are any less likely to judge the girls' behaviour according to limited visions of what is appropriate behaviour for girls. Stubbs (in Baines 1996) notes that alternatives may simply reproduce such practices in the absence of the checks and balances of the formal court system such as public records and the prospect of appeal (Warner, 1994).

Community understandings of gender appropriate behaviour and appropriate response can be expected to affect not only the decision-making process, but also the outcomes of any such decision-making. Restorative justice might be about reintegrating the offender into the community, but it is not always the most welcoming of young women offenders.

People attempting community integration projects for girls have indicated that community attitudes and responses present them with some of their greatest difficulties. In commenting on the early days of Family Group Conferencing in South Australia, a co-ordinator, Jan Kitcher noted that 'different standards of behaviour for girls and boys still exist' and that girls themselves believed that it was 'worse for a girl to commit an offence than a boy' (Kitcher in Baines, 1996). Also in South Australia, the coordinator of a community work program, noting the difficulties her program had in placing young women, commented, 'Young women referred with community service orders are often stigmatised in the community as being "very bad".... there is greater acceptance in the community of offending by young males'. She found that workers needed to undertake more intensive networking to gain relevant and appropriate work opportunities for young women (Althorpe, 1996: 68).

Community understandings and reactions to them are not trifling matters for young women trying to establish themselves in a community. Negative interactions with those in the community setting in which they have been placed may significantly affect the young woman's successful completion of community based activities. In Queensland girls are twice as likely to be breached for non-compliance with the conditions of a community service order (Beikoff, 1996: 20). Also, in the United States a higher proportion of girls than boys are institutionalised for justice violations including parole and probation violations (Poe-Yamagata and Butts, 1996).

In summary, what little evidence we have about women serving community based orders suggests that they have difficulty successfully completing such orders. While at this point there is little research to draw upon to help us understand this situation, it does suggest that we have to think carefully about the form and nature of the expectations we place upon young women offenders in the community. It is probably the case that the placement of offending girls in the community will require considerable effort be undertaken to prepare not only the young woman concerned, but also the setting, including others with whom she will be working.

Again it is potentially the case that the very process of conferencing, if it were to involve a range of supportive individuals from the community, could by its very nature begin to address negative community attitudes towards young women offenders. However, unless this issue is first acknowledged, it cannot be addressed and thought will not be given to how community integration can best be accomplished for young women.

Considering Girls' Experiences

Girls' offending is less accepted by the community and by both their male and female peers, than it is for boys. Thus for girls, their offending challenges their status and value as a "woman", and thereby has significant negative implications for their sense of identity and self-worth. This has consequences for girls' expectations of others' reactions to them and girls' reactions to others' understandings and expectations of them. The implications of these need to be considered in the development of programs for offending girls.

Shame and Self-Harm

In part as a consequence of the expectation of strong negative reactions to their behaviour, and also because of a tendency for young women to self-blame, some girls feel guilt and "shame" about their actions in a way that makes it difficult for them to talk about their offending. Some conferences require not only that the offender talks about their offending, but that they acknowledge "shame" and contrition. Danny Sandor questions processes that entail young women publicly confronting or acknowledging their guilt, and in particular those processes that intend the young person to experience "shame". In relation to conferences, he comments:

> In a culture where shame has been a powerful tool of domestic control over women, this assumed pathway to reintegration has to be questioned. We know for example that self harm rather than violence towards others is a particularly likely response to emotional pain and frustration among young

women and any assessment of how conferences work need to consider this gender difference (Sandor in Baines, 1996: 45).

For some girls, there may be a delicate balance between exhibiting contrition and remorse, and feelings of guilt and self-blame and self-harm. Conferencing systems differ in the degree to which they expect to establish "shame", or elicit expressions of contrition, as opposed to establishing outcomes. The implications of these differences for girls need to be examined.

Managing their own Stories

It is not only their offending that girls may be reluctant to talk about in a conference setting. Managing their own life history, their "story", is for some girls in juvenile justice an important part of a process of both self-protection and of establishing their independence and their self-sufficiency. This is particularly true for those young women who have had extensive involvement with both the juvenile justice and welfare systems. Girls' offending continues to be understood predominantly within a pathological framework. This is evidenced by a preoccupation with girls' past experiences. Young women with more extensive experiences with juvenile justice and welfare become fed up with being asked about very personal issues by a seemingly never-ending stream of workers. Their privacy and their independence are highly valued by these young women and managing their own stories becomes a significant mechanism for asserting both of these. They become very careful about how much and what they tell, to whom and when. Some girls may refuse to access services if they believe they are going to have to tell their story once again, or they refuse to communicate, or they manage the content they do reveal. All of these actions may be understood by others as recalcitrance, "being difficult", or of reflecting a lack of humility, or of a failure to show remorse.

Again, conferences differ in the significance they give to examination of the offender's personal circumstances and background. The ramifications for girls of these differences warrant investigation.

Establishing Trust

A not unrelated issue for some young women in the juvenile justice system is the issue of trust. Who they will talk to and what they will talk with them about is related to the extent to which they believe they can trust a person. Given the backgrounds of many of the young women, they are justifiably cautious about trusting people to understand them or to do the right thing by them. The expectation that a young woman will be forthright and honest when confronted by a group including strangers, no matter how well intentioned, may be unrealistic. The establishment and maintenance of "trustworthiness" needs to be acknowledged as significant for girls and a key objective of processes involving young women in juvenile justice.

'Girls are Harder to Work With'

In general those working with delinquent youth find girls more difficult to work with than boys (Baines and Alder, 1996; Kersten, 1990). This is an often heard, but rarely examined, lament among youth workers. The implications of this observation for everyday practice in juvenile justice and related areas require further investigation. Girls are described as 'verbally aggressive', 'hysterical', 'manipulative', 'dishonest' and 'untrusting'. Boys, on the other hand, are described as 'honest', 'open', 'less complex' and 'easier to manage'. Workers are also frustrated by their lack of experience and the lack of suitable service options for them to draw upon in addressing girls' problems.

Young women in the juvenile justice system may very well be "in your face" young women, feisty, and "difficult". Some may have had to develop these characteristics in order to survive. Most young women in the "deep end" of the juvenile justice system are no longer living at home. It takes a good deal of courage to leave home and then to survive as a single young woman forced to live on the margins of our society. Other young women may always have been very assertive, independently minded, and "wilful" young women. It may well be this "attitude", unacceptable for girls, that caused them to be labelled as "trouble" from a very early age by their family, schools, and neighbours. Whatever the precursor, this combination of having been in "trouble", and their assertiveness, along with an increasing reserve and reluctance to engage with authoritative elders means that people find them "difficult to work with" and may interpret their behaviour as uncooperative, or lacking the required subservience or contrition.

Concerns regarding sexuality and emotionality run through youth workers' reasons for why they find girls more difficult to work with. Many young women in the juvenile justice system have been, and may be in a situation where they continue to be, physically and sexually abused. Increasing public acknowledgment and awareness of this situation has meant in recent years that it has become one of the generally understood explanations for young women's "troublesome behaviour". While on the one hand recognition of this as a problem for some girls is a step forward, on the other, uncertainty surrounding sexual abuse has meant that it has become a catch all explanation for girls' problems.

Few young women readily reveal the full nature and circumstance of their abuse. As a result, even in circumstances in which the girl has not acknowledged it herself, sexual abuse is sometimes presumed to be an underlying factor in her "troublesome" behaviour. In fact, it has been argued that sexual abuse has become the concept around which the tendency to pathologise girls' behaviour has coalesced in recent years. Baines (1997) considers data suggesting that insinuations of sexual abuse are invoked in ways which pathologise girls' problems, constitute them as a victim and obscure their agency, and limit the range of options considered (see also Haaken, 1994). Sexual abuse thereby becomes another of the 'deficit discourses' (Carrington, 1993) framing responses to female delinquency.

Few people feel comfortable dealing with issues of sexuality, and especially with issues such as abuse which can be related to complex personal problems. To some extent workers can feel intimidated by their inability to deal with the girls' problems when they are understood in these terms. The tendency to define young women's problems in psychological and emotional terms related to sexual abuse, can leave workers feeling as though they as individuals do not have the skills to deal with these sorts of problems. It also defines the range and nature of responses that are considered for addressing the situation of young women.

At the same time, it is nevertheless the case that many young women in the juvenile justice system have been physically and sexually abused, and that many of them have not disclosed this fact, or the name of their abuser, to anyone. One would want to avoid the situation where a conference involved a girl's abuser participating in the determination of her penalty for an alleged offence. As Sandor notes, in such a circumstance, 'Her experience as a victim is then powerfully denied by the perpetrators participation' (Sandor in Baines, 1996: 45).

There is clearly no easy resolution to this potential, unwanted situation. However, its identification indicates the need for consideration of this potential problem in decisions regarding the composition of conferences. It has been suggested that a practice of having as many carers as possible involved in a conference may be a way of ameliorating or avoiding this situation. The point of this chapter is to indicate the need for identification of the particular situation of young women and issues such as these so that they can be acknowledged, and measures to address them can be identified and evaluated.

Some conferencing models emphasise their role in educating the offender about the inconvenience and pain they have caused the victim.

The rhetoric of such models draws clear distinctions between victims and offenders. Recent feminist literature has challenged the form of this dichotomy, noting that women and girls are often both victims and offenders (Gilfus, 1992; Daly and Chesney-Lind, 1988; Maher, 1992). The framing of restorative justice practices such as conferencing in terms of victim awareness strategies becomes questionable when so many girls are themselves victims. Further, as noted above, a problem confronting those working with young women is not that these young women are not aware of the pain that they have caused or that they are not ready to take responsibility or blame for their actions, in fact, the problem is the reverse.

In summary, research in various countries (England, Germany, Canada and the United States) indicates that experienced juvenile justice workers find girls more difficult to work with. The reasons for this are complex and in need of further exploration. Nevertheless, it does suggest that in considering new practices in juvenile justice, the implications of the sex of the offender need to be taken in consideration.

What are the Objectives for Work with Young Women in Juvenile Justice?

The implications of conferencing for young women in the juvenile justice system need to be considered in light of overall objectives of juvenile justice practice with young women offenders. I have argued (Alder, 1993) that key objectives must relate to facilitating and enabling young women: 1) To lead safe, secure and independent lives; and 2) To participate as citizens of their community, that is, to be able to participate and contribute to their community in meaningful ways that provide them with a sense of self-worth.

Essential to this scenario are economic independence by virtue of paid, meaningful employment and suitable long-term living accommodation. When young women in the juvenile justice system are asked about their most pressing needs, they will talk about their desperate need to find economic means of independent survival. Their need to be able to live independent lives, including independence from "social services", comes through very clearly and strongly in young women's comments (Alder and Hunter, 1999; Department of Community Services, Victoria, 1992).

However, providing young women offenders with educational options, accredited training, vocational planning and employment which leads a career, have not been a priority of policies and programs for young women. A review of vocational programs and services in

Australia in 1995 indicated that very few specifically addressed the needs of young women. If we are serious about assisting young women to move to real independence, to establish legitimate identities, to attain a meaningful role in the community, to have some choices about the direction and form of their lives, we have to look at developing this aspect of our policies for young women in the future.

In 1992, the then Department of Community Services in Victoria developed a young women's policy with overall objectives that I would argue are worthy of further consideration.

> Help young women become independent in ways which recognise the inequalities which have shaped their development as children and young women and have an impact on their ongoing opportunities for independent adulthood.
>
> Ensure safe environments for young women while they achieve greater independence and participation in their communities.
>
> Change those conditions (policies, service distribution, administrative and professional practices) which act to exclude young women from mainstream services and supports.
>
> Provide programs promoting personal and social growth and increasing young women's skills in controlling their experiences and utilising opportunities.
>
> Ensure that programs are accessible and relevant to the experiences of young women, particularly in terms of their geographic location and the way in which they are provided. (Community Services Victoria, 1992: 1)

The achievement of this goal requires working not only with individual girls. In part workers find girls more difficult to work with because the programs and services available for them to draw upon to meet girls' needs are limited and their efforts are often frustrated. The available options and possibilities for both workers and the young women with whom they work, are structured by broader legislative and policy frameworks that also need to be the targets of change strategies.

At another level, we cannot begin to take on the issues that need to be addressed if we are genuinely concerned with enabling girls to lead independent lives until we challenge longstanding understandings of femininity and what it is to be a young woman. We have tended to understand girlhood in terms of pathology and protection. Our responses to girls have been founded in understandings of girl-as-victim, girl-as-dependent/passive which have evoked coercive restrictive responses to signs of girls' wilfulness and passion. Our responses have consequently been constraining and controlling of girls' efforts at independence, rather than empowering and enabling.

Aspiring to and achieving the sorts of objectives with girls that I have outlined requires directing our efforts at a number of different levels. In considering what restorative justice practices have to offer young women, we need to consider their potential contribution to the achievement of these sorts of objectives. In principle, with the emphasis placed in some restorative justice models on the responsibilities of the community as well as the offender for the resolution of the situation, it is possible to envisage restorative justice practices that could well contribute to the achievement of these objectives. However, the achievement of such objectives for girls will require first and foremost that those framing theories, policies and practices, recognise and consider the situation of young women. Only then will we be able to both implement restorative justice practices sensitive to the needs and interests of girls, and to monitor the processes and outcomes in this light.

Conceptual Dilemmas

The situation and experiences of young women in the juvenile justice system raise a number of issues in relation to key concepts of restorative justice that are worthy of further consideration if we are to develop restorative justice practices that address the needs and interests of young women.

The term "community" is central to the notion of restorative justice, and many other commentators have indicated the complexities of meanings of this term. One aspect of this discussion that is raised for me by the situation of young women, is the need to acknowledge that there is not a single, unified community to which everyone relates or of which everyone is a member. Young women who have left home and have been living "on the streets" for some time, have often developed a "community" of their own. Often in order to survive, they have a relatively loose association of peers and others who they look to for protection, shelter, conversation, and advice (Hagan and McCarthy, 1997).

Their "street" community, if you like, is the one to which they feel closest; it is members from this community that they are more likely to trust. From their perspective, it is the "community" of their parents, teachers and welfare workers perspective that has harmed them, and continues to harm them.   They feel, and in fact, have been ostracised, cast out of that community.   A dilemma for young women is the often contradictory expectations of them in these two communities.

To date, in many discussions of restorative justice the use of the term "community" does not appear to take into account these "street" communities (as an example of a diversity of communities), but rather refers to restoring "the" community, of holding offenders accountable to, or making amends to "the" community.   The literature on restorative justice in relation to practice recommendations for juveniles, generally assumes a single community of shared values and commitments from which the young offender is marginalised and has harmed in some way.

"Harm" is a second concept that is often used in statements of restorative justice.   In general talk of "repairing harm" refers to either the harm suffered by the community or the victim.   For example, Bazemore (1997: 195) notes that 'Restorative justice views crime primarily as harm to victims and the justice response should, through restitution, community service, and victim offender dialogue and related processes, seek to repair this harm and actively involve victims and communities'.   The situation of young women draws our attention to the fact that we also need to acknowledge and address the "harm" caused to the offender, perhaps especially by the community.   In particular, young women with extensive juvenile justice and/or welfare backgrounds, generally have long experience of being ostracised and stigmatised in a wide variety of both direct and indirect, personal and more general ways by organisations and individuals in the community. If we are interested in "reintegrating" young women, this will have to be acknowledged and addressed.   This requires addressing aspects of the community's actions that cause ongoing "harm" to young women.

"Repairing the harm" is also a notion that causes some concern when it comes to young women: what does "repairing" mean?   In the case of young women, it is evident that the "harm" caused to the "community", that is, parents, teachers, social workers and neighbours, is often not so much the criminality of her actions as it is that her actions contravene dominant understandings of acceptable feminine behaviour. Does repairing the harm in this case, entail reinforcement of the communities traditional expectations of young women?   Does this mean that restorative justice is by its very principles, inherently conservative on these dimensions?

On the other hand, is there room for the processes of restorative justice, to repair the harm done to young women by conservative expectations, by challenging traditional expectations and understandings of what it is to be a "good girl"?   Civic republican discourse holds that confronting such forms of domination is a central value of restorative justice. In relation to racist attitudes, Hudson (1998) is hopeful about the 'norm-creating' role of conferences. Drawing on the work of Habermas, Hudson considers whether 'in the exposition of views, the listening to accounts of harm, the attempting to justify prejudice, that more progressive moral consensus can be reached' (Hudson, 1998: 250). The theoretical foundation for this to occur assumes a situation in which people participate without constraint or oppression, and are power equals or can equally contribute to the discussion (Habermas, 1984: 8-42). Achieving this situation is a challenge for conferences and we await the evidence that it can be achieved, especially in situations involving young people as offenders. Whether or not conferences are able to achieve this level of equality has significant implications for the possibilities that restorative justice may, or may not, offer young women.

"Accountability" is a final concept used in some models of restorative justice that has some significance for young women. In general this term is used in relation to holding the young offender accountable for her actions. However, it is not clear that issues of proportionality and equity are necessarily achieved through informal group processes (Warner, 1994). Further, the history of the outcomes of decision-making in relation to young women's troublesome behaviour across a range of organisations including juvenile justice, welfare, mental health, medicine and education (Heidensohn, 1985; Carrington, 1993; Alder, 1998; Chesney-Lind and Joe, 1996), indicates the need for some level of community accountability, or decision-making accountability.

Conclusion

Overall the principles of some restorative justice models suggest potential benefits for young women in the juvenile justice system. Particularly worthy contributions would be the potential for community change and development, and the possibility for respecting young women's contribution to decision-making regarding the most appropriate outcome for their offending behaviour. On the other hand, if young women's needs and interests are to be addressed by restorative justice practice, they have first to be acknowledged. There remain a number of unanswered questions about restorative justice practices in relation to young women offenders. Before we can feel comfortable about the use of restorative justice practices with young women in the juvenile justice system, these questions and the issues raised in this chapter, need to be acknowledged and addressed. Most urgently, the practices of restorative justice need to be evaluated and monitored in regard to their implications for young women.

References

Alder, C. (1998), 'Passionate and Wilful Girls', *Women and Criminal Justice*, vol. 9, pp. 81-101.

Alder, C. M. (1993), 'Programs and Services for Young Women: Future Directions', in S. Gerull and L. Atkinson (eds), *National Conference on Juvenile Justice*, Australian Institute of Criminology, Canberra, pp. 305-11.

Alder, C. and Hunter, N. (1999), '"Not Worse, Just Different?" Working with Girls in Juvenile Justice. A Report submitted to the Criminology Research Council, Canberra, Australia', Criminology Department, The University of Melbourne, Melbourne.

Althorpe, G. (1996), 'Young Women and Community Service Orders', in C. Alder and M. Baines (eds), " ... *and when she was bad?" Working with Young Women in Juvenile Justice and Related Areas*, National Clearinghouse for Youth Studies, Hobart, pp. 73-79.

Baines, M. (1996), 'Viewpoints on Young Women and Family Group Conferences', in C. Alder and M. Baines (eds), " ... *and when she was bad?" Working with Young Women in Juvenile Justice and Related Areas*, National Clearinghouse for Youth Studies, Hobart, pp. 41-47.

Baines, M. and Alder, C. (1996), 'Are Girls more Difficult to Work with? Youth Worker's Perspectives in Juvenile Justice and Related Areas', *Crime and Delinquency*, vol. 42, pp. 467-85.

Baines, M. (1997), 'Mad, Bad or Angry?', *Youth Studies Australia*, vol. 16, pp. 19-23.

Beikoff, L. (1996), 'Queensland's Juvenile Justice System: Equity, Access and Justice for Young Women', in C. Alder and M. Baines (eds), "... *and when she was bad?" Working with Young Women in Juvenile Justice and Related Areas*, National Clearinghouse for Youth Studies, Hobart, pp. 15-25.

Carrington, K. (1993), *Offending Girls: Sex, Youth and Justice*, Allen and Unwin, Sydney.

Chesney-Lind, M. and Joe, Karen A. (1996), 'Official Rhetoric and Persistent Realities in Troublesome Behavior: The Case of Running Away', *Journal of Contemporary Criminal Justice*, vol. 12, pp. 121-50.

Chesney-Lind, M. and Sheldon, R. (1992), 'Girls, Delinquency and Juvenile Justice', Brooks/Cole Publishing, Pacific Grove, Ca.

Daly, K. and Chesney-Lind, M. (1988), 'Feminism and Criminology', *Justice Quarterly*, vol. 5, pp. 497-538.

Daly, K. and Immarigeon, R. (1998), 'The Past, Present and Future of Restorative Justice: Some Critical Reflections', *Contemporary Justice Review*, vol. 1, pp. 21-45.

Department of Community Services Victoria (1992), *Becoming Stronger: An Action Plan for Young Women*, Community Services, Melbourne, Victoria.

Department of Youth and Community Care (1999), *What About the Girls? Young Women's Perceptions of Juvenile Justice Programs and Services*, Department of Youth and Community Care, Brisbane.

Gelsthorpe, L. (1986), 'Towards a Sceptical Look at Sexism', *International Journal of the Sociology of Law*, vol. 14, pp. 125-53.

Gilfus, M. E. (1992), 'From Victims to Survivors to Offenders: Women's Routes of Entry and Immersion into Street Life', *Women and Criminal Justice*, vol. 4, pp. 63-89.

Haaken, J. (1994), 'Sexual Abuse, Recovered Memory and Therapeutic Practices', *Social Text*, vol. 40, pp. 115-45.

Habermas, J. (1984), *The Theory of Communicative Action. Vol. 1. Reason and Rationalisation of Society*, Heinemann Educational Books, London.

Hagan, J. and McCarthy, B. (1997), *Mean Streets: Youth Crime and Homelessness*, Cambridge University Press, New York.

Heidensohn, F. (1985), *Women and Crime*, New York University Free Press, New York.

Hudson, B. (1998), 'Restorative Justice: The Challenge of Sexual and Racial Violence', *Journal of Law and Society*, vol. 25, pp. 237-56.

Hudson, B. (1984), 'Femininity and Adolescence', in Angela McRobbie and Mica Nava (eds), *Gender and Generation*, McMillan, London, pp. 31-54.

Kersten, J. (1990), 'A Gender-Specific Look at Patterns of Violence in Juvenile Institutions: Or are Girls Really more "Difficult to Handle"', *International Journal of the Sociology of Law*, vol. 18, pp. 473-93.

Maher, L. (1992), 'Reconstructing the Female Criminal: Women and Crack Cocaine', *University of Southern California Review of Law and Women's Studies*, vol. 2, pp. 131-54.

Phillips, L. (1998), *The Girls Report. What We Know and Need to Know about Growing up Female*, The National Council on Research on Women, New York.

Poe-Yamagata, E. and Butts, J. A. (1996), *Female Offenders in the Juvenile Justice System. Statistics Summary*, National Centre for Juvenile Justice, Pittsburg, PA.

Stubbs, J. (1995), 'Communitarian Conferencing and Violence against Women: A Cautionary Note', in M. Valverde, L. MacLeod, and K. Johnson, (eds), *Wife Assault and the Canadian Criminal Justice System: Issues and Policies*, Centre of Criminology, University of Toronto, Toronto, pp. 260-89.

Stubbs, J. (1997), 'Shame, Defiance and Violence against Women: A Critical Analysis of "Communitarian" Conferencing', in S. Cook and J. Bessant (eds), *Women's Encounters with Violence: Australian Experiences*, Sage, Thousand Oaks, Ca., pp. 109-26.

Warner, K. (1994), 'The Rights of the Offender in Family Conferences', in C. Alder and J. Wundersitz (eds), *Family Conferences and Juvenile Justice*, Australian Institute of Criminology, Canberra, pp. 141-53.

8   Values and Restorative Justice in Schools

VALERIE BRAITHWAITE

Morris and Young conclude their essay in this collection recognising that punishment processes and practices are a reflection of the sort of society we are and want to be. The connection between punishment institutions and a society's values extends from the macro level discussed by Morris and Young to the micro level where connections are mirrored in the belief systems of ordinary people. The belief systems of individuals allow experiences, observations and aspirations to be connected in personally meaningful ways. At the heart of these connections are basic beliefs and values about individuals, social relations, and institutions.

Morris and Young along with Daly provide some clues as to how restorative justice connects with the belief systems of individuals. Morris and Young refer to restorative justice in terms of a new set of values and priorities. Daly suggests that restorative justice is a package that brings retributive and rehabilitative notions of justice together with an extra quality that is relational and that extends beyond victim and offender to include community. These accounts have been defended in this volume through teasing out the features of restorative justice and traditional justice in action.

The present chapter shifts the frame of analysis in two respects. First, the focus changes from what happens, to what people think should happen when rules have been broken and others harmed. Perceptions and expectations that individuals have of justice practices is a topic that Daly touches upon in her argument why retributive and restorative practices should not be conceptualised as oppositional forms of justice. Second, this chapter looks behind the practices that individuals favour in particular situations, and seeks to identify broad and widely held value systems that explain why certain justice practices resonate more strongly with some constituencies than with others. In the process, the age-old question of personal experiences versus social ideals as shapers of our policy preferences is addressed.

Context of the Study

The social context in which justice practices are examined is school bullying, and the perceptions that are measured are those held by parents in relation to how a child who bullies another should be treated. This setting, while removed from the legal domain of courts and conferences, is interesting in a number of respects.   First, bullying, its causes and its consequences, touches the lives of the majority of parents at one point or another to varying degrees.   As such, views about how bullying should be handled are widespread and strongly held.   School bullying therefore provides an interesting context in which to examine the tussle that one might expect at the individual level between responding in terms of principles and responding from personal experience.

The second attraction in searching for the value base to a restorative justice approach in the school context is that restorative justice was not recognised in this population as a "social movement" at the time the data were collected. The value base therefore is not one that has been imposed through organised public discussion about this type of justice. There is scope to understand the way in which individuals give meaning to restorative justice actions from the perspective of their own value systems.

Several practices recommended for dealing with bullying behaviour in schools capture one of the distinctive elements of restorative justice, its inclusiveness of community in the process of acknowledging and making amends for wrongdoing.   This set of practices, that place importance on building and restoring positive relationships within the community are referred to in this chapter as dialogic.   Dialogic relational practices are compared with traditional practices that have a punitive individualised orientation.   The basis of comparison are the values that underlie preferences for dialogic or punitive approaches to dealing with bullying. The purpose is to find out if the value base for dialogic practices is unique or if it represents a combination of more traditional values.

The Values Base

An argument to support the view that the values underlying restorative justice are not unique but rather combine a set of traditional values that are expressed more generally in socialisation practices has been put forward by Ted Wachtel (1999).   Wachtel draws upon the work of Glaser (1969) and Baumrind (1968) and proposes that effective social control can be understood in terms of two dimensions.   One dimension, 'control', is defined in terms of discipline or limit setting. The second, 'support', is defined as encouragement or nurturing. Restorative justice practices employ high control (confronts and disapproves of wrongdoing) and high support (valuing the intrinsic worth of the wrongdoer).

Restorative justice, conceptualised in this way, has a counterpart in the effective parenting literature, Baumrind's (1968) notion of authoritative parenting. Authoritative parenting involves a combination of affection and attentive responsiveness to individual needs along with clear requirements for responsible, pro-social behaviour. Baumrind's prescription for good parenting has been widely recognised as requiring not only negotiation but also confrontation. Empirical work conducted since Baumrind's initial formulation has resulted in parenting styles being conceptualised in terms of two basic approaches (Amato, 1987; Block, 1984; Kochanska, Kuczynski, and Radke-Yarrow, 1989). The authoritative style encompasses expressions of love, praise, independence, and responsibility, the setting of standards for behaviour and performance, and the enforcement of these standards. The authoritarian style is characterised by regulating through control, restrictiveness, and criticism, the use of punishment, and insistence on obedience to authority.

Should views that individuals hold about effective parenting be associated with the views they hold about systems of justice? Goodnow (1988) argues that the ideas that people have about parenting are driven by societal expectations and standards as well as individual experiences. Parenting norms are learnt, contested, and discussed at length in our society in public and private settings. Whether or not we are influenced by the knowledge and opinions we hear depends on how we filter and process the information available to us. Framing schema play an important role in how we interpret the world around us (Tversky and Kahneman, 1981). One schema for cueing us as to society's expectations is our socially transmitted, internalised value system (Rokeach, 1973). This value system comprises socially shared goals and modes of behaviour that have legitimacy across situations and across time (Kluckhohn, 1951; Rokeach, 1973; Schwartz, 1994; Scott, 1965). Such value systems help us decide what is a desirable course of action to follow and what is not, for ourselves, groups or society. If we believe in freedom or in equal opportunity, certain practices become more acceptable than others, regardless of whether we are considering the justice system, the school system, or parenting.

A conceptualisation of broad widely-held value systems that appears relevant to discussions of restorative versus traditional justice practices is the value balance model (Braithwaite, 1998a). The value balance model emerged from an empirical study of the values expressed by a random sample of the Australian population in 1974.   The first study involved semi-structured interviews in which participants were invited to express their views on what values were important to them personally and to Australians generally.   The 125 values generated by this study have been the basis for measuring values of Australian students and citizens over a 25 year period (Braithwaite, 1982; Braithwaite and Law, 1985; Braithwaite, 1994; Blamey and Braithwaite, 1997; Braithwaite and Blamey, 1998). The patterns of interrelationships among these values have been relatively stable over time and across populations, with a series of factor analytic studies producing remarkably consistent conclusions.   Most of the variation among individuals in human valuing can be explained by the pursuit of two major value orientations or value systems, one representing harmony, the other security (Braithwaite, 1998b).

The security value system brings together guiding principles that ensure that one is well positioned to protect one's interests and further them within the existing social order.   Security values guide us in deciding how we divide up limited resources, what kinds of competition between groups and individuals is legitimate, and how we define winners and losers.   The principles apply at a personal or societal level.   At the societal level, values such as the rule of law, national economic development, and national greatness are socially sanctioned goals for ensuring the safety of one's group and individuals within it.   At a personal level, security values include having authority, social recognition, economic prosperity, and being competitive (see Appendix I for sample items).

In contrast, the harmony value system brings together societal and personal values that aim to further peaceful coexistence through a social order that shares resources, communicates mutual respect, and cooperates to allow individuals to develop their potential to the full. Harmony values orient us toward establishing connections to others, transcending our individual grievances and dissatisfactions, and finding peace within ourselves and with our world.   Harmony values for society include a good life for others, rule by the people, international cooperation, a world at peace, human dignity, greater economic equality, and preserving the natural environment.   Harmony values for the individual include self-insight, inner harmony, the pursuit of knowledge, self-respect, and wisdom, as well as being tolerant, generous, forgiving, helpful, and loving (see Appendix I for sample items).

The security and harmony systems are stable, enduring, and valued at some level by the vast majority of the population (Braithwaite and Blamey, 1998).   In spite of very high levels of acceptance of these values in the community, individuals differ in how they prioritise them (Braithwaite, 1994, 1997, 1998a).   Values are useful, therefore, for explaining how different individuals see their obligations to the collectivity (Blamey and Braithwaite, 1997; Dryzek and Braithwaite, 1999).

The value balance model identifies four different value constituencies within the population. The security oriented prioritise security over harmony values. For this group, winning resources in an orderly fashion takes precedence over harmonious relationships and spiritual well-being. The priorities are reversed for the harmony oriented: they prioritise harmony over security values. Value relativists differ from both groups: they downplay the importance of either security or harmony values as a framework for decision-making, preferring to be responsive to context. In contrast, dualists profess to wanting it all, committing to both security and harmony values as guiding principles in their lives. A series of studies have shown these groups to differ in their responses to policy issues (Braithwaite, 1994, 1998a). In the context of this chapter, it is of interest that the security oriented are most likely to be in favour of tougher law enforcement and harsher penalties. The harmony oriented oppose increasing police powers and stiffer sentencing (Braithwaite, 1998a).

Just as individuals differ in their value priorities, institutions differ in the values that frame their social interactions (Braithwaite, 1998c; Rokeach, 1979). Charitable institutions, for instance, speak to the harmony values of the community, the stock exchange speaks to security values. Within different institutional settings, different values frame the ways in which business is conducted, and such institutions, in turn, appeal to different sections of the population for support and affirmation. Elsewhere it has been suggested that institutional resilience and adaptability may be derived through harnessing practices that speak to both security and harmony values (Braithwaite, 1998c). Nowhere is this more apparent than in the school system, where competition and cooperation are institutionalised side by side.

Harmony values are hypothesised as the frame for developing strategies that encourage collective responsibility and shared decision making. School actions within a harmony framework are likely to include dialogue among all parts of the school, and the building of a strong community around the prevention of bullying practices. The actions are likely to have a strong relational focus. These actions are hypothesised as being most strongly supported by those who place high importance on harmony values as guiding principles in life.

While harmony values set standards that allow for the identification of wrongdoing, they do not, in themselves, give guidance for the allocation of blame or fault toward an individual. Decisions about who wins and who loses, who is to be punished and who is to be rewarded are made within a security value framework. Security values involve rules and the enforcement of rules that set limits on legitimate competitive struggle.   School actions within a security framework therefore take the form of having rules against bullying, formally confronting bullies with their wrongdoing, and sanctioning bullies in public ways through suspensions and expulsions.   These actions are hypothesised as being most strongly endorsed by those who place high importance on security values as guiding principles in life.

The Relevance of Parenting Styles

If harmony values predict parental support for dialogic relational strategies to prevent school bullying, and security values predict support for punitive individualised strategies, do parental styles of child-rearing have a role to play in this study? Parental styles of being authoritative and authoritarian may overlap too much with harmony and security values, if they are regarded as merely a contextualised representation of the more abstract principles. Not everyone, however, relies on broad abstract principles to guide their policy preferences in a specific context, particularly if they have not been engaged in public debate that might draw such linkages to their attention. Furthermore, the information that shapes the child rearing practices adopted by parents comes from many sources, including experience, family traditions, norms, fashions and the ideas of significant others (Goodnow, 1988).   A strong case can be made, therefore, for expecting child rearing practices to have an influence on school disciplinary practices that is independent of their value base.

At this point, the question that needs to be asked is why child-rearing styles should influence parents' views in a different domain, that is, school disciplinary policy?   In general, individuals strive for consistency among different parts of their belief system (Abelson, 1983). If these parts are closely related, the pressure for consistency is greater. When children go to primary school, parents are trusting others with their care.   It is reasonable to expect parents to approve of care practices in the school that reflect their values and their child rearing practices at home.   Indeed, the degree to which parents favour parental styles of being authoritative or authoritarian in dealing with their children may be a stronger predictor of favoured strategies for dealing with bullying than abstract and generalised values. Therefore, the model tested in this chapter includes both the abstract harmony and security value orientations and the child rearing styles of being authoritative and authoritarian.   Child rearing styles are conceptualised as action-based composites of values, experience, knowledge, habits, and mores.

Contextual Personal Experiences

Values and general styles do not always guide our decision-making (Ajzen, 1991). In a specific context, feelings, beliefs and attitudes can come into play to exert influences on how we respond to certain issues. When wrongdoing harms others, being the victim or the offender, or a member of either's intimate network, is bound to shape one's views about how matters should be dealt with. Personal experience is likely to impact on notions of fairness and legitimacy, which in turn will shape sympathy or antipathy for certain regulatory strategies. In this study, intermediate variables of fairness and legitimacy were not measured, but experience as a parent of a victim or bully was measured.

From a self-interest perspective (Downs, 1957), parents of children who have been accused of being a bully or who have experienced victimisation, are likely to respond in a way that advantages them. Parents of victims are most likely to want the threat to their child removed immediately, that is, to favour suspension or expulsion, and in more extreme cases, desire compensation or revenge. Parents of bullies are most likely to want to protect their child and themselves from further stigmatisation and punishment, and to shift the blame elsewhere. The parents of victims and bullies are, therefore, most likely to favour punitive individualised strategies and dialogic relational strategies respectively.

For parents whose children are not in the bullying and victimisation category, but who are struggling to cope with the demands of parenting, self-interest may loom large in their expectations of the school and its disciplining policies. Parents who are struggling may see the school system as a place for support and assistance in disciplining children. Whether they would favour a punitive or dialogic approach to bullying is difficult to say. But to the extent that the dialogic relational strategies include and assist parents with parenting, one might expect parents who are experiencing considerable parenting burden to favour the dialogic approach.

First hand experience with bullying or parenting difficulties is not the only factor that results in our supporting a policy initiative that may be inconsistent with our values. Psychological theory alerts us to the importance of having achievable goals as well as the capacity to achieve them (Feather, 1982). If the goal is to stop a child from being a bully, one has to believe that children who bully can change. If one believes a child can change, some strategies for preventing bullying make more sense than others. Alternatively, if one believes a child cannot change, options are more limited.

Values represent hopes and aspirations. The capacity to achieve them at a societal level often rests on others. If we do not have confidence that our hopes and aspirations can be realised through the commitments and actions of others, values may not predict our policy preferences very well. A concept which captures our belief that others can deliver the goals we want is trust. In policy matters, trust in those with decision-making power to realise our aspirations is critically important. If parents do not feel that they can trust teachers, students, other parents, school boards, and education departments to implement strategies to control bullying, disillusionment with the strategies may be expressed, even if such strategies are consonant with their personal values.

Thus, the model used to explain support for restorative justice and subsequently, retributive justice, can be summarised as follows. Public support for dialogic collective strategies (restorative justice) and punitive individualised strategies (retributive justice) are hypothesised as a function of (a) abstract values (security and harmony), (b) parenting styles (authoritative and authoritarian), (c) belief that a child who bullies can change, (d) experience as a parent of a bully, (e) experience as a parent of a victim of bullying, (f) parenting burden, and (g) trust in members of the school community. The major focus of this study are the values that underlie a restorative or retributive approach: are these values different or are they the same, and do values retain their importance when personal experiences of bullying, schools, and parenting are taken into account?

The Data Base

The 'Life at School Survey' (Ahmed, 1999) involved the participation of 1402 students, and 978 of their parents or guardians. Of the 96 schools contacted in the Australian Capital Territory, 32 public and private schools agreed to take part. The sample comprised those families who had volunteered after receiving a letter outlining the purpose of the study and a permission slip for participation. The overall rate of participation was 47%. The sample was restricted to grades 4 to 6 in the primary schools, except in a few schools which were unusual in having a grade 7 class for inclusion. The ages of the children ranged from 9 to 13 years (mean = 10.86 years). The sample comprised 54% girls, 46% boys.

The questionnaires were self-completion, designed for a child and the parent or guardian with whom the child was most involved on a daily basis. Children filled out their 'Life at School Survey' in class. Questionnaires were sent home with the children for parents to complete and return to the school.

Parent or guardian data were available for 70% of the children who participated and took home a questionnaire. Of this sample of 978 respondents, 845 (86%) were mothers, 132 (14%) fathers and 1 was a guardian. Self-identified non-Australians comprised 25% of the sample.

Measures

Values and Parenting Styles

The Goal, Mode and Social Values Inventories comprise 14 subscales, 4 of which measure a security value orientation and 3 a harmony value orientation (Braithwaite and Law, 1985, Braithwaite and Scott, 1991, Braithwaite, 1997, 1998b). The security value orientation scale comprises the subscales 'national strength and order', 'social standing', 'getting ahead' and 'propriety in dress and manners'. The harmony value orientation scale comprises 'international harmony and equality', 'a positive orientation to others' and 'inner harmony and equality'. Sample value items for both orientations are given in Appendix I. Respondents are asked to rate each value item in terms of its importance as a guiding principle in life from 1 meaning 'I reject this' to 7 meaning 'I accept this as of the greatest importance'.

Parenting styles were measured through a modified version of the Child-Rearing Practices Report (Block, 1965). The CRPR is a self-report inventory that requires parents to sort a set of statements about child-rearing values, attitudes and behaviours into categories that provide a personal profile of how each respondent thinks and behaves in relation to their child. A subset of the items was selected and the methodology was altered from a sorting task to one in which respondents rated each item on a 6-point scale from strongly disagree to strongly agree.[1] The modified format and item set were piloted in the same population from which the sample was drawn and scales to measure authoritarian and authoritative parenting were developed (Huntley, 1995).

In the present larger scale study, further modifications to the scales were made on the basis of a psychometric analysis of the items. The scales used to measure parenting styles in this paper are more limited than implied by the labels of authoritarian and authoritative parenting. Consequently, the parenting scales used in the present analyses are called the "command and control" style and the "supportive and self-regulatory" style.

Command and control represents a parenting style that is protective and restrictive, induces guilt to regulate behaviour, and insists on achievement, self-discipline and obedience in the child. The command and control scale does not include items referring to physical punishment and the expression of negative emotions toward the child, as might have been expected in an authoritarian parenting scale.

The supportive self-regulatory scale represents the expression of positive affect and openness in the parent-child relationship, fostering autonomy and exploration, and guiding children's behaviour through positive feedback and affirmation. The supportive self-regulatory scale does not include insistence on the child undertaking duties and family responsibilities, one facet of Baumrind's (1968) initial formulation of authoritative parenting. The items used in the parenting scales are included in Appendix II.

Contextual Personal Experience

The experience of having a child who has been accused of bullying was assessed through a single question, 'How often has your child been accused of being a bully?' The response categories were 'more than once' (scored 3 for this analysis), 'it has happened' (2), and 'never' or 'don't know' (1).

Parents were also asked if they were aware of their child having a problem with bullying: 'How often has your child been bullied by another student or a group of students in the last year (1995-96)?' Response categories ranged from 'most days' (scored 6 for this analysis) to 'never' (1).

Both of the above personal experience measures reflect the parent's world view. In other words, children could be bullies or victims, unbeknown to their parents. The measures chosen are consistent with the argument of this paper, that support for justice practices can be understood in terms of the values and interpretations of reality made by individuals, in this case parents, regardless of whether or not these understandings are externally validated.

In order to measure the degree to which parents believed change was possible among individual bullies, parents were asked 'What do you think are the chances of changing children who bully others into good citizens in the school?' The response categories ranged from 1 to 5 and were labelled 10%, 25%, 50%, 75% and 90% chance.

Trust was measured through asking respondents: 'How much can you trust the following groups to control the problem of school bullying?' Groups such as students, parents of bullies, parents of victims, school teachers, and school disciplinary boards were rated on a four point scale from 'not at all' (1) to 'a great deal' (4). A principal components analysis followed by a varimax rotation resulted in 9 items being collapsed into three trust scales. Trust in authorities involved summing responses to the amount of trust placed in the following groups: (a) Parents and Citizens Associations, (b) School Disciplinary Boards, and (c) the Australian Capital Territory (ACT) Department of Education and Training. Trust in professionals involved summing responses to the amount of trust placed in (a) school teachers and (b) school principals. Trust in the community involved summing responses to the amount of trust placed in the following groups: (a) students, (b) parents of bullies, and (c) parents of victims.

Parenting burden was measured with a multi-item scale adapted from the Threat to Basic Needs Scale and the Time Constraints Scale in caregiving (Braithwaite, 1990). Respondents were asked how often their parenting responsibilities produced the following experiences: (a) having too little time to myself, (b) giving up interests, leisure activities or hobbies that I enjoy, (c) being unable to get my household chores done, (d) losing patience with the family, (e) being unable to rest when ill myself, (f) feeling that I cannot get on top of all the things I have to do, (g) being unable to get enough sleep, (h) feeling that I have lost control over my life, (i) feeling guilty about what I have or have not done for my child(ren), and (j) feeling that I am not doing anything as well as I should. Responses to these 10 items were given on a 5 point scale from 1 meaning 'never' to 5 meaning 'a lot of the time'. Responses were added to produce a total parenting burden scale score for each respondent.

Outcome Measures

The outcome measures used in this study were dialogic relational strategies and punitive individualised strategies. Parents were asked 'How important would you consider each of the following school actions to be in dealing with bullying?'. Response categories ranged from 1 meaning 'undesirable, would make things worse' to 5 meaning 'essential, the highest priority'.

The dialogic relational strategies were: (a) Role-playing and story-telling which explains why bullying is bad; (b) Meetings that make bullies commit to changing their behaviour and playing a constructive role in the school rather than a destructive one; (c) Organising discussion groups for parents of students who bully or are bullied; (d) Consulting with parents and children to develop guidelines for how bullying should be handled; (e) Training courses for parents to improve parenting skills; (f) A school contract signed by each student and their parents not to be involved in bullying in any form; and (g) Encouragement of 'neutral' students to help break up fights in the playground.

The punitive individualised strategies were (a) Class rules against bullying, e.g., taking away privileges from children who bully others;

(b) Formal confrontation of students who bully others by the principal in her/his office; (c) Expulsion of children who have repeatedly been reported as bullies of other children; and (d) Suspension for a week or two of children who have bullied other children.

Responses to each set of items were summed to create the outcome measures. The basis for the construction of these scales was a principal components analysis and varimax rotation of 16 possible intervention strategies. This analysis produced a three factor solution. The third factor has not been included in this analysis because it related to avoidance, rather than dealing with a bullying problem once it had occurred.

Results

The central hypotheses of this study are that:

A: Dialogic relational strategies for dealing with bullying (a) belong to the domain of the harmony value orientation, (b) are linked with supportive self-regulatory parenting and (c) are shaped by personal experiences with bullying, parenting and schools.
B: Punitive individualised strategies for dealing with bullying (a) belong to the domain of the security value orientation, (b) are linked with command and control parenting and (c) are shaped by personal experiences with bullying, parenting and schools.

These hypotheses were tested using a hierarchical regression analysis in which values and parenting styles were entered first as a block, followed by personal experiences. This approach gives us insight into how the more stable and enduring values fare as predictors of policy preferences, and how their influence is modified when personal experiences are added to the equation. The results of these analyses are presented in Table 8.1.

The strongest predictor of support for dialogic relational strategies is commitment to the harmony value system. This is the value system that guides us in the cooperative side of social life, setting markers for sharing resources, resolving differences, and preserving our interdependency. Interestingly, this variable remains the dominant predictor even when personal experiences are added to the equation. In Table 8.1, the change in the beta weights for harmony values from Model 1 to 2 in the prediction of dialogic relational strategies is minor.

By the same token, personal experiences also predict our preferences for models of social control as self-interest theorists claim

Table 8.1: Results of the Hierarchical Regression Analyses Predicting Support for Dialogic Relational Strategies and Punitive Individualised Strategies among Parents of Primary School Children (minimum N = 919)

Predictors	Mean[a] (SD)	Dialogic			Punitive		
		r	b Model 1	b Model 2	r	b Model 1	b Model 2
harmony	5.77 (.61)	.37**	.32**	.27**	.11**	-.07	-.07
security	4.93 (.76)	.21**	.04	.01	.38**	.36**	.35**
supportive self-regulatory	5.02 (.49)	.19**	.07*	.09**	.03	.07*	.07*
command & control	3.54 (.55)	.09**	.08*	.07*	.27**	.13**	.11**
trust in authority	2.24 (.70)	.25**		.17**	.15**		.04
trust in professionals	3.23 (.65)	.10**		-.07*	.09**		.05
trust in community	2.47 (.56)	.24**		.16**	-.01		-.04
parent of perpetrator	1.18 (.47)	-.04		-.05	-.09**		-.09**
parent of victim	1.97 (1.28)	.13**		.10**	.08*		.07*
parental burden	2.84 (.58)	.05		.07*	-.02		.02
likelihood of change	3.39 (1.00)	.10**		.01	-.10**		-.09**
Adj. R^2			.14**	.21**		.16**	.18**
Change in R^2				.07**			.02**

a Total scale scores for each individual were divided by the number of items in the scale so that means could be interpreted in terms of the original metric.

*   p < .05

** p < .01

and as Goodnow (1988) argues in her paper on how parenting practices come into being. The change in R^2 of 7% shows that personal experience is an additional influence in shaping preferences on how schools should handle problems of bullying. Parents who have a child who has been victimised and parents who report high parenting burden favour the use of a dialogic relational approach, possibly in the hope that others can assist in bringing about changes that they alone are unable to effect.

Trust in others and expectations of behaviour change in bullies were also elements in supporting a dialogic relational approach. Although not significant in the final regression equation, parents who believed children who bully others could change were more likely to favour dialogue. Trust in all groups was positively related to favouring a dialogic approach at the bivariate level, although the variables behaved a little differently in the regression model. Trust in both authorities and in the community increased support for a dialogic approach, trust in teachers reduced it. Possibly this reflects an individualised view of behaviour management: in the absence of other kinds of trust, trust in teachers to solve bullying may accompany the expectation that teachers are responsible for and capable of controlling the behaviour of difficult children. In such circumstances, a dialogic approach oriented to all children is unnecessary.

Interestingly, both supportive self-regulatory and command and control parenting styles were positively associated with a dialogic approach. This outcome was unexpected. The hypothesis was that supportive self-regulatory parenting would be correlated with the harmony value system, and both would constitute foundational beliefs for a dialogic approach to dealing with bullying in the school. Command and control parenting was expected to be associated with the security value system and both were expected to underlie a punitive approach.

Original expectations were confirmed in so far as supportive and self-regulatory parenting was positively correlated with commitment to a harmony value system ($r = .40$, $p < .01$), but not the security value system ($r = .00$, ns). Command and control parenting was positively correlated with commitment to a security value system ($r = .41$, $p < .01$), but not the harmony value system ($r = .02$, ns). What then is the explanation for why parents who subscribe to command and control parenting also support dialogue?

Possibly, the common element is desire for intervention in the school setting. Parents who use supportive self-regulation and parents who use command and control regulation both want to see the school take action to contain bullying. In contrast, parents who subscribe to neither command and control nor supportive self-regulatory styles prefer a permissive approach to bullying in schools, and favour non-intervention. In school policy terms, a permissive response is likely to be expressed as "kids will be kids" and "let them sort it out". Those who adopt this view are likely to be low scorers on both command and control parenting and supportive and self-regulatory parenting, and are the most likely to say that proposed school interventions that involve meetings, rules and lessons in responsibility and accountability will make things worse.

Support for punitive individualised strategies followed the same general pattern to that described above. Values were the most important predictor of policy preference, in this case, commitment to the security value system. Those who place great store in principles for regulating competition and establishing order were the most supportive of a retributive approach to dealing with bullying, an approach that targets the perpetrator, isolates him/her from the community, and punishes him/her for wrongdoing. Personal experience extended understanding of the sources of support for the retributive system. Parents of children accused of bullying were less enthusiastic about a punitive individualised approach, whereas parents of victims expressed positive reactions, as did those who had little confidence that bullies could change their ways.

Trust did not predict support for punitive individualised strategies in the regression model, although at the bivariate level, trust in authorities and trust in professionals were positively associated with support for a retributive approach to dealing with bullying. It is of note that trust in the community was not relevant to the question of support for a punitive individualised approach.

Just as command and control and supportive and self-regulatory parenting both predicted a dialogic approach in the previous set of analyses, both parenting styles predicted support for a punitive individualised approach to bullying. Parents who believe in actively guiding the development of children, regardless of their preferred orientation, concur in giving support to punitive individualised strategies in the school's disciplinary portfolio.

Where to From Here?

These findings explain the diversity of views among parents in how to deal with bullying. Security values direct some parents in one direction, harmony values in the other. Personal experiences in dealing with bullies, victims and the school also have an effect. Most interestingly, and most unexpectedly, parents who actively socialise children, regardless of whether their strategy is command and control or supportive and self-regulatory favour strategies for dealing with bullying that span the restorative and retributive divide.

The notion of a portfolio of strategies raises the interesting question of how this range of options should be organised so as to be mutually reinforcing. It is not unusual for educationalists to advocate a system that prioritises strategies that fall under the restorative/rehabilitative umbrella and to discourage escalation up the punishment ladder until cooperative efforts to regulate behaviour have been fully explored (Johnson and Johnson, 1995). This approach is formalised in the arena of business regulation through the concept of an enforcement pyramid. Cooperative problem solving and strategies of education and persuasion should be tried first against a backdrop of penalties that can be used sequentially and that escalate in severity until there is no option other than incapacitation (Ayres and Braithwaite, 1992).

Both these literatures suggest a model for institutionalising strategies for dealing with bullying behaviour, a model that gives precedence to a dialogic relational approach (restorative justice) with a punitive individualised approach (retributive justice) being used as the last resort. This model is consistent with the way in which Braithwaite (1999) envisages restorative justice processes operating within a traditional legal framework.

With this in mind, additional data were collected in the 'Life at School Survey' to explore parents' reactions to an enforcement pyramid that combines key elements of the restorative and retributive approaches. Parents were asked the extent to which they agreed or disagreed with the following three models for bringing bullying under control:

1. Through discussions involving teachers, students and parents to sort out problems between children who bully and the children who are bullied.
2. Through enforcing strict rules that forbid bullying and through disciplining guilty parties.
3. Through discussions first and then through stricter enforcement of rules if the problem is not resolved.

Parents responded to each on a scale from 1 (strongly disagree) to 5 (strongly agree). The breakdown across categories is given in Table 8.2. More than three quarters of the parents agreed or strongly agreed with each option, but the most strongly endorsed was option 3. Strong agreement was expressed by 53% of the sample, and agreement by a further 40% for trying a restorative approach prior to a punitive approach.

Table 8.2: Breakdown of Responses and Means (Standard Deviations) for Three Approaches to Controlling Bullying

Approach	Response categories					Mean (SD)
	1	2	3	4	5	
Discussions involving teachers, students and parents to sort out problems between children who bully and the children who are bullied.	1%	4%	10%	51%	34%	4.12 (.83)
Enforcing strict rules that forbid bullying and through disciplining guilty parties.	2%	7%	13%	44%	34%	4.01 (.96)
Discussions first and then through stricter enforcement of rules if the problem is not resolved.	1%	3%	3%	40%	53%	4.42 (.76)

Conclusion

This study examined the value base underlying restorative and retributive approaches to dealing with bullying in schools. Values were examined at the abstract level as principles that guide behaviour across contexts and situations. These same values were hypothesised as underlying child-rearing styles, and these styles were expected to shape parents' preferences for how disciplinary problems should be handled in the school setting.

The hypotheses were largely confirmed, but with some surprises. Values were conceptualised in terms of a security value system and a harmony value system. Both value systems are familiar and deeply embedded in society's institutions. As suggested by previous work, favouring punitive individualised strategies for dealing with bullying was an expression of the security value system. The dialogic relational strategies, in contrast, were an expression of the harmony value system. This finding suggests that restorative justice is not so much founded on new values, as being a new form of expression for some rather old and familiar values in the community.

The harmony value system was linked with supportive self-regulatory parenting, while the security value system was linked with command and control parenting as expected. Particular parenting styles, however, did not predict the kind of disciplinary strategy preferred at school. Parents who practised command and control regulation and parents who practised supportive self-regulation concurred in recommending that schools have both punitive individualised strategies and dialogic relational strategies at their disposal. This result, together with the other findings of the study, point to directions for school policy on bullying that should meet with tolerance, if not approval, from the vast majority of the school community.

The model that meets with most approval from parents is that which uses a restorative justice approach, while giving schools the capacity to move to retributive measures in the event that restorative strategies fail. It appears that parents are willing to prioritise harmony values, as long as measures are in place to give expression to security values should that be necessary. This is not to deny that there are parents who would prefer to go straight to punitive individualised measures and opt for a security approach before anything else. Similarly, there are harmony oriented parents who resist contemplating failure of a dialogic relational approach, and who are horrified at the prospect of escalation to punitive individualised strategies. But both these ideological groups (the security oriented and the harmony oriented) need to accommodate the world views of the other, and these data suggest that such accommodation is not only desirable, but achievable.

The security oriented and the harmony oriented are likely to represent politically active and vocal groups in society. They may engage in adversarial wrangles over policy, but these data suggest that such conflicts should have a constructive rather than destructive end point. First, it is significant that while the security oriented favour a retributive approach and the harmony oriented a restorative approach, they are not strong opponents of each other's preferred strategies. Their understanding of the world and their views on how to make it a better place are not in opposition to each other, just different. Second, most individuals in society are neither security oriented nor harmony oriented, but are dualists (Braithwaite, 1994, 1998a). As such, they want their institutions to deliver harmony, while providing security against those who threaten harm or disruption. Ultimately, the anti-bullying policies adopted by schools will need to meet these expectations. Often we think of a school favouring a particular philosophy in designing its anti-bullying policy, and we think of schools with different philosophies and policies catering for different constituencies. Rigby's (1996) distinction between moralistic, legalistic and humanistic approaches can be readily used to classify schools in terms of how they address bullying.

What is being advocated in this paper, however, is a break from "pure" types that rest on a particular educational or regulatory philosophy. Different strategies make sense to different people, and the diversity among individuals, both students and parents, demands a mix-and-match approach whereby each school has a basket of tools that span the dialogic-relational and punitive-individualised divide.

How the strategies in the basket are put together to be mutually reinforcing needs to be considered within particular contexts, and requires considerably more research. Other contributions in this volume outline some of the principles that need to be considered in designing mixed regulatory approaches. What the current findings can contribute to this debate is an assurance that involving ordinary citizens in the process need not necessarily polarise the debate between retributivists and restorative justice advocates. The findings of this chapter show that in school communities, most parents endorse a dual system. Second, while security and harmony value systems may point parents in different directions, neither group systematically opposes the others' preferred approach. Third, while values may result in different perspectives, these differences are reduced by the experience of parenting. Those who engage with parenting styles in a bid to regulate their child at home are sympathetic to the need for a range of skills at school that answer security and harmony needs. It seems that being a parent can de-politicise problem solving considerably and help us understand the need for compromise and balance in the rules and policies that operate in schools.

Being a parent does not just cover general parenting styles, but specific experiences of feeling over-burdened, dealing with a child accused of bullying, or protecting a child who has been victimised. These experiences shape preferences, but again, in most cases, they do not systematically give rise to opposition to retributive or restorative processes. Victims prefer punitive individualised strategies, but do not oppose dialogic relational ones. Indeed, they support dialogue, along with parents who are stressed by parenting. The only instance where we see systematic opposition to a disciplinary approach is in the case of parents of children accused of bullying. These parents are more likely to regard punitive individualised strategies as counterproductive, and are therefore likely to take an adversarial position in relation to parents of children who are victims. Such conflict is less likely to occur, however, when dialogic relational processes are used. This last finding lends some support to the argument that restorative processes should precede punitive ones.

Note

1   In this way, the measurement of parenting styles departed from the Q-methodology employed by Block (1965) and followed the R-methodology tradition.

References

Abelson, R. P. (1983), 'Whatever Became of Consistency Theory?', *Personality and Social Psychology Bulletin*, vol. 9, pp. 37-54.

Ahmed, E. (1999), *Shame Management and Bullying*, PhD Thesis, Australian National University, Canberra.

Ajzen, I. (1991), 'The Theory of Planned Behavior', *Organizational Behavior and Human Decision Processes*, vol. 50, pp. 179-211.

Amato, P. (1987), *Children in Australian Families: The Growth and Competence*, Prentice Hall, New York.

Ayres, I. and Braithwaite, J. (1992), *Responsive Regulation: Transcending the De-regulation Debate*, Oxford University Press, Oxford.

Baumrind, D. (1968), 'Authoritarian Vs. Authoritative Parental Control', *Adolescence*, vol. 3, pp. 255-72.

Blamey, R. and Braithwaite, V. (1997), 'The Validity of the Security-Harmony Social Values Model in the General Population', *Australian Journal of Psychology*, vol. 49, pp. 71-7.

Block, J. H. (1984), *Sex Role Identity and Ego Development*, Jossey-Bass, San Francisco.

Braithwaite, J. (1999), 'Restorative Justice: Assessing Optimistic and Pessimistic Accounts', in M. Tonry (ed.), *Crime and Justice: A Review of Research*, vol. 25, University of Chicago Press, Chicago.

Braithwaite, V. A. (1982), 'The Structure of Social Values: Validation of Rokeach's Two Value Model', *British Journal of Social Psychology*, vol. 21, pp. 203-11.

Braithwaite, V. (1990), *Bound to Care*, Allen & Unwin, Sydney.

Braithwaite, V. A. (1994), 'Beyond Rokeach's Equality – Freedom Model: Two-dimensional Values in a One-dimensional World', *Journal of Social Issues*, vol. 50, pp. 67-94.

Braithwaite, V. A. (1997), 'Harmony and Security Value Orientations in Political Evaluation', *Personality and Social Psychology Bulletin*, vol. 23, pp. 401-14.

Braithwaite, V. (1998a), 'The Value Balance Model of Political Evaluations', *British Journal of Psychology*, vol. 89, pp. 223-47.

Braithwaite, V. A. (1998b), 'The Value Orientations Underlying Liberalism-Conservatism', *Personality - Individual Differences*, vol. 25, pp. 575-89.

Braithwaite, V. A. (1998c), 'Communal and Exchange Trust Norms, their Value Base and Relevance to Institutional Trust', in V. Braithwaite and M. Levi (eds), *Trust and Governance*, Russell Sage, New York, pp. 46-74.

Braithwaite, V. A. and Blamey, R. (1998), 'Consensus, Stability and Meaning in Abstract Social Values', *Australian Journal of Political Science*, vol. 33, pp. 363-80.

Braithwaite, V. A. and Law, H. G. (1985), 'Structure of Human Values: Testing the Adequacy of the Rokeach Value Survey', *Journal of Personality and Social Psychology*, vol. 49, pp. 250-63.

Braithwaite, V. A. and Scott, W. A. (1991), 'Values', in J. P. Robinson, P. R. Shaver and L. S. Wrightsman (eds), *Measures of Personality and Social Psychological Attitudes*, Academic Press, San Deigo, pp. 661-753.

Daly, K., 'Revisiting the Relationship between Retributive and Restorative Justice' (see Chapter 3 of this volume).

Downs, A. (1957), *An Economic Theory of Democracy*, Harper and Row, New York.

Dryzek, J. and Braithwaite, V. (forthcoming), 'On the Prospects for Democratic Deliberation: Values Analysis Applied to Australian Politics', *Political Psychology*, vol. 20.

Feather, N. T. (1982), *Expectations and Actions: Expectancy-Value Models in Psychology*, Erlbaum, Hillsdale, NJ.

Glaser, D. (1969), *The Effectiveness of a Prison and Parole System*, Bobbs-Merrill, Indianapolis, Indiana.

Goodnow, J. (1988), 'Parents' Ideas, Actions, and Feelings: Models and Methods from Developmental and Social Psychology', *Child Development*, vol. 59, pp. 286-320.

Huntley, S. (1995), *The Socialisation of Pride, Shame and Guilt*, Honours Thesis, Division of Psychology, The Australian National University.

Johnson, D. W. and Johnson, R. T. (1995), *Reducing School Violence through Conflict Resolution*, Association for Supervision and Curriculum Development, Alexandria, Virginia.

Kluckhohn, C. (1951), 'Values and Value Orientations in the Theory of Action', in T. Parsons and E. Shils (eds), *Toward a General Theory of Action*, Harvard University Press, Cambridge, MA, pp. 388-433.

Kocanska, G., Kuczynski, L. and Radke-Yarrow, M. (1989), 'Correspondence between Mothers Self-reported and Observed Child-Rearing Practices', *Child Development*, vol. 60, pp. 56-63.

Morris, A. and Young, W., 'Reforming Criminal Justice: the Potential of Restorative Justice', (see Chapter 2 of this volume).

Rigby, K. (1996), *Bullying in Schools: And What to Do About It*, ACER, Melbourne.

Rokeach, M. (1973), *The Nature of Human Values*, Free Press, New York.

Rokeach, M. (1979), *Understanding Human Values: Human and Societal*, Free Press, New York.

Schwartz, S. H. (1994), 'Are there Universal Aspects in the Structure and Contents of Human Values?', *Journal of Social Issues*, vol. 50, pp. 19-45.

Scott, W. A. (1965), *Values and Organizations: A Study of Fraternities and Sororities*, Rand McNally, Chicago.

Tversky, A. and Kahneman, D. (1986), 'The Framing of Decisions. The Psychology of Choice', *Science*, 211, pp. 453-458.

Wachtel, T. (1999), 'Restorative Justice in Everyday Life: Beyond the Formal Ritual', Paper presented at the Reshaping Australian Institutions Conference, Restorative Justice and Civil Society, The Australian National University, Canberra, February 16-18.

Appendix I

Sample Items for the Security Value System:

National strength and order
> national greatness (being a united, strong, independent, and powerful nation)
> national economic development   (greater economic progress and prosperity for the nation)
> the rule of law (punishing the guilty and protecting the innocent)
> national security (protection of your nation from enemies)

Social standing
> economic prosperity (being financially well off)
> authority (having power to influence others and control decisions)

Getting ahead
> ambitious (being eager to do well)
> competitive (always trying to do better than others)

Propriety in dress and manners
> polite (being well-mannered)
> neat (being tidy)
> reliable (being dependable)

Sample Items for the Harmony Value System:

International harmony and equality
> a good life for others (improving the welfare of all people in need)
> rule by the people (involvement by all citizens in decisions that affect their community)
> international cooperation (having all nations working together to help each other)
> greater economic equality (lessening the gap between the rich and the poor)

Personal growth and inner harmony
> the pursuit of knowledge (always trying to find out new things about the world we live in)
> inner harmony (feeling free of conflict within yourself)

A positive orientation to others
> tolerant (accepting others even though they are different from you)
> helpful (always ready to assist others)
> trusting (having faith in others)

Appendix II

Parenting Styles

Supportive Self-Regulatory Parenting (Authoritative)

1. I make sure my child knows that I appreciate what he/she tries to accomplish.
2. I encourage my child to be curious, to explore and question things.
3. My child and I have warm intimate times together.
4. I let my child make many decisions for him/herself.
5. I find some of my greatest satisfactions in my child.
6. I feel a child should have time to think, daydream, and even loaf sometimes.
7. I joke and play with my child.
8. I believe in praising a child when he/she is good and think it gets better results than punishing him/her when he/she is bad.
9. I encourage my child to wonder and think about life.
10. I am easy-going and relaxed with my child.

Command and Control Parenting (Authoritarian)

1. I try to stop my child from playing rough games or doing things where he/she might get hurt.
2. I do not allow my child to question my decisions.
3. I do not allow my child to say bad things about his/her teachers.
4. I teach my child to keep control of his/her feelings at all times.
5. I let my child know how ashamed and disappointed I am when he/she misbehaves.
6. I try to keep my child away from children of families who have different ideas or values from my own.
7. I believe my child should be aware of how much I sacrifice for him/her.
8. I expect my child to be grateful and appreciate all the advantages he/she has.
9. I believe children should not have secrets from their parents.
10. I do not allow my child to get angry with me.
11. I want my child to make a good impression on others.
12. I believe it is unwise to let children play a lot by themselves without supervision from grown-ups.
13. I expect a great deal from my child.
14. I think it is good practice for a child to perform in front of others.
15. I think a child should be encouraged to do things better than others.

9 Republicanism and Restorative Justice: An Explanatory and Normative Connection

JOHN BRAITHWAITE AND PHILIP PETTIT

Take any normative ideal for how society should be organised and directed. If its defenders wish to make a claim on its behalf, arguing that the ideal is of sufficient importance and attraction to command general allegiance, then they must presumably think that it is intimately related to the things for which people reveal a concern and capacity in their own actions and lives. But if a normative ideal can be shown to have a psychological resonance of this kind, then presumably it must point us towards a basis on which to explain many of the things that people individually do and many of the patterns to which they collectively give rise. It must point us towards a useful explanatory category.

If this thought is correct, then any normative proposal should be subjected to the test of seeing whether it points us towards a plausible explanatory category. Indeed, if the thought is correct, then equally any explanatory category - or at least any that is based in a story about human psychology - should be subjected to the corresponding test of seeing whether it directs us towards a plausible normative ideal: to an ideal that people can be brought, on reflection, to find significantly attractive.

But if an ideal or category proves persuasive on both normative and explanatory fronts, then presumably it may be equipped to serve in both roles to support certain institutional arrangements. It will provide a basis on which to argue that such an arrangement is normatively attractive and it will serve at the same time to show us why the arrangement should work well: it will be able to represent the behaviours required for the arrangement as explicable and reliable.

The paper is designed, following this pattern, to look at the explanatory aspect of the republican ideal of freedom as non-domination, and to explore how far the arrangement for which it provides a normative argument in the area of criminal justice - broadly, a dispensation of restorative justice - is an arrangement for which it also provides explanatory support. The first section focuses on the two aspects of the ideal, comparing it with the two aspects of rival political ideals, and the second turns to the normative-cum-explanatory lessons of the ideal in the area of criminal justice.

Freedom as Non-Domination: Normative Ideal, Explanatory Category

Before coming to the republican ideal and its normative-cum-explanatory dimensions, it may first be useful to look at how the two dimensions show up with some other social and political ideals. This will give us an idea of what we should be looking for with the ideal of freedom as non-domination.

Utilitarianism

Take the most familiar of political ideals to begin with: the utilitarian ideal of maximising overall happiness, in particular in its interpretation as the ideal of maximising overall preference-satisfaction. It is very striking that this ideal does indeed point us towards a more or less plausible explanatory category and that, to that extent at least, it has something to be said in its favour.

The utilitarian ideal, by most accounts, is not one of maximising the satisfaction of just any preferences that people may prove to have. Some of those preferences will be nosy preferences as to what others should do or will derive from non-utilitarian ideas as to how things should be (Dworkin, 1978). Others will be preferences that are formed on a self-sacrificing basis, as in the mannerly preference for giving the better of two options to another and taking the worse oneself (Sen, 1982). The ideal, most plausibly construed, is that of maximising the satisfaction of those preferences that people have which intuitively concern themselves rather than others and which are sourced in a concern for their own fortunes.

But why, a utilitarian may be asked, should we find this ideal even half-way persuasive? The answer that surfaces continually in the literature - most famously or infamously with J. S. Mill's 'proof' of utilitarianism (Mill, 1969) - is that people individually care about the satisfaction of such preferences in their own case. It may not follow from the fact of this self-centred care, contrary to some readings of Mill's argument, that all ought to care about the satisfaction of such preferences in their own case, let alone that all ought to care about the satisfaction of such preferences on the part of people generally. But the existence of the self-centred care does at least make sense of why utilitarians might hope to carry people along with them. They can argue that in the cooperative efforts that people make with one another - particularly, in the cooperative efforts that a democratic state might be thought to represent - the guiding star should be something that all individually care about in their own case. There may be other things that all individually care about but utilitarians can claim that their ideal answers at least to one and that to that extent it proves to be an eligible ideal.

The normative enterprise of utilitarianism may be expected, in view of this argument, to pair off with an explanatory enterprise that seeks to make sense of people's choices by reference to a concern for the satisfaction of their self-regarding preferences. And that enterprise is represented of course in the project of providing economistic or rational choice explanations of people's behaviour in the market, in the polity and in social life more generally. While many economists maintain that they do not assume that the preferences by which behaviour can be explained are mainly self-regarding, this claim is flouted in practice; "homo economicus", in almost all plausible incarnations, proves to be precisely the relatively self-regarding creature that our argument would lead us to expect (Pettit, 1995). We do not pass judgment here on the effectiveness of rational choice theory but we do note that it is to the credit of utilitarianism that it can plausibly claim that its ideal satisfies the explanatory constraint that we have identified.

Rawlsianism

In contemporary political philosophy, the approach that is often set off most forcibly against utilitarianism is the sort of liberalism represented by John Rawls (1971). This breaks with utilitarianism in two ways. First of all, it notes that we may assess the basic structure of a society, not just for how much of something it produces, but also for how it distributes it among members of the society and it argues that the primary concern should be with fair distribution, not maximal production: the primary virtue of institutions, as Rawls puts it, is justice as fairness. And then it says, second, that in identifying the appropriate maximand or rather distribuend, we should not privilege any of the different conceptions of the good that prevail in most societies. We should rather take our starting point from those 'primary goods' that are supposed to be the sorts of things that people will need, no matter what else they happen to desire.

How does the Rawlsian theory of justice fare with the explanatory constraint? If the theory is well grounded - if it is likely to appeal to people as something that they can cooperatively endorse - then two things must hold. First, people must care about how well they do relative to others, as well as about how they do in absolute terms: otherwise the focus on distribution would be misplaced. And second, people must care in particular about how they do in respect of the primary goods: the list that Rawls gives includes income and wealth, freedom and opportunity, and a basis for self-respect.

There is no particular explanatory theory that corresponds to Rawlsianism in the way that rational choice theory answers to utilitarianism. But there are resources in the psychological research tradition on distributive justice (Gergen et al., 1980) and in social science more generally (Cook and Hegtvedt, 1983) to support the claim that people care about how they compare with others as well as about how they do in absolute terms; Bob Frank (1985) has provided ample arguments, for example, in support of the thesis. And it is intuitively plausible to hold, as Rawls does, that people care in particular about how they do in respect of his rather heterogeneous list of primary goods. The only question we would raise here bears on how far they care for freedom in the way in which Rawls articulates it: essentially, in the mould of freedom as non-interference (Pettit, 1997: 50, 301). But that question will arise naturally in the context of our discussion of the republican ideal.

Republicanism

And so, finally, to the republican ideal of freedom as non-domination. Think of how you feel when your welfare depends on the decision of another and you have no come-back against that decision. You are in a position where you will sink or swim, depending on the other's say-so. And you have no physical or legal recourse, no recourse even in a network of mutual friends, against that other. You are in the other's hands; you are at their mercy.

This experience of domination by another comes in many forms. Think of the child of the emotionally volatile parent; the wife of the occasionally violent husband; or the pupil of the teacher who forms arbitrary likes and dislikes. Think of the employee whose security requires keeping the boss or manager sweet; the debtor whose fortunes depend on the caprice of money-lender or bank-manager; or the small business owner whose viability depends on the attitude taken by a bigger competitor or a union boss. Think of the welfare recipient whose fortunes turn on the mood of the counter-clerk; the immigrant or indigenous person whose standing is vulnerable to the whims that rule politics and talk-back radio; or the public employee whose future depends, not on performance, but on the political profile that an ambitious minister happens to find electorally most useful. Think of the older person who is vulnerable to the culturally and institutionally unrestrained gang of youths in her area. Or think indeed of the young offender whose level of punishment depends on how far politicians or newspapers choose to whip up a culture of vengeance.

In all of these cases someone lives at the mercy of others. That person is dominated by those others in the sense that even if they don't interfere in his or her life, they have the power to do so: there are few restraints or costs to inhibit them. If the dominated person escapes ill treatment, that is by the grace or favour of the powerful. The person lives in their power or under the mastery of those others: they occupy the position of a "dominus" - the Latin word for master - in his or her life.

The republican ideal of freedom as non-domination is the ideal of organising society and politics in such a way that this domination - this subjection to the arbitrary will of another - is minimised. A republican arrangement will have to struggle to ensure non-domination on two fronts: first, by restraining the private power associated with "dominium", as the Romans called it; and second, by restraining the public power - the "imperium" - of those in government. On the first front the republican ideal provides a basis for devising policies whereby people can be effectively protected, informed and empowered in relation to one another. On the second it provides a basis for devising constitutional and democratic constraints whereby people can be assured of not being dominated by the very government that is supposed to protect them from domination by others. Such an assurance of non-domination will be forthcoming to the extent and only to the extent - a big and difficult qualification - that government is forced, when it interferes in people's lives, to do so in a way that is not arbitrary: in a way that tracks their common perceived interests.

So much for the nature of the republican ideal of non-domination that we endorse (Braithwaite and Pettit, 1990; Pettit, 1997). The question that we now want to ask is how far it points us towards a plausible explanatory category: how far it satisfies the sort of explanatory constraint that we think any plausible ideal should be able to satisfy.

If freedom as non-domination is maximised in a society then, for reasons given elsewhere, we think that it will also tend to be equally distributed (Braithwaite and Pettit, 1990: Ch. 5; Pettit, 1999: Ch. 4). The main thread in the argument goes roughly like this. Suppose that people fare equally well in non-domination terms, enjoying equivalent resources of empowerment relative to each other. It is extremely unlikely that the quantum of non-domination can be increased overall by giving one of these people further resources still, thereby introducing an inequality. For any move that gives one person extra resources will affect others negatively and will reduce their freedom as non-domination at the very moment that it increases the freedom as non-domination of the original person.

If this claim about maximisation and equalisation is sound, as we think it is, then there is no issue raised for the approach as to whether people are as fundamentally concerned with distribution as with overall production of non-domination. Let people be concerned about either, or about both, and our approach will be to that extent vindicated.

But the more telling question is whether it is plausible to think that people are concerned, each in his or her own case, with how far they enjoy non-domination. Enjoying non-domination will have two sides to it. On the one hand, it will mean not having another agent or agency stand over you, in a position to interfere in your life without regard to your perceived interests. And on the other hand, it will mean not being so constrained by non-dominating restrictions - natural obstacles and limitations, and the restraints of a non-dominating law or culture - that there is very little undominated choice to enjoy. So the question is whether people care in their own case, first for the absence of the domination of others, and second for the presence of opportunities in which undominated choice can be exercised. Almost everyone nowadays is happy to assume that people care about the second sort of factor and we shall concentrate here on the first.

We have a three-stage argument for holding that people care very deeply about not being dominated by others (cf. Pettit, 1997: Ch. 3). The first stage in the argument is that people care much more about a harm that they suffer at the hands of another than they care about a harm that they suffer as a result of natural misfortune. The consideration that reveals the depth of that care is this: that in such cases people generally feel resentment at the action of the other as well as the loss that they would feel had the cause been just a natural accident. And resentment, by a long tradition of thought, is one of the very deepest and most disturbing of human emotions (Strawson, 1982). There are many theories as to why resentment at harm done by others is nearly universal among humans. Alfred Adler, for example, argues that the will to struggle against inferiority and to escape adult domination is born of the need to survive at the stage when dependency on parents ends and we are left to our own resources (Ansbacher and Ansbacher, 1956). But we do not need to pronounce on the origins of resentment; it is sufficient for our purposes that we can plausibly postulate it.

As against this emphasis on resentment, some may point out we don't feel resentment if the person who interferes in our life is not negligent or deliberate, or if the interference has in some way been licensed by us: if we are like Ulysses in relation to the sailors who keep him bound. But that is no objection in the present case, because interference will not be an exercise of domination if it is not intentional or negligent. And neither will it be an exercise of domination if it tracks the perceived interests of the interferee, as it would in the Ulysses-type case. Indeed that is why republicans think that the law, if it is a proper republican law, will not dominate those in whose lives it interferes.

The first stage of argument gives grounds for thinking that we care much more about the sort of actual interference that domination makes possible than we would care about a corresponding natural restriction. But we need also to show that we care about domination, even when there is no restriction imposed: even when the "dominus" in our lives happens not to use their power against us.

The second stage in our argument says that we do indeed care about such domination and for just the same reason: it too gives rise to resentment; or at least it gives rise to resentment in anyone of the kind we are likely to admire. Think about how you must feel towards another to the extent that there is no physical difficulty, no legal risk, no cultural inhibition, no moral commitment, and no prospect of retaliation that might stop them from exercising a certain form of arbitrary interference in your life. You may be able to escape such interference, say by means of keeping your head down, or by currying the favour of that person, by cultivating in yourself the sorts of preferences they approve of, or by being lucky enough to have achieved such results without trying. But even if you do those things, you are surely likely to resent the need to do them. Certainly you will resent the need to do them unless you are the servile sort who has lost a sense of self, as we would say: the sort of person who has internalised their subjection and identified with someone on whose mercy they depend.

The upshot of these two stages of argument is that the ideal of freedom as non-domination has deep psychological roots in the resentment that we would all feel, short of being self-abasing types, at another's having arbitrary power to interfere in our lives in some way and at our being required therefore to take precautionary measures. The third stage in the argument complements this conclusion about the negative resonance of domination by drawing attention to the positive resonance that non-domination, in particular conscious non-domination, has in our psychology.

Imagine that you are in a position where no one else is able to interfere on an arbitrary basis in your life, or at least where you are as well off as anyone else in this respect. Imagine that you are aware of this, that it is a matter of which you may expect others to be aware, and indeed that it is likely to be a matter of common or mutual awareness. Since being non-dominated requires public resources of empowerment, it is by no means unlikely that those conditions will be fulfilled (Pettit, 1997: Ch. 2). In such a case you will enjoy what is most properly described as standing or status in the eyes of others. You will not just be treated respectfully by them; you will command their respect, so far as they are forced to recognise your power. You will be able to look each of them in the eye, in a shared awareness that you cannot be denied a voice or a hearing or a response in the general run of exchanges that constitute social life. You will be a somebody, not a nobody.

So much for the motivational roots that make it plausible for republicans like us to say that an ideal for social and political life is that things be organised so that domination is minimised, and minimised in such a way that people retain significant room for the enjoyment of undominated choice (on the balance between these dimensions see Pettit, 1999: Ch. 3). If those roots have a real hold in human psychology, then we should expect that there will be an explanatory category or categories corresponding to the republican ideal. And of course that category is not hard to find. It is marked in the widespread recognition of the desire for empowerment - having control over one's life with others - and of the aversion to powerlessness and subordination. The literature of psychology and sociology, history and political theory gives sustained testimony to the importance of this desire and this aversion in human life.

To sum up, then, the connection between being dominated and feeling resentful, and the emotional power of resentment in our lives, makes it entirely plausible by our lights to claim that the republican ideal has deep psychological roots. That in turn implies, then, that it ought to prove possible to explain many human responses by the desire to express or avoid resentment and its associated ailments. And this, we think, is borne out in much contemporary work in the psychological and social sciences, as well as in the wisdom - and common sense - of the ages.

The Normative and Explanatory Connection to Restorative Justice

We have looked elsewhere at the normative implications of the republican standpoint for the design of a criminal justice system (Braithwaite and Pettit, 1990). While we didn't make a case for a system of restorative justice as such, the features that we said should be incorporated in any republican system of criminal justice are all characteristic of restorative justice. In this second section what we would like to do is show that not only does republicanism provide a normative case for promoting those features (and make thereby for a normative connection with restorative justice) but also that the case is supported by empirical considerations in a way that makes equally for an explanatory connection between republicanism and restorative justice.

The features that we identified as essential to any republican system of criminal justice are: a preference for parsimony in criminal justice interventions, particularly in the sanctions imposed on offenders; a commitment to seeing that whatever power is given within the criminal justice system to different agents and agencies, that power is never arbitrary but is subject to systematic checks; and an orientation towards reprobation of offending and towards the ultimate reintegration of both offenders and victims. We propose to look at each of these headings in turn, showing in each case how the normative argument that republicanism provides is buttressed or likely to be buttressed by an argument that derives from the explanatory significance of the republican ideal of non-domination.

Parsimony

The normative preference for parsimony arises because any criminal justice intervention involves initial and near-certain costs to freedom as non-domination. This is true of criminalisation, surveillance, arrest or punishment. In contrast, the benefits of such interventions are more distant and probabilistic. Hence the prescription: if in doubt, intervene less in peoples' lives. Where intervention is parsimonious, people are likely to feel and be less dominated (Braithwaite and Pettit, 1990: 87).

But is this prescription really a sensible approach? Isn't it likely to err always on the side of leniency, confronting potential offenders with lower expected costs that are needed to dissuade them from crime? The theory of rational choice that is associated with utilitarianism would argue that we ought to go straight for those interventions that would have the effect of making the expected costs of a life of crime exceed the expected benefits. Thus, many will say that while parsimony may have a normative appeal for republicans, the likelihood is that it will not work as well in practice as a policy that is more firmly rooted in an explanatory theory such as rational choice.

This line of thought, however, is profoundly mistaken. For it turns out that the empirical evidence supports a presumption - an overridable presumption - in favour of parsimony; and that this evidence fits with the explanatory perspective provided by republicanism.

The relevant evidence is best encapsulated in Brehm and Brehm's (1981) theory of psychological reactance. Figure 9.1 summarises the patterns of results from a number of experiments on the effect of force against the exercise of a freedom. More force produces more deterrence. However, it simultaneously produces more "reactance". Reactance is loosely what the criminological literature refers to as defiance effects (Sherman, 1992). What is the net effect - the net social control - secured by a given use of force. That is given by measuring the deterrence effect and then subtracting from it the reactance effect of the intervention in question.

Figure 9.1: The Interaction between the Importance of a Freedom and the Contest between Deterrence and Reactance
(from Brehm and Brehm, 1981: 60)

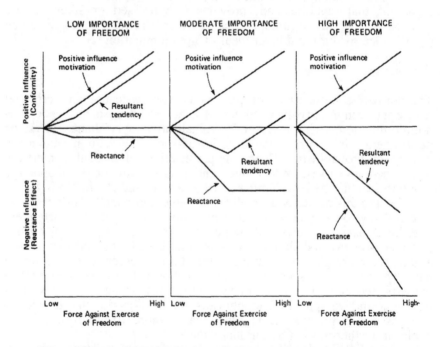

What Figure 9.1 illustrates is that reactance is greatest when controlling force is used against a freedom of high importance to the citizen, as in the right hand panel. Let freedom of religion be involved, for example, and any attempt at regulation is likely to have enormous reactance effects: throwing more Christians to the lions may only increase the resolve of Christians. In the left hand panel, the freedom that is subjected to regulation is of low importance to the citizen: it may be the freedom to park a car wherever one wants. As the force used against the exercise of that freedom increases - as parking fines are raised, for example - reactance is low and the net social control achieved by the intervention will be mainly determined by its deterrence effect and the result will be as rational choice theory would predict.

These results should not be surprising, in light of the explanatory category to which republicanism points us: the concern of people not to be stood over by others. For it is precisely in cases where freedom is important to people, that any attempt to regulate it will have the aspect of domination. From their point of view, it will represent the presence in their lives of an arbitrary power of interference that is not itself forced to track their common perceived interests. And the results that support this lesson are not an isolated set of findings. More than 50 studies in a related tradition of psychological research shows that extrinsic rewards or punishments that are viewed as dominating or controlling tend to undermine intrinsic motivation to act in the direction commended by the incentives (Boggiano et al., 1987: 867).

The presumption in favour of parsimony is supported, then, not just by normative republican arguments but also by the explanatory considerations to which republicanism points us. That presumption is well respected in the idea of a restorative justice conference of a sort that republicanism commends and so we see here a tight explanatory as well as normative connection between republicanism and restorative justice. The idea behind the conference is that it should reach a non-dominated consensus as to what the offender or offenders should have to do, in the circle of all those affected by a crime: victim, offenders, family, peers, police and so on. To be non-dominated, it should be a consensus reached by moral reasoning, in particular moral reasoning about the harm that has been suffered as a result of the crime. To the extent that this is achieved by restorative justice, the prediction is that restorative justice should be more effective at securing subsequent compliance with the law than coercion that involves no attempt to persuade the offender. Deliberative regulation of crime will not only be more normatively decent, but partly because it is more decent, it will be more effective.

Of course Figure 9.1 also reveals that there will be contexts where this will not be true. For example, in the context of the middle panel of Figure 9.1 (moderate importance of freedom) it can be seen that if dialogue and low-level sanctions have failed, escalating to tough deterrent sanctions may have a positive influence on compliance. The reason for this is the shape of the reactance curve when freedoms are moderately important. With an escalating threat people dig their heels in more and more until the point is reached where the coercive force confronting them becomes so severe that they give up on escalating their resistance. As deterrence effects then outstrip reactance effects, we find a context where escalating deterrence works. With the right hand panel, we find contexts where no amount of persuasion nor any amount of deterrence will work: the man who views it as his inalienable right of fatherhood to physically abuse his children may be unpersuadable and undeterrable. Then we may need to incapacitate his criminality by taking his children away from him or even locking him up.

Parsimony is commended by the results of the reactance experiments and the experiments on extrinsic threat and intrinsic motivation. They show why coercion is more likely to be counterproductive than productive, complementing criminological research on the various counterproductive effects of imprisonment and other forms of degradation (Gendreau, Goggin and Cullen, 1999), of punitive authoritarian parenting compared to authoritative parenting (Baumrind, 1978; Sampson and Laub, 1995). However, the pattern of the results of the reactance experiments also shows why there will be contexts where deterrence will work when the deliberative regulation of restorative justice fails and contexts where incapacitation will be needed because both deliberation and deterrence fail. So we see the empirical evidence as grounding a normative preference for parsimony as a presumption that can be overridden. If in doubt about what to do, our presumption will be to try deliberative regulation (restorative justice) first even with very serious kinds of crime. We will only opt for deterrent regulation in light of clear evidence that restorative justice will fail, or direct experience of trying it and failing. Similarly, we will be parsimonious in escalating from deterrence to more draconian incapacitative regulation. Both the normative story and the explanatory story about parsimony can ultimately be traced back to the fact that freedom as non-domination is an idea with both explanatory and normative purchase.

Checking of Power

Freedom as non-domination achieves its full value for those who possess it to the extent that it is common knowledge in their society that they do indeed possess the relative immunity it confers against arbitrary interference. To that extent it will require the provision of both objective and subjective assurance that those who have power in the society - in particular, power that comes from public office - cannot exercise that power arbitrarily against others. There are checks on the exercise of the power that guarantee or militate against arbitrariness.

It is this line of thought that motivates one of the most striking institutional prescriptions associated with the republican tradition: that public power should be placed in many hands, so far as that is possible, and not given in monopoly measure to any one individual or group (Pettit, 1997: Ch. 2). This prescription lies behind the age-old republican preference for having more than one assembly - Rome had four; for having a representation of different classes within those assemblies; for dividing up public responsibilities between different officials, even investing some officials or bodies with a power of challenging or vetoing or reviewing the actions of others; and for separating out the basic government functions: the functions, as identified in Montesquieu's (1989) magisterial and distinctively republican work, of legislation, administration and adjudication.

In our original analysis of the normative significance of republicanism for criminal justice, we emphasised the need to introduce this emphasis on the importance of checking public power to the design of the criminal justice system (Braithwaite and Pettit, 1990) and in later work one of us extended this emphasis to separating and mutual checking of private powers (Braithwaite, 1997). Not only should it be invoked in arguing against unchecked power on the part of police, prosecutors, and prison warders, for example; it should also be invoked in considering how we can guard against crime in the world of potential offenders, particularly the corporate world.

State power is often less profound than private corporate power, especially in weaker states than France, the United Kingdom and the United States, where so much republican theory has been written. If we want to check the criminal abuse of power, therefore, we must pluralise our conception of the separation of powers and look for devices for checking corporate power and, in particular, for guarding against collusion between business and government. The introduction of independent accountants and auditors - in particular, auditors who had statutory duties beyond responsibilities to their clients - was a nineteenth century innovation that carried the principle of the separation of powers into the corporate world, after the English Registered Companies Act of 1862. Independent auditors may be a weak force in themselves but they are not negligible, especially when they are one strand in a web of controls. It was Arthur Young, the auditors, who effectively blew the whistle when the Lockheed corporation was bribing the Prime Minister of Japan and others to buy military aircraft (Boulton, 1978).

So much for the normative connection between the republican ideal of non-domination and the need for checking power in the world of criminal justice, broadly conceived. But that connection, it now transpires, is reinforced by an explanatory connection in just the way that the connection with a presumption in favour of parsimony is reinforced. Some critics might have thought that enforcing procedures for checking power would hamper the state's attempt to regulate and reduce crime and that, notwithstanding the normative republican case for doing so, it would not represent a sensible policy. But that, it turns out, is not so, at least by some evidence currently available in criminology.

There are many types of criminological literatures which suggest both that powerlessness over one's own life promotes crime and that extreme levels of unchecked power over the lives of others is a cause of a different kind of crime (see particularly the debates around Charles Tittle's (1995) control balance theory) (Piquero and Hickman, 1999). The key idea of our republican reading of this criminological tradition is that extremes of unchecked power engender two kinds of crime problems. First, crimes of exploitation that are made possible by the unchecked power of those who dominate; and, second, crimes on the part of those who suffer from this domination to such an extent that they feel they have little to lose and much to resent. In the worst cases of domination, we find intergenerational criminality in families so deflated by their powerlessness that they give up on the idea that they can regulate their children (Weatherburn, forthcoming) or even perhaps themselves. These twin explanatory stories explain why republican checks on the wealth and power of the powerful can simultaneously help control crimes of exploitation and crimes of the exploited (see Braithwaite, 1991).

These results should not be surprising, if we are persuaded of the importance of the explanatory category highlighted in republicanism. If people are averse to being stood over, then a chronic exposure to such domination is likely to demoralise them so that they no longer care about the costs associated with crime. And if people are allowed dominating power, then it will be no surprise for a republican if they exercise it. The emphasis on the importance of ensuring against domination is inspired by a belief that domination represents an attractive temptation for those who can have it. Lord Acton was drawing on deep themes in the republican tradition when he said that all power corrupts and that absolute power corrupts absolutely.

What is the lesson for restorative justice? As we have seen in other contributions in this book, the restorative justice approach holds to the regulative ideal that all stakeholders affected by a breach of the law have an opportunity to participate in deciding what to do about it. This implies a major difference from old-fashioned statist regulation: from a regime, for example, where a nursing home inspector meets with the manager of the facility at the end of an inspection to tell her what has to be done to come into compliance and whether there will be any prosecution. At a restorative exit conference, there can be representatives present from nursing home residents, relatives, staff, advocacy groups, outside directors as well as different levels of management. Resolving matters through the payment of a business-government bribe is more difficult in the context of these more richly separated powers that inhere in a more deliberative restorative justice process. In the best case, it would be necessary to bribe a roomful of people all digging into what went on, all with a more direct stake in a decent outcome than the government inspector.

This line of thought shows that in this respect, as in respect of the presumption in favour of parsimony, republicanism gives explanatory as well as normative support to restorative justice. It shows that restorative justice can serve to prevent the abuse of power. And it probably helps to explain why the empirical research shows that citizens mostly prefer restorative justice conferences to the courtroom adjudication of disputes (Braithwaite, 1999). It may be that consensus decisionmaking in restorative justice is a reason for this, though there is no empirical evidence to support this yet. That is, if participants keep talking until a consensus agreement is reached that they all will voluntarily sign, they are likely to feel less dominated than if the judge slams his hammer at some point to impose a decision. Process control (e.g. the control of the offender and victim over who is to be invited to the conference) is particularly important in driving citizen perceptions of fairness here. Indeed, process control may also be the facet of procedural justice that best explains subsequent compliance with the law by offenders (Makkai and Braithwaite, 1996; see generally Tyler, 1990). Empowerment prevents crime; dominated process causes it.

Reprobation and Reintegration

The reprobative ideal in criminal justice is that whatever process someone charged with an offence receives, and whatever remedy is meted out to an offender, it should be designed to communicate in the fashion of a piece of moral reasoning the grounds for taking the offence seriously and condemning it (Duff, 1986). The process and the remedy should not be mechanical or merely punitive procedures, without moral significance. The reintegrative ideal, closely tied to this, is that whatever process and treatment is involved, it should so far as possible promote the prospect that the victim and the offender are each reintegrated into society as recognised, respected members.

These ideals derive straightforwardly from the republican ideal of non-domination. For criminal process and criminal punishment will succeed in avoiding domination only so far as it is clear to all that they are guided by perceived interests that the offender shares with others in the society. And it is only so far as victim and offender are fully reintegrated into society that either can hope to enjoy their status as non-dominated members. Unless offenders can return to a situation where they can enjoy social support from those they care about, for example, their prospects of not being dominated and of not trying to dominate others are poor. Frank Cullen (1984) has reviewed the considerable empirical evidence that social support is associated with reduced prospects of reoffending.

In supporting the ideals of reprobation and reintegration, republicanism makes its closest normative contact with restorative justice. Restorative justice conferences offer the best prospect of achieving a process, and an agreed outcome, that will communicate the reason why the offence is objectionable. And they also promise the best chance of reintegration. They are designed to maximise social support for both offenders and victims, particularly through selecting for attendance those supporters enjoying the strongest relationships of trust or love with them.

But are restorative justice conferences likely to be effective? From the perspective of rational choice theory, it may seem not; after all, they would seem to reduce the expected costs of committing those crimes that will go to conference. Here once again, however, it turns out that the empirical evidence on restorative justice, while preliminary, is encouraging (Braithwaite, 1999) and that the explanatory category to which republicanism points us - the importance for people of not being stood over by others - helps to make sense of that evidence.

Nathan Harris's (1999) research, for example, shows that the only kind of disapproval arising from court and conference cases that arouses shame is perceived disapproval of the act by those whose respect the offender values very highly. The disapproval of judges, policemen or other people the offender does not greatly respect fails to induce remorse. One reason may be that their attempts at control are (rightly) seen as motivated by domination rather than by love or friendship. It follows that a restorative conference design that assures the attendance of those who love and respect the offender most has the best chance of inducing remorse.

The impact of restorative justice conferences will be particularly positive if reintegrative shaming theory is correct (Braithwaite, 1989). And there is some evidence that reintegrative shaming does reduce lawbreaking (Braithwaite, 1999). But it is early days in the empirical assessment of this theory; in fact, our Restorative Justice Group colleagues at ANU will over the next two years publish data that will demonstrate a need for some important revisions to the theory of reintegrative shaming, while still supporting many key aspects of its explanatory claims.

٦

Conclusion

Freedom as non-domination is a compelling normative ideal for a criminal justice system and domination is also important to explaining crime and what kind of crime prevention works. The republican normative theory of non-domination commends restorative justice as an attractive way of dealing with known criminal offenders and victims. The explanatory theory of domination and crime explains why restorative justice may be more effective in preventing crime than punishment by courts. Restorative justice is of course neither the most important implication of republican normative theory nor the most important implication of explanatory theories of domination and crime. But its convergence as a corollary of potent normative and explanatory theories speaks to the importance of restorative justice.

But our paper also underlines a more general conclusion. This is that in doing social theory we should look for an adjustment between normative and explanatory categories of analysis and that, if we do so, we are likely to reach a higher level of performance on both fronts (Parker, 1999). Any normative theory that works with a category that lacks explanatory resonance is likely to be utopian and it will serve our policy-making badly. Any explanatory theory that fails to connect with a normative concern is likely to be unguided and it will be incapable of serving policy-making at all. Normative theory without explanatory theory is empty; explanatory theory without normative theory is blind, often dangerously so.

References

Ansbacher, H. and Ansbacher, R. (1956), *The Individual Psychology of Alfred Adler*, Basic Books, New York.

Baumrind, D. (1978), 'Parental Disciplinary Patterns and Social Competence in Children', *Youth and Society*, vol. 9, pp. 239-76.

Boggiano, Ann K., Barrett, Mary, Weiher, Anne W., McLelland, Anne W. and Lusk, Cynthia M. (1987), 'Use of the Maximal Operant Principle to Motivate Children's Intrinsic Interest', *Journal of Personality and Social Psychology*, vol. 53, pp. 866-79.

Boulton, D. (1978), *The Grease Machine*, Harper and Row, New York.

Braithwaite, J. (1989), *Crime, Shame and Reintegration*, Cambridge University Press, Cambridge.

Braithwaite, J. (1997), 'On Speaking Softly and Carrying Big Sticks: Neglected Dimensions of a Republican Separation of Powers', *University of Toronto Law Journal*, vol. 47, pp. 305-61.

Braithwaite, John (1999), 'Restorative Justice: Assessing Optimistic and Pessimistic Accounts', in M. Tonry (ed.), *Crime and Justice: A Review of Research,* vol. 25, University of Chicago Press, Chicago.

Braithwaite, J. and Pettit, P. (1990), *Not Just Deserts: A Republican Theory of Criminal Justice,* Oxford University Press, Oxford.

Brehm, Sharon S. and Brehm, Jack W. (1981), *Psychological Reactance: A Theory of Freedom and Control,* Academic Press, New York.

Cook, K. S. and Hegvedt, K. A. (1983), 'Distributive Justice, Equity, and Equality', *Annual Review of Sociology,* vol. 9, pp. 217-41.

Cullen, Francis T. (1994), 'Social Support as an Organizing Concept for Criminology: Presidential Address to the Academy of Criminal Justice Sciences', *Justice Quarterly,* vol. 11, pp. 527-59.

Duff, R. A. (1986), *Trials and Punishments,* Cambridge University Press, Cambridge.

Dworkin, R. (1978), *Taking Rights Seriously,* Duckworth, London.

Frank, R. (1985), *Choosing the Right Pond,* Oxford University Press, New York.

Gendreau, Paul, Goggin, Claire and Cullen, Francis T. (1999), *The Effects of Prison Sentences on Recidivism,* A Report to the Corrections Research and Development and Aboriginal Policy Branch, Solicitor General of Canada, Ottawa.

Gergen, K. J., Greenberg, M. S. and Willis, R. H. (1980), *Social Exchange: Advances in Theory and Research,* Plenum, New York.

Harris, Nathan (1999), 'Shame and Shaming: An Empirical Analysis', PhD Dissertation, Law Program, Australian National University.

Makkai, Toni and Braithwaite, John (1996), 'Procedural Justice and Regulatory Compliance', *Law and Human Behavior,* vol. 20, pp. 83-98.

Mill, J. S. (1969), *Essays on Ethics, Religion and Society (Collected Works, Vol. 10),* Routledge, London.

Montesquieu, C. d. S. (1989), *The Spirit of the Laws,* Cambridge University Press, Cambridge.

Parker, Christine (1999), *Just Lawyers,* Oxford University Press, Oxford.

Pettit, P. (1995), 'The Virtual Reality of Homo Economicus', *Monist,* vol. 78, pp. 308-29.

Pettit, P. (1997), *Republicanism: A Theory of Freedom and Government,* Oxford University Press, Oxford.

Piquero, Alex R., Hickman, Matthew (1999), 'An Empirical Test of Tittle's Control Balance Theory', *Criminology,* vol. 37, pp. 319-43.

Rawls, J. (1971), *A Theory of Justice,* Oxford University Press, Oxford.

Sampson, Robert and Laub, John H. (1995), *Crime in the Making: Pathways and Turning Points Through Life,* Harvard University Press, Cambridge, Mass.

Sen, A. (1982), *Choice, Welfare and Measurement,* Blackwell, Oxford.

Sherman, L. W. (1992), *Policing Domestic Violence,* Free Press, New York.

Strawson, P. (1974), *Freedom and Resentment, and Other Essays,* Methuen, London.

Tittle, Charles (1995), *Control Balance: Toward a General Theory of Deviance,* Westview Press, Boulder, Co.

Tyler, Tom, (1990), *Why People Obey the Law,* Yale University Press, New Haven, CT.

Watson, G. (1982), *Free Will*, Oxford University Press, Oxford.

Weatherburn, Don and Lind, Bronwyn (forthcoming), *The Economic and Social Antecedents of Delinquent-Prone Communities*, Cambridge University Press, Cambridge.

10 Restorative Justice and the Republican Theory of Criminal Justice: An Exercise in Normative Theorising on Restorative Justice[1]

LODE WALGRAVE

Restorative justice techniques seem to leave gradually their "research and development" phase and to evolve in many countries towards being a "normalised" routine activity. One of the main risks of thoughtless enthusiasm is possible negligence of the legal rights of those involved. However, settling the aftermath of a crime without respect for human rights and the essential freedoms due to all citizens involved would be detrimental to society and its communities.

Till now, restorative theory has focused more on psycho-social and ethical aspects than on legal thinking. Not surprisingly, because restorative justice has emerged partly out of dissatisfaction with formal juridical procedures. Most restorative interventions favour informalism, in order to promote 'encounter' and 'participation' (van Ness and Heetderks Strong, 1997), and that is often difficult to combine with strict legal procedures. Prominent scholars even claim that only restorative justice can include voluntary settlements (e.g. Marshall, 1996). They consider free participation in the process and voluntary compliance with the agreements as satisfying replacements for legal safeguards. If not, it is feared, legal formalism and rule setting would hinder the healing and encountering character of the sessions.

However, the restorative option on doing justice cannot be restricted to voluntary processes only. A 'maximalist view' on restorative justice includes also the use of coercion, to be implemented by a 'restorative justice system', and that should guarantee all legal safeguards[2] (Walgrave, 1995; Bazemore and Walgrave, 1999a). But voluntary sessions need to be checked as to their respect for legal rights (Warner, 1994; Wright, 1998; Trépanier, 1998). The voluntariness of the participation, the power balance in the negotiations, the reasonableness of the agreed compensation and the true commitment to comply are elements to be checked and assured. This is not to say that legal formalism should intrude into the restorative process, but that this process should take place in a 'legalised context'.

Restorative justice proponents must reflect intensely on the question of how to construct a system that would combine maximal openness for informal encounters of those 'with a stake in the aftermath of a particular offence' (Marshall, 1996: 37), with maximal guarantees for their rights and freedoms. Some consider legal problems with restorative justice as being insurmountable. This makes them very sceptical with regard to the feasibility of a restorative justice system (Ashworth, 1993; Feld, 1999). Others, however, take up the challenge, and reflect on the possible insertion of restorative justice into the principles of the democratic constitutional state (van Ness, 1993, 1996, 1997 with Heetderks Strong, and 1999).

In this text, I will focus on legal theorising about a coercive justice system that would be oriented towards doing justice through restoration, as the feasibility of this is the litmus test for the maximalist option on restorative justice. Referral to voluntary settlements will only happen occasionally.

Searching for a Foundation

Several countries and states have partly legislated restorative justice practices. New Zealand is often quoted as the most far-reaching example (Brown and McElrea, 1993), but also some states in Australia and the United States states have legislated restorative interventions towards crime. The majority of Western industrialised countries provide in their justice systems opportunities for mediation, group conferencing and/or community service, as a pathway for diversion or as an intra judicial intervention scheme (Schelkens, 1998).

Restorative Justice is not a New Version of Punitive Justice

For our undertaking it is appropriate to start with a discussion on legal theory and legal principles. The existing legal theories do not deal with restorative justice, but with penal law. Restorative justice, however, claims to be more than just another version of existing juridical approaches, but to be another paradigm (Bazemore and Walgrave, 1999a). That provokes the need for at least a fundamental rethinking of the existing theories.

The paradigm-claim is a matter of discussion. Some authors are of the opinion that restorative justice offers nothing more than another version of the same basic retributive option of doing justice. Restorative justice then is no 'alternative to punishment', but an 'alternative punishment' (Duff, 1992). The differences in character between retributivist and restorative approaches would better be forgotten, is their opinion (Daly and Immarigeon, 1998; Daly, 1999). These authors seem to overlook an essential element in conceptualising punishment. For Daly (1999), for example, everything that is unpleasant is a punishment. In such a vision, there is indeed no principled reason to distinguish properly between punishment and restoration, because an obligation to restore may be very unpleasant.

However, we must regard punishment in a more specific way. Punishment only occurs when the pain is willingly inflicted, and is inflicted on a person because of the wrongfulness of the behaviour he/she has done. In von Hirsch's words, 'punishing someone consists of visiting a deprivation (hard treatment) on him, because he supposedly has committed a wrong, in a manner that expresses disapprobation of the person for his conduct' (von Hirsch, 1993: 9). Punishment and restoration differ fundamentally then, despite some similarities. Both retributive and restorative responses can provide clear limits to social tolerance, base the intervention on the accountability of the offender, can use force upon him, and may be painful. But the restorative response to a crime does not aim at censuring through hard treatment, but at being restorative, which may be painful though. The outcome is meant to be beneficial for the victim, constructive for society and more reintegrative for the offender. Painfulness only applies when it is needed to achieve restoration. It is subordinated to the aim of restoration.

We therefore maintain the necessity to reflect on a legal theory that addresses the specific characteristics of the restorative approach to doing justice, as distinguished from the traditional criminal justice theories.

For a Consequentionalist Approach

Literature often distinguishes between two different types of legal theories on criminal justice (Braithwaite and Pettit, 1990). Deontological theorists look for intrinsic values and how to make them operational through a set of constraints for the criminal justice system. They do not ask questions about possible targets, because they do not believe in the "engineerability" of society through legislation and legal intervention. Constraints cannot be subordinated to goals, because that would subordinate the values, intrinsically linked with the constraints, to the goals set forward (like in rehabilitative justice, for example). In a deontological option, we would enlist a series of prescriptions to which penal law is subjected, such as the legality principle, the due process principle, the proportionality principle, and then examine if these constraints also apply to restorative justice, possibly in an adjusted or reformulated form (Warner, 1994). That is what van Ness has done (1999) and what we also have tried with regard to proportionality (Walgrave and Geudens, 1996).

Consequentionalist theories, on the contrary, do reflect on for what purpose the criminal justice system exists, and derive the constraints from the target put forward. Adherents of such a theoretical approach consider that criminal justice inevitably serves a purpose.

The contradiction between both theoretical models seems to be sometimes exaggerated. A purely deontological theory does not exist. They mostly hide some consequentionalist presuppositions. Von Hirsch (1993), for example, stresses the need for punishment, because of the need for censure, and censure is needed to keep morality. But why should we keep morality? Can we still maintain that morality is given by nature, or do we accept that it is a pragmatist social construction, based on civilisation, to keep life in community livable? Morality as such serves a target and preserving morality through censure indirectly serves the same target.

On the other hand, a purely consequentionalist theory would mean that the end justifies the means, and that is unacceptable. The aim of rehabilitation, for example, as put forward for juvenile justice, cannot justify endless intervention. Juveniles, their families and victims have rights to be respected, regardless of the rehabilitative purpose. Here, principled (often deontological) reasons seem to overrule the rehabilitative purpose.

We therefore must start our theorising toward such apparently deontological principles by reflecting on targets. If we would not indicate a target for the criminal justice system, why would we keep it? If we do not expect any positive effect from that system, what should we fear from abolishing it? Criminal justice must deserve its right to exist through the target it promotes. There is a deep tension between the fundamentals of our democratic constitutional states, i.e. the protection and promotion of the citizens' rights and freedoms, on the one hand, and the essentials of the coercive judicial system, being the reduction of citizens' freedoms, on the other. That is why the criminal justice system must be used carefully and only in clearly defined exceptional situations. Intervening by coercion and reduction of freedom can only apply in a situation of emergency. These situations must be clearly defined, referring to commonly acceptable goals.

Restoring the Harm to Dominion as the Target

Defining the Target

Though Braithwaite and Pettit's 'Republican Theory of Criminal Justice' (1990) deals with a punitive criminal justice system, it does reject the retributive starting point of most traditional criminal justice theories and it searches for a more constructive response to crime. That makes it an attractive basis for opening reflection on a model for legalising restorative justice. Second, it is based on a communitarian view of humankind, and that is a view to which I am sympathetic. Third, the formulation of the republican theory explicitly refers to restoration at several passages; and, finally, the theory is still open enough to allow reformulations and adjustments.

Braithwaite and Pettit opt for 'promoting dominion' as the target for the criminal justice system (1990). Dominion is a republican concept and it refers to a set of assured rights and freedoms. Contrary to the purely liberal concept of freedom, dominion essentially is a social concept. In the assurance lies the reference to the community in which we live. 'Assurance' means that I know that I have these rights and freedoms, that I know that the others know it, and that my dominion will be defended by my fellows, if it would eventually be threatened or intruded upon. I need to live in a community to have dominion. Fellow citizens are companions in the promotion and the protection of my and their dominion. In the liberal concept of freedom, on the contrary, the other is a rival in the struggle for expanding maximally the scope of my freedom.

The question now is if 'promoting dominion' could apply as a target for restorative justice. We cannot imagine preserving or promoting dominion after the occurrence of a crime without restoring and repairing the harm. Dominion cannot be promoted, unless the harm done to it has been restored. Restoring invaded dominion comes before promoting dominion. Inversely, there might be restoration without caring for dominion as a whole if, for example, restoration were limited to purely material restitution, reparation or compensation. But the harm under consideration by the restorative justice theory includes a much larger scope of possible harms and sufferings.

The target 'repairing the harm' is a specification of 'promoting dominion'. Restoration only happens after damage has been done to dominion and it aims at re-establishing dominion in its formerly existing scope and quality of assured rights and freedom. Promotion always can happen, and aims at expanding the scope and improving the quality of the assured rights and freedoms. Promotion therefore includes restoration if damage has been done, but restoration is not necessarily promotion. Restoring the harm is the defensive side of the aim of promoting dominion (see Figure 10.1).

Figure 10.1   Restoring vs. Promoting Dominion

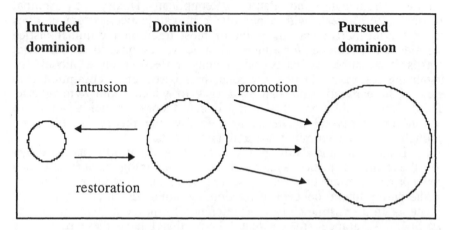

Yet surely repairing the harm appears to be a more adequate target for criminal justice than promoting dominion. Promoting dominion may be advanced as the central target of a good society, but that does not mean that it should be the overall target of all societal institutions. Society should pursue the maximising of citizens' dominion through socio-economic and cultural policies, integration policies, education and welfare. But not all societal institutions do the same. There is rightly a division of tasks, according to which specific power and equipment is given to each institution. Criminal justice is a very specific societal institution.

Braithwaite and Pettit distinguish between coercive and socialising institutions (1990, 80-85), Polk between developmental and coercive justice institutions (Polk, 1994). The French philosopher Althusser points to the difference between '*les institutions idéologiques de l'état*' (in plural form) and '*l'institution répressif de l'état*' (in singular form) (1980). According to Althusser, the state uses most of its institutions to 'seduce', 'convince' or 'motivate' its citizens to accept the dominant norms and values and to behave accordingly. Only when these institutions fail for one or another reason, does the state openly rely on its coercive power through its repressive institution, the criminal justice system. It then forces the citizens to conformity, or excludes them temporarily or permanently from community.[3]

In this view, criminal justice only intervenes as a last resort, when all other possibilities to nurture law-abiding citizens have proven unsuccessful. And rightly so, because criminal justice is the system of coercion and repression, and, as we mentioned earlier, that is in tension with the fundamentals of a democratic constitutional state, and of course also with the aim of promoting dominion. Coercion essentially reduces freedom and this should only be permitted in exceptional situations of emergency. Criminal justice is a defensive system, that only intervenes after a crime has been committed, when harm has already been done to dominion. It is crucial to stick to the defensive role of the criminal justice system. That is also why the target of its interventions should be defined in defensive terms. The target must be limited to repairing the harm done to dominion, rather than expanding or promoting dominion. If promoting dominion would be the target of criminal justice, there would be no reason for it to wait reactively until damage has been done, but it could proactively seek out possible threats to dominion, and possibilities for promoting it. The pathway to preventionism would be open, and that is not what we want for the coercive and potentially intrusive system that is the criminal justice system (Braithwaite and Pettit, 1990: 45-48).

Checking Three Desidarata

For a target to be appropriate for the criminal justice system, it must meet some conditions. Braithwaite and Pettit list three 'desiderata'.

Uncontroversial The damage and suffering caused by a crime are the essential reasons to find crime undesirable. Von Hirsch considers 'the harm to the standard of living' (1993: 30) as the basic measure to estimate the seriousness of a crime. If harm is so crucial, its repair must be uncontroversial as a target for the intervention.

However, unlike Braithwaite and Pettit, I do not think that uncontroversiality is sufficient. Caring for wounded victims after a violent assault certainly is uncontroversial, but it would not be accepted if the societal response were restricted to that. Besides being uncontroversial, the target must meet maximally the full range of uncontroversial expectations.

Can restoration do this? Difficult to say, as the full range of uncontroversial expectations is unknown. We provisionally have to rely on some research on victims' experiences (Umbreit, 1994) and on public opinion (Sessar, 1999) to suggest that restoration probably does better meet general expectations than punishment. Probably, the public expects the criminal justice system to act against crime rather than to intervene broadly and intrusively for promoting dominion in general. For the latter goal, the public will look to other institutions.

Focusing the target on repairing the harm provokes questions with regard to crimes without victims, without harm, such as drug use, drink driving without causing an accident, and unsuccessful attempts. If there is no harm to concrete victims, how could the focus of the judicial intervention be on repairing the (absent) harm (Ashworth, 1986, 1993)? Perhaps drug use should be decriminalised, but taken seriously as a problem for socialisation and health prevention. In drink driving and unsuccessful attempts, however, the value of introducing the concept of dominion clearly appears. The restoration pursued is not only about sufferings and losses by individual victims, but also about the dominion of all citizens. It is part of my dominion to have the assured right and freedom to circulate safely on public roads. The presence of a drink driver is a threat to that. If authorities would not intervene, it would mean that they do not take my right seriously. The "common-knowledge" of dominion would be damaged. In the same sense it is my right to be safe from being victimised by an offence. Therefore, the authorities can intervene after an unsuccessful attempt also. Recognition, recompense and reassurance are all vital to dominion, according to Braithwaite and Pettit (1990).

This analysis takes republican theory close to preventionism. Intervention against drink driving is not meant for being drunk, but because of the risks it implies for potential victims. Shouldn't we accept then also coercive preventive interventions in families at risk for example? I would not think so, because there are essential differences between a family at risk and drink driving. Drink driving (or unsuccessful attempt) is a deliberate act, posed by an accountable person, whereas a family at risk is a situation, not chosen by the family members. Moreover, drink driving is well defined, even objectively assessable, whereas defining a family at risk is itself a risky undertaking, as prediction research demonstrates. We would not accept prosecution for drink driving to be dependent on the police officer's feeling that the driver looked a bit too cheerful or that his/her breath had a suspicious smell. Leaving drink driving and unsuccessful attempts under criminal law has a lightly preventionist flavour, indeed, but it is under control and does not undermine the stability nor the satiability of the system's target, which are the two other desiderata to be commented on.

Stabilising   The stability of the target refers to obligations of the authorities to take the uncontroversial target seriously in all circumstances. In the original formulation of the republican theory of criminal justice, this means a commitment to promote in any case the dominion of all citizens concerned. In our emerging theory on restorative justice, we would say that the state should always take seriously the rights of citizens for their dominion to be restored, if invaded. The state has to set the conditions for restoration and it can use force for that aim by referring to the justice system. The citizens considered here are not only the concrete victim, but all citizens. If indeed the state would not take seriously the right of the concrete victim that his/her dominion be restored, it would affect the dominion of all citizens, as they would understand that, as with their unlucky fellow citizen, their rights to be restored in case of intrusion are not assured either.

Does the target of restoring dominion also affect the action towards the offender? It is questionable because the offender's dominion has not been invaded, so there seems nothing to be restored. The answer nevertheless is yes. The very idea that the restoration of the invaded dominion is the primary target for the criminal justice system can only be sustained if the dominion of citizens is considered as a crucial intrinsic value in itself. Accordingly, dominion should always be respected as much as possible. Promoting dominion may be too ambitious a target for criminal justice, but respect for dominion, thus aiming at a status quo as a minimum, should be a basic principle in criminal justice intervention. Restoring dominion is its target; respect for dominion is its bottomline constraint. Also the dominion of the intruder is thus to be taken into account when a restorative intervention is planned, together with the needs for restoration of the victim and of all other possibly involved citizens.

Satiable Restoring dominion might very well be a more satiable target than promoting dominion.

Society and community are entities in action. From this point of view, promoting dominion never ends, because the scope of dominion should in principle always be subject to possible expansion. This is a task for the societal organisation as a whole, through refinement of democratic rules, socio-economic equity, cultural differentiation, opportunities for education, etc... For criminal justice, it is not. As we already noted above, criminal justice plays on the defence, because it only intervenes after intrusion into a dominion, never before. It seems obvious then that repairing what has been damaged, certifying what is threatened allows a better delimitation than promoting what is not there yet and what in fact should be expanded endlessly. The target of repairing the harm to dominion offers a better stake to put an upper limit to the intervention than promoting it.

Through all these comments, it is clear that I favour a more restricted view on the function of a coercive justice system into society than the original republican theory of criminal justice does. The use of force against citizens should be delimited in as secure a way possible.

Therefore, it seems preferable to formulate the target of the restorative justice system more defensively: it aims to restore the harm, instead of promoting dominion. This reformulation seems to offer better stakes for assuring the satiability of the system.

Derived Constraints

Repairing the harm to dominion as the target for a criminal justice system (being viewed now as a restorative justice system) brings about derived obligations to which the system has to respond. In their republican theory of criminal justice, Braithwaite and Pettit, distinguish four presumptions.

The Criminal Justice System must be Parsimonious with Punishment

The meaning of parsimony is close to that of satiability, but it is more restricting. We can eat until full satiation, but we can parsimoniously do with less to survive. Satiability restricts the possible coercive intervention by an upper limit. Parsimony actually limits the coercive intervention to what is strictly needed. Its prescription is: "If in doubt, do less". That can be less than would be acceptable according to the satiability requirement.

The satiability/parsimony couple is close to the retributivist issue of proportionality, in that both do limit the quantum of intervention permissible. There is however a crucial difference. Satiability obliges us to set an upper limit, as required by the proportionality principle in retributive justice. Parsimony, however, excludes the setting of a lower limit, as would be required by the same principle. The parsimony constraint requires an active involvement to search for non-coercive ways to restore dominion. For parsimony reasons, the opportunities for non-coercive restorative processes are of crucial importance. The more voluntary restorative processes can lead to satisfying and balanced outcomes, the less appeal to the coercive judicial system will be needed and thus, the more the parsimony principle will be realised. A fully fledged restorative justice system should fulfil its parsimony obligation by leaving space for, or by diverting to voluntary processes, wherein victim, offender and community can seek together an agreed settlement in the aftermath of a crime that maximally restores the dominion injured.

There is another important difference between retributive proportionality and parsimony in restorative justice: the nature of the 'entities' to be related to each other. Retributive proportionality relates the seriousness of the crime to the amount of punishment ('Seriousness and Severity', von Hirsch, 1993: 29-35) whereas restorative theory links the amount of harm to dominion[4] with the amount of restorative efforts (Walgrave and Geudens, 1996). There may be some comparability between the seriousness of the crime and the harm to dominion,[5] but the nature of the response is quite different. In retributivism, the reaction is 'hard treatment'; the pain is willingly inflicted (von Hirsch, 1993: 12-13). In restorative justice, it is an obligation to contribute to restoration; as discussed above, that may be hard to comply with, but the hardness of the treatment is not willingly inflicted.

The System must Allow the Checking of the Authorities' Use of Power

Checking of power is the "pendant" of the stabilising desideratum described before. Stabilising means the assurance that intrusion into dominion will be a stable reason for the power to act in view of restoring the harm done to dominion. Checking of power is about the other side: it is necessary to assure that the power will not 'exaggerate' in its zeal to restore the harmed dominions, nor will it be guided by prejudice against certain citizens. The dominion also holds assured rights not to be abused by the state's power. Van Ness (1999) lists the rights for equal protection before the law, to freedom from torture and cruel, inhuman and degrading treatment, to be presumed innocent, to a fair trial and to assistance of counsel. Juridical and institutional "handles" must be provided for the citizens and their counsel to check whether these rights are respected through the restorative procedure.

The rights listed by van Ness are derived from the traditional penal law procedural dispositions, and it seems that they could be maintained in view of a restorative version. Van Ness explores the respect for these rights especially with regard to voluntary mediation and family group conferences. His conclusion that 'there is no reason to conclude that restorative processes will inherently result in due process violations' (p. 9), is in fact insufficient. The conclusion should be much more affirmative, for example, that the restorative processes offer sufficient (juridical) tools for the participants to check the power exercised on them and to counterbalance it if they consider this necessary.

A special problem with regard to participatory processes is the right to a defence. Many lawyers are not inclined so much to promoting peace, but rather to trying to win the war. The presence of a lawyer in the process, or even as a counsel before or after the meetings, often makes the exchanges more complicated and disadvantageous even for their own client. On the other hand, people need support by counsel, in order to be informed correctly about their rights.

The Intervention must Disapprove the Criminal Act

Societies cannot function without social disapproval.   If socialising institutions would not express disapproval for harmful behaviour, there would be no internalisation of norms, and societies would degrade into being arenas of permanent risk and benefit calculations, without commitment to life in community.

Reprobation also is important for the target of restoring the harm to dominion.   Reprobation by officials confirms the authorities' commitment to dominion, not only the concrete victim's dominion, but also all citizens' dominion.   It adds to the assurance that dominion is taken seriously and that intrusion into it are responded to by reprobation (and obligation to restore).   Interventions to repairing the harm can go along with 'moral reasoning with offenders' (Braithwaite and Pettit, 1990: 90), including shaming and provoking guilt feelings within the offender.   This holds an important dominion-reinforcing impact on the victim and the community and may be a powerful incentive for the offender to accept restorative actions.

However, this will preferably occur in informal processes, involving only victims, offenders and other persons who have freely agreed to participate (Walgrave and Aertsen, 1996).   The free acceptance demonstrates the participants' sharing of at least an elementary 'communitarian feeling' or 'bonds', that can serve as a common base for exchanges and seeking agreement.   What binds these people is more important than what has split them as victim vs. offender.   In moralising with an offender, one tries to motivate him/her to conform to a common set of values and norms. The commonality of values about crime is the main ground for shaming and motivating the offender to respond positively to the gestures of reacceptance (Braithwaite, 1989).

In coercive judicial interventions, however, the situation is quite different.   Participation is not free, so the common ground for shaming and moralising is far from evident.   The coerciveness provokes a stringent need for checking of power, mostly through some formalism and publicity.   Two reasons make it difficult to see judges engage in moralising rhetoric towards the offender.

First, formal moralising has no great chance of affecting the offender positively.   In a family situation, moralising occurs in a context of affection and support.   The child takes the moralising seriously because he/she is convinced of his/her parents' commitment to him/her, as he/she can experience every day.   The parents' reproving message is accepted because the child perceives them as having the moral authority to do so.   More or less, the same can apply to freely accepted restorative processes, as we mentioned just before.   With the judiciary, on the contrary, many offenders have already experienced a career of social exclusion and failures. Society and its (judicial) representatives are looked at as hostile and unjust. Unlike the parents towards the child, the judge has no moral authority in the eyes of many offenders. He/she is seen as a professional who is paid to do his/her ("further excluding", "unjust") job. There is no space for moralising comments. On the contrary, if there would be tendencies to do so, it would be felt as an additional, unnecessary insult and humiliation, that may contribute to the hardening of the offender's hostile attitude towards society and its institutions. Therefore, judges need to be polite, correct, respectful to the citizen in front of them, but not to moralise.

Second, judicial trials rightly are public, but that entails great risks in moralising. Whether or not moralising the person through shaming has a reintegrative or disintegrative effect, depends on how the community will receive the shamed person. In the closed situation of informal processing, including only victim, offenders and proximates, the impact of shaming can be controlled and gestures of reintegration can be provoked in the session itself. But as soon as shaming goes beyond the informal and enclosed environment, there is no longer any control over what "people" at large will do with that shaming process. The risk is that "the public", not being involved in the exchange of feelings and opinions, will adopt a position towards the offence (and the offender) that is relatively unrelated to the reintegrative aims of the process. Stigmatisation of the offender then would become an obvious consequence.

Restraining the judiciary from moralising to the offender does not exclude its reprobatory function as a whole. The judicial intervention does issue a reprobative message, but I would rather see it in the sense indicated by von Hirsch (1993: 9-12). Censure proclaims that the behaviour was wrong. It is not aimed at changing the offender's attitude ('the condemner is no mentor or a priest': 10), but to confirm him/her as a responsible person who has committed a wrongful act. It may give the 'actor' a reason for acknowledgment of the wrongfulness of his/her act and to try to avoid such acts in the future, but censuring is 'not a technique for evoking specified sentiments' (1993: 10). The censure also addresses the public to provide them with moral reason for desistance. The act is punished and therefore clearly charged with blame. Censure just confirms that the act is reprehensible.

In short, the justice system has no explicit moralising mission towards the offender. It has to confront him/her by force (when the offer for voluntary participation does not function) with his/her obligation to take responsibility for the wrong, and to oblige him/her to contribute reasonably to the restoration of the harm caused by that. By doing so, the justice system issues a reprobative message, demonstrating that such acts cannot be tolerated, because they are harmful to the dominion of citizens.

It is a theme for debate whether or not reprobation necessarily includes punishment. The relation between both is to be considered in two directions. First, not all punishments express blame. Punishment actually is sometimes seen as a cost to be added to the commitment of an offence. Many professional criminals and white collar criminals consider it not as blame, but as a rationally balanced risk to take when they go for a benefit by criminal action. For juveniles involved in subcultures, being arrested and condemned is often a reason for pride towards peers. Some scholars even argue that the decrease of social blaming in the community provokes an increasing need for penal punishment (Boutellier, 1996): because people do not feel blamed anymore, you have to augment the 'objective risks' for potentially criminal behaviour.

But the other direction is more complicated. Do we need punishment to express blame? Braithwaite and Pettit (1990) clearly uncouple this relation, whereas von Hirsch's (1993) standpoint is complicated. Punishment is linked to censure via a detour in four steps. (1) Behaviour is wrong, because it causes harm to 'a person's standard of living'. (2) The wrongfulness needs to be censured, as a moral message, and to be prevented, as a prudential message. (3) Although the censure can also be expressed in other ways, the punitive way is chosen, because of its preventive (deterrent) impact. (4) To decide upon the amount of punishment, however, only the degree of blameworthiness (and not the preventive aims) is the reference. Von Hirsch therefore does not consider punishment as the only way to express blame, but he needs punishment for preventive reasons. Reference to blameworthiness is needed in punishment because of the need for proportionality.

That means in fact that if a way can be found to assure proportionality, or a satisfying version of it, without punishing, the relation between censure and punishment drops off. We consider the satiability/parsimony couple described above as a satisfying alternative to proportionality and we do not therefore need punishment in that version.

The Intervention must Contribute to the Reintegration of the Parties Affected by the Crime

Whereas the three formerly mentioned constraints deal with process and procedure, this one explicitly is about the target. It confirms that it is not sufficient that the judicial intervention be just but that it should also be constructive for social life. The notion of reintegration focuses on the relation between the individual and community, contrary to the notions of rehabilitation or treatment, which focus on the individual. Braithwaite and Pettit write '... the restoration of victims and ex-offenders to the enjoyment of full dominion must be a priority' (1990: 91). This sentence confirms restoration of dominion (and not its promotion) as the highway to reintegration.

Restoration of the victim's dominion is achieved by the authorities' clear message that it takes the intrusion seriously and by the offender's restorative gestures. The intervention also is a message to citizens as a whole that the concrete victim is an example of how societal institutions intervene restoratively when an intrusion into dominion occurs. Restoration also gives the offender the opportunity to take responsibility and to make up for what he/she has harmed. All this contributes to the reintegration of all parties concerned into a restored peaceful community and ordered society (as van Ness, 1996, distinguishes the roles of community and society).

Such restorative actions are more integrative than punishment. In the retributive option, censuring is the primary function, including prevention as a secondary goal (von Hirsch, 1993). For reintegration (something that is not the retributivists' concern in fact), all has to be expected from the clear, formal and deterrent confirmation of the rules. As a reintegrative effort, this is meagre indeed. In its instrumentalist version, punishment is seen as being 'communicative', in order to provoke feelings of guilt and repentance within the offender (Duff, 1996). Guilt feelings may encourage accepting to do restoration, but punishment is not the only way to provoke guilt feelings (Walgrave and Braithwaite, 1999). Sticking to punishment as a wilful infliction of pain may have more negative side effects than the positive ones supposed by Duff. Punishment mostly enhances stigmatisation and other social exclusion of the offender. Therefore, it is restoration that promotes reintegration, not punishment.

Coercive restorative interventions and sanctions (like a restorative community service, imposed by court) may be painful, but as argued before, they are not punishments, because the pain is not deliberately inflicted. They also have a more reintegrative impact than traditional punishments. Even if the offender does not freely accept the accomplishment of a restorative action, he/she may in the longer term understand the sanction constructively and the chances for him/her to be reaccepted by the community are greater than after a retributive action. This is also true in comparison with rehabilitative measures, as appears through research on the impact of restorative sanctions on the offender (Geudens, 1998; Walgrave and Geudens, 1997; see also Schiff, 1999). Moreover, the carrying out of restorative sanctions within the community is also educational for the community itself. It has the opportunity to observe young offenders doing constructive service, which, if done well, may contribute to the deconstruction of stereotyped images.

Conclusion

The republican theory of criminal justice, as formulated by Braithwaite and Pettit, has been explored for its usefulness to lay theoretical fundamentals for legalising restorative justice.

The republican theory of criminal justice appeared to offer an excellent ground for thinking about putting restorative justice into a legal framework that is open enough to safeguard space for free informal processing and, at the same time, carefully guarantees legal safeguards.

However, a more accurate definition of the target is needed. Instead of promoting dominion, restoring the harm to dominion seems to be a more appropriate target, and more satiable, which is an essential condition for being suitable as a target for a coercive system in a society that guarantees a complete set of freedoms and liberties to its citizens. The constraint of parsimony motivates a linkage of the coercive justice system to the circuit of extra-judicial restorative settlements. This circuit must be maximally developed, but also legally checked. The reprobative presumption, however, is a cause for concern. In the coercive system, reprobation towards the individual and/or his/her act, is to be handled very carefully, if not to be avoided. The presumption of reintegration fits perfectly into the restorative option, but it is unclear why the notion of restoration is not advanced as the ideal. It would be more accurate and – in a sense – again more delimiting.

Clearly, the remarks added to the republican theory of criminal justice, to orient it more openly towards being a theory of restorative justice, depart from a more restricted, purely defensive view on the role of the coercive justice system in the constitutional democratic state.

Notes

1   This paper has been written during a stay as a visiting fellow, granted by the Research School of Social Sciences, Australian National University, Canberra. I thank the RSSS board, and like to witness that ANU is a wonderful place to be and to study. Thanks also to my colleagues and friends John Braithwaite and Kathy Daly for their thoughtful comments.

2 A maximalist perspective in restorative justice opts for developing restorative justice into being a fully fledged systemic alternative to both the retributive and rehabilitative approaches to crime. This is contrary to the diversionist perspective, that aims at diverting as many cases as possible to restorative solutions, leaving the traditional models in place (see Walgrave, 1998).

3 Althusser was a marxist. In his vision, he would not agree that the State promotes dominion, but it would only function to preserve the existing hegemony.

4 Referral to harm and not relying on penal law may evoke the notion of civil law tort (Barnett and Hagel, 1977; Feld, 1999). There is however a distinction between dealing with conduct that results in tort to an individual person and an act that does more, by causing harm also to public life (Ashworth, 1986). That is the essential distinction between tort and crime. In the latter cases, the harm done to the individual victim does not merge with the harm done to community. Community also is in need of restoration and neither the victim nor the community necessarily speak for each other (van Ness and Heetderks Strong, 1997; van Ness, 1999).

5 Von Hirsch (1993: 29-33), for example, defines the seriousness of crime in terms of harm, namely harm to the standard of living (also, von Hirsch and Jareborg, 1991).

References

Alder, C. and Wundersitz, J. (eds) (1994), *Family Conferencing and Juvenile Justice. The Way Forward or Misplaced Optimism?*, Australian Institute of Criminology, Canberra.

Althusser, L. (1980), *Positions*, Hachette, Paris.

Ashworth, A. (1986), 'Punishment and Compensation: Victims, Offenders and the State', *Oxford Journal of Legal Studies*, vol. 6, pp. 86-122.

Ashworth, A. (1993), 'Some Doubts about Restorative Justice', *Criminal Law Forum*, vol. 4, pp. 277-99.

Bazemore, G. and Walgrave, L. (eds) (1999), *Restorative Juvenile Justice. Restoring the Harm by Youth Crime*, Criminal Justice Press, Monsey (New York).

Bazemore, G. and Walgrave, L. (1999a), 'Restorative Juvenile Justice. In Search of Fundamentals and an Outline for Systemic Reform', in G. Bazemore and L. Walgrave (eds), *Restorative Juvenile Justice. Restoring the Harm by Youth Crime*, Criminal Justice Press, Monsey (New York), pp. 45-74.

Braithwaite, J. (1989), *Crime, Shame and Reintegration*, Cambridge University Press, Cambridge.

Braithwaite, J. and Pettit, P. (1990), *Not Just Desert. A Republican Theory of Criminal Justice*, Clarendon, Oxford.

Brown, B. and McElrea, F. (eds) (1993), *The Youth Court in New Zealand: a New Model of Justice*, Legal Research Foundation, Publ. 34.

Boutellier, H. (1996), 'Beyond the Criminal Justice Paradox. Alternatives between Law and Morality', *European Journal of Criminal Policy and Research*, vol. 4, pp. 7-20.

Daly, K. and Immarigeon, R. (1998), 'The Past, Present and Future of Restorative Justice: Some Critical Reflections', *Contemporary Justice Review*, vol. 1, pp. 21-45.

Daly, K. (1999), 'Revisiting the Relationship Between Retributive and Restorative Justice', Paper prepared for the conference Restorative Justice and Civil Society, ANU, Canberra, 16-18 Feb.

Duff, A. (1992), 'Alternatives to Punishment – or Alternative Punishments?', in W. Cragg (ed.), *Retributivism and its Critics*, Steiner, Stuttgart, pp. 44-68.

Duff, A. (1996), 'Penal Communications: Recent Work in the Philosophy of Punishment', in M. Tonry (ed.), *Crime and Justice. A Review of Research*, Chicago University Press, Chicago, pp. 1-97.

Feld, B. (1999), 'Rehabilitation, Retribution and Restorative Justice: Alternative Conceptions of Juvenile Justice', in G. Bazemore and L. Walgrave (eds), *Restorative Juvenile Justice. Restoring the Harm by Youth Crime*, Criminal Justice Press, Monsey (New York), pp. 17-44.

Geudens, H. (1998), 'Recidivism Rate of Community Service as a Restorative Judicial Sanction as Compared with the Traditional Juvenile Justice Measures', in L. Walgrave (ed.), *Restorative Justice for Juveniles. Potentials, Risks and Problems for Research*, University Press, Leuven, pp. 335-50.

Hirschi, T. (1969), *Causes of Delinquency*, University of California Press, Berkeley.

Marshall, T. (1996), 'The Evolution of Restorative Justice in Britain', *European Journal of Criminal Policy and Research*, vol. 4, pp. 21-43.

Polk, K. (1994), 'Family Conferencing: Theoretical and Evaluative Concerns', in C. Alder and J. Wundersitz (eds), *Family Conferencing and Juvenile Justice. The Way Forward or Misplaced Optimism?* Australian Institute of Criminology, Canberra, pp. 123-40.

Schelkens, W. (1998), 'Mediation and Community Service in the Juvenile Justice Legislation in Europe', in L. Walgrave (ed.), *Restorative Justice for Juveniles. Potentials, Risks and Problems for Research*, University Press, Leuven, pp. 159-83.

Schiff, M. (1999), 'The Impact of Restorative Interventions on Juvenile Offenders', in G. Bazemore and L. Walgrave (eds), *Restorative Juvenile Justice. Restoring the Harm by Youth Crime*, Criminal Justice Press, Monsey (New York), pp. 327-56.

Sessar, K. (1999), 'Punitive Attitudes of the Public: Reality and Myth', in G. Bazemore and L. Walgrave (eds), *Restorative Juvenile Justice. Restoring the Harm by Youth Crime*, Criminal Justice Press, Monsey (New York), pp. 287-304.

Sinkinson, H. and Broderick, J. (1998), 'A Case Study of Restorative Justice: The Vermont Reparative Probation Program', in L. Walgrave (ed.), *Restorative Justice for Juveniles. Potentials, Risks and Problems for Research*, University Press, Leuven, pp. 301-15.

Trepanier, J. (1998), 'Restorative Justice: a Question of Legitimacy', in L. Walgrave (ed.), *Restorative Justice for Juveniles. Potentials, Risks and Problems for Research*, University Press, Leuven, pp. 55-73.

Umbreit, M. (1994), *Victim Meets Offender: the Impact of Restorative Justice and Mediation*, Criminal Justice Press, Monsey (New York).

Van Ness, D. (1993), 'New Wines in Old Wineskins: Four Challenges of Restorative Justice', *Criminal Law Forum*, vol. 4, pp. 251-76.

Van Ness, D. (1996), 'Restorative Justice and International Human Rights', in B. Galaway and J. Hudson (eds), *Restorative Justice. International Perspectives*, Kugler/Criminal Justice Press, Amsterdam /Monsey, pp. 17-35.

Van Ness, D. and Heetderks Strong, K. (1997), *Restoring Justice*, Anderson, Cincinnati.

Van Ness, D. (1999), 'Legal Issues of Restorative Justice', in G. Bazemore and L. Walgrave (eds), *Restorative Juvenile Justice. Restoring the Harm by Youth Crime*, Criminal Justice Press, Monsey (New York), pp. 263-84.

Von Hirsch, A. and Jareborg, N. (1991), 'Gauging Criminal Harm: A Living-Standard Analysis', *Oxford Journal of Legal Studies*, vol. 11, pp. 1-38.

Von Hirsch, A. (1993), *Censure and Sanctions*, Clarendon, Oxford.

Walgrave, L. (1995), 'Restorative Justice for Juveniles: Just a Technique or a Fully-fledged Alternative?', *The Howard Journal of Criminal Justice*, vol. 34, pp. 228-49.

Walgrave, L. and Geudens, H. (1996), 'The Restorative Proportionality of Community Service for Juveniles', *European Journal of Crime, Criminal Law and Criminal Justice*, vol. 4, pp. 361-80.

Walgrave, L. and Aertsen, I. (1996), 'Reintegrative Shaming and Restorative Justice: Interchangeable, Complementary or Different?', *European Journal on Criminal Policy and Research*, vol. 4, pp. 67-85.

Walgrave, L. and Geudens, H. (1997), 'Restorative Community Service in Belgium', *Overcrowded Times*, vol. 8, pp. 3 + 12-15.

Walgrave, L. (1998), 'What is at Stake in Restorative Justice for Juveniles?', in L. Walgrave (ed.), *Restorative Justice for Juveniles. Potentials, Risks and Problems for Research*, University Press, Leuven, pp. 11-16.

Walgrave, L. (1999), 'Community Service as a Cornerstone within a Systemic Restorative Response to (Juvenile) Crime' in G. Bazemore and L. Walgrave (eds), *Restorative Juvenile Justice. Restoring the Harm by Youth Crime*, Criminal Justice Press, Monsey (New York), pp. 129-54.

Walgrave, L. and Braithwaite, J. (1999), 'Guilt, Shame and Restoration', *Justitiële Verkenningen*, vol. 25, pp. 71-81.

Warner, K. (1994), 'Family Group Conferences and the Rights of the Offender', in C. Alder and J. Wundersitz (eds), *Family Conferencing and Juvenile Justice. The Way Forward or Misplaced Optimism?*, Australian Institute of Criminology, Canberra, pp. 141-52.

Wright, M. (1998), 'Victim/Offender Conferencing: the Need for Safeguards', in L. Walgrave (ed.), *Restorative Justice for Juveniles. Potentials, Risks and Problems for Research*, University Press, Leuven, pp. 75-91.

11 Decolonising Restoration and Justice in Transitional Cultures

MARK FINDLAY

The Comparative Project

Recently, when examining the relationship between crime and globalisation (Findlay, 1999), I argued the virtues of comparative contextual analysis. This means an interactive project where context is employed over *community* or *culture,* to enable comparative analysis without sacrificing specificity. Comparative contextual analysis provides the potential to reconcile 'an acute sensitivity to the peculiarities of the local', with 'the universalising imperative'. The novelty in this approach to comparative analysis is not the rediscovery of context. Rather it is in the multi-levelled applications which context invites.

> To achieve its fullest potential ... comparative research should, therefore, concentrate within a nominated cultural context; across two or more contexts within the same culture; across time and space within a culture in transition; culture to culture; and (or not) simultaneously at the local and global levels (Findlay, 1999: vii).

Nelken identifies the need to ensure, when analysing any feature of criminal justice, that it 'resonates' with the rest of the culture in context before a comparison is advanced.

> Cultural ideals and values of criminal justice do not necessarily reflect their wider diffusion in the culture. In many societies there is a wide gulf between legal and general culture, as where the criminal law purports to maintain principles of impersonal equality before the law in societies where clientilistic and other particular practices are widespread (Nelken, 1997: 563; also Findlay, 1997b).

The recognition of difference is crucial to the success of comparative contextual analysis. So too is there potential through comparison, to understand the complexity of culture and not only seek explanations for features of culture, such as crime.

> Comparative investigation turns into the hermeneutic exercise of trying to use evidence about crime and its control to resolve puzzles about culture (Nelken, 1994: 225).

Comparative contextual analysis should not be bound by dichotomous methodologies, (see Sztompka, 1990) or divergent outcomes (see Beirne, 1983). Its focus on interaction within contexts, opens up to understanding dynamic relationships such as crime and control, and trends in these. The perennial problem of comparing like with like or a common concept within different contexts is surpassed when the analysis is of interaction and transition. Further, the concerns for comparison in terms of motivation or expectation are less likely to be discussed as stark dichotomies if the analysis unfolds through various levels and dimensions.

Comparative contextual analysis does not focus on the boundaries of crime and control in order to seek their explanation. It is more likely to explore the relationships within these boundaries, and the manner in which new or transitional contexts impact on and transform these relationships.

An enlivening, if underdeveloped capacity of comparative analysis is to move away from "cause and effect" as a narrow frame of analytical reference. When examining institutions and strategies of crime control, a causal focus tends both to distort the place and purpose of criminal justice, as well as the motivations for the analytical project. Comparative contextual analysis recognises the possibility of simultaneously viewing crime and control from several dimensions, as 'multiple, overlapping and interconnecting socio-spatial connections of power' (Mann, 1986: 1). This emphasis on interaction and transition avoids simplistic assumptions about criminal justice, and the unfounded construction of policy. It should also prevent the abstraction of effective social control mechanisms from their essential contextual supports, to the extent where an appreciation of the impact of context over control is lost.

An example of this is the examination of restorative justice mechanisms from the culture out of which they emerge, then the introduced culture into which they are adapted, and finally in the context of their representation. As instanced above, however, it is necessary to dispel the impediments to this analysis by exposing some of the interests which advance more limited approaches to comparative analysis (e.g. where one form of justice seeks its legitimacy from the other, or its validation from the other's failure).

Restorative justice as a focus for comparative cultural analysis has regularly suffered from what David Nelken refers to as 'comparison by juxtaposition' (Nelken, 1997). This may be explained through answers to Nelken's question about what the comparison is supposed to be achieving. Particularly in the literature supporting the policy of conferencing, the relentless reference back to methods and experiments in a specific cultural context so as to justify their adoption and promotion in others, exposes comparative analysis to criticisms for which it should not be held responsible. Rather than the style of analysis, it might be 'the disguised hegemonic project and the avowed search for global legal concepts' (Zedner, 1995: 519), which is laid open to criticism.

The inclusion of comparative analysis amongst the characteristics of intellectual and administrative imperialism is only to be expected when contextual actuality is overlooked or under-played. Where the comparative project breaks down into an exercise in justification rather than analysis is when context is marginalised. Therefore, the insights into restorative justice, for instance, offered by comparative analysis are no longer sufficiently critical or analytical, unless they recognise levels of cultural context and transition.

Restorative Justice and Colonisation

Restorative justice may be understood as a new wave of colonialism in the current domain of social control. When examined against the cultural roots of certain restorative justice strategies[1] this potential to colonise is especially poignant. Constitutional legality and legal formalism were crucial to political and economic colonialism of the 'new worlds' (when introduced law and legal institutions repressed the impact of custom) (see Findlay, 1997a). More recently, claims for 'informal justice'[2] and its potential to remedy the failings of bureaucratised crime control have tended to legitimate the capture by communitarians of juvenile justice in particular. As with the colonisation of social control through legal and constitutional formalism, restorative justice has, in some instances, failed to respect the limitations of the models it promotes, as well as the tensions with the systems it replaces (see Cunneen, 1997).

Colonisation through restorative justice is more complex than the triumph of the informal over the formal. Claims for restorative justice, and its mechanisms have led to change in both custom-based and bureaucratised criminal justice, as the case-studies to come suggest. A consequence of these changes has been that bureaucratised justice is buffered from challenge by the incorporation and cooption of alternative modes of resolution. Also, custom-based control can be drawn closer to the command of the state through recognition and integration.

Advocates of restorative justice argue that less formal justice resolutions must replace moribund and dysfunctional bureaucratised strategies for control. Beyond the justification of failure theory (see Cohen, 1995) restorative justice is commended as a means for modifying and augmenting pre-existing control mechanisms. Kathleen Daly (see Daly, 1998) suggests the exploration of 'spliced justice forms'. By this, Daly recognises the potential of collaboration, 'where an informal, restorative justice process was piggybacked on a formal, traditional method of prosecuting and sanctioning serious offences' (Daly, 1998: 10). In advancing this position, Daly identifies the merits of an interrelationship between formal and informal justice. She notes Roger Matthews' view (see Matthews, 1988) that formal and informal justice are neither dichotomous nor a matter of choosing one or the other, but of examining how they worked together (see Findlay and Zvekic, 1988). While this is true, it does not invite anything but the most sensitive and contextually aware intersection between justice models with differing features of formalisation.

Experience in transitional cultures, such as those in the South Pacific (see Findlay, 1999: 203-17) suggests caution when considering the grafting of a more formal institutionalised mechanism of justice onto pre-existing, and customary restorative practices. In this respect 'restorative' is not so much the description of an 'alternative process for resolving disputes' but one in which it is both customary and traditional for victims, offenders and communities to accept responsibility for the resolution of crime-based problems. Harry Blagg challenges 'orientalist' appropriations of culturally specific reintegration endeavours (see Blagg, 1997, 1998). Blagg argues that the colonisation of customary ceremonies and resolutions may be more about the securing of the hegemony of introduced systems of justice, rather than the reassertion and recognition of custom-based alternatives. Scholarly support for a synthesis of custom and introduced systems may, as Blagg criticises, endorse and confirm Eurocentric 'devices of destructuring the totality and context' of customary resolutions.

While justifying Daly's interest in a synthesis between formal and informal criminal justice, recent work on the transitional relationships of crime in a global context (see Findlay, 1999: Ch. 1 and 4) confirms the significance of Blagg's injunction. Attempts to 'splice' justice forms in certain South Pacific jurisdictions reveal the danger of cultural abstraction, and the potential to compromise the essential and potent contextual elements of customary justice resolution mechanisms.

In order to appreciate the dangers involved in any mindless merging of justice resolution mechanisms, it is useful to examine these both from local and more global perspectives. The imperatives and interests behind the move to integrate may reflect a crisis in local control strategies, as well as wider claims for legitimacy across control agendas, beyond local, jurisdictional or immediate demands.

A blatant example of the colonising potential of 'spliced' justice forms is demonstrated through reconciliation in the criminal courts of Fiji. This also provides a local level of analysis for restoration as a justice paradigm.

i) Local Level of Analysis

Section 163 of the *Criminal Procedure Code* 1978, of Fiji, provides that where charges for criminal trespass, common assault, assault occasioning actual bodily harm, or malicious damage to property are brought under the *Penal Code*:

> the Court may in such cases which are substantially of a personal or private nature and which are not aggravated in degree, promote reconciliation and encourage and facilitate the settlement in an amicable way on terms of payment of compensation or other terms approved by the Court, and may thereupon order the proceedings to be stayed or terminated.

While having regard to the court's role as a "facilitator" in the reconciliation process, this section operates on the understanding that the sanction is in the hands of the accused. To that extent, the Court disposes itself of "ownership" of the penalty beyond its role in promoting settlements of this form.

The state constrains the use of such penalty, or at least limits the situations in which reconciliation may be recognised by the court, by designating the offences to which it may relate. This is important in terms of a purpose for reconciliation; that being the staying or terminating of other penalty options.

Reconciliation has long existed as a feature of the restitution and compensation dimensions of customary punishments in the Pacific. Even so, its punitive potential is recognised in Section 163, through the reference to 'payment of compensation or any other terms approved by the court'. Moreover, by providing for an avoidance of any further State-based penalty by achieving reconciliation, the institutions of legal formalism have incorporated this penalty within their own sentencing options.

The operation of reconciliation under the sponsorship of the state courts differs from "self-help", customary resolutions. The consequences of modern reconciliation as a penalty option within the formal courts are interesting. In its custom-based context, reconciliation is governed by three factors,

- the public nature of the settlement,
- the collective nature of its terms and
- the relative expectations of parties involved.

In its contemporary context within the formal legal framework of the Fijian courts it would appear that reconciliation has been removed from an open, accountable, and relative penalty where the community has an investment, into a far more private and localised settlement. In Fiji today it is common, when domestic violence comes before the court, to see reconciliation promoted as an appropriate penalty. However, between the unequal power positions of persons negotiating domestic reconciliations, the private nature of their terms, and the application of expectations which may go well beyond an immediate issue of the assault or future threats of violence, reconciliation may become more of an avoidance of penalty rather than a penalty. For instance, where a complainant withdraws her allegation of assault as a result of reconciliation, this may be the consequence of threats from the husband to throw the wife out into the street if she does not 'reconcile' rather than any genuine rapprochement. The court would not become aware of this by simply seeking an assurance on reconciliation from the accused, and the court may not examine the complainant in this regard. The community, the traditional witness and enforcer of reconciliation also has no voice in the court hearing.

A key problem with the 're-culturising' of such resolutions or penalties is the realisation that the state is not the community and vice versa (see Abel, 1995). While the state may need to take responsibility (and hence sponsor criminal justice initiatives) for those crimes which the community should not own, there exists a significant array of crime situations and crime choices where community ownership and involvement is appropriate. However, these situations may not regularly overlap. Therefore, legal formalism as a feature of the state may not be supportive of customary penalty. Those features of customary penalty which seem appealing when compared with the formalised justice structures of introduced law, (such as openness and accountability) are often compromised or corrupted within state-centred environments. Further, the essential sanctioning impact of customary penalties may be lost as they are required to address new aspirations from within the formal justice process.

By identifying the difficulties facing the integration of formalised and custom-based resolution, it should not be assumed that attempts at such integration are either fruitless or flawed. In fact, some of the problems associated with the intersection of formal and informal justice mechanisms may have been overcome with the assistance of a more detailed and considered analysis of the consequences of such integration.

The Indigenisation of Justice

The influence of customary penalty over the control process of formalised legality means more than the recognition of custom through mitigation, or acceptance through judicial notice. Across the Pacific the penalties which now emerge from the state-centred judicial system often incorporate features of customary penalty. Considering the penalty of banishment, speculation on the development of 'hybrid' and culturally sensitive penalties in terms of their ownership, object and purpose is possible. In so doing, Garland's (1990) emphasis on the cultural essence of penalty is confirmed.

Banishment, an extreme custom sanction in Western Samoa, might provide an instance where a less formalised control mechanism may be extrapolated from a uniquely local and relative cultural context into an application where the level of analysis is potentially global. In this regard, the more universal potential of the sanction is available for comparative analysis and cultural transportation only after the original custom context (and its relationship with the sanction) is appreciated.

Potentially Global Level of Analysis

With banishment, the state in Western Samoa recognises the resilience, popularity and utility, of community-centred control. It also appreciates the dangers inherent in a challenge from constitutional legality which will expose its peripheral and symbolic presence. Finally, through the tolerance and even celebration of banishment the state, and its constitutional legality, share the legitimacy of indigenised justice forms and outcomes.

In Western Samoa, where today structures of custom-based social order remain intact, banishment is a powerful penalty available to village communities. Beyond this both the formalised state-sponsored processes of dispute resolution and introduced law have borrowed and endorsed banishment.

The history of banishment as penalty in Western Samoa was interestingly reviewed in the recent decision of *Italia Taamale and Taamale Toelau v Attorney General of Western Samoa* (Court of Appeal – CA. 2/95B). This was an appeal from a decision of the Land and Titles Court, a court in the state judicial hierarchy, ordering the appellants and their children to leave their village by a nominated date. The appellants argued on appeal that they could not be in contempt of the original court order through non-compliance because the penalty itself contravened Article 13 (1 (d) and 4), the freedom of movement and association provisions of the Constitution. They further argued that it was clear from earlier decisions of the Supreme Court, the penalty of banishment was not to be recognised by the courts of Western Samoa. It is worthy of note here, that in attempting to defeat the jurisdiction of the custom penalty the appellants not only had recourse to the courts of introduced law, they also relied on constitutional legality, and colonial law doctrines of precedent.

The tenure of the earlier courts' argument against banishment as "law" was that "ownership" of the penalty remained within customary tribunals, directed against traditional relationships and for the purpose of enforcing customary obligations. None of these therefore should be legitimised at the level of the state through its legal formalism or constitutional legality.

The appeal court in *Taamale* rejected such submissions. Banishment was historically rooted, as the court saw it:

> there is no doubt that banishment from the village has long been an established custom in Western Samoa.

Further, the court went on to review the place of banishment within the law of the colony, and following on from independence. In 1822 the German Administration of Western Samoa passed an Ordinance *to Control Certain Samoan Customs.* The Ordinance prevented Samoans of any station from 'expelling any person from his village or district, under penalty of imprisonment...'. The penalty of banishment was then reserved to the Administrator.

With the introduction of independent constitutional legality in Western Samoa, the status of banishment as a penalty became ambiguous in terms of ownership and objective. The appeal court drew from earlier decisions of the Supreme Court the view that:

> undoubtedly the customs and usages of Samoa in the past acknowledged the rights of village councils and the court to make banishment orders, but that custom ceased on 28 October 1960 when the Constitution was adopted.

Several judgments of the Supreme Court in the 1970s and 1980s endorsed appeal points that such banishment orders were in violation of the Constitutional rights of freedom of movement and residence.

In *Taamale* the appeal court acknowledged that currently, for many village councils in Western Samoa, banishment was the 'most important sanction vested by custom in the village council'. Banishment is usually employed when other forms of customary penalty such as fines and ostracism from village affairs had failed.

A further argument in favour of the continued significance of banishment was that as an effective general deterrent at a village level, it was rarely necessary to employ state-centred crime control resources such as the police to back up the enforcement of customary orders.

The appeal decision recognised the Land and Titles Court as the only judicial 'site' from where banishment as a penalty may emerge:

> While upholding the jurisdiction of the Land and Titles Court to order banishment we do so on the express basis that the jurisdiction can only lawfully be exercised in accordance with the principles and safeguards identified in the present judgment.

The purpose of the penalty was said to be 'limited to the interests of public order - meaning to prevent disturbances, violence or the commission of offences against the law'. The Land and Titles Court has taken from the village council the responsibility for the banishment penalty, making it a formal court order. The councils are left with their ultimate penalty of ostracising a person within the village.

The appeal court in *Taamale* endorsed the Court's assumption of banishment, and the monopoly over this sanction as within its jurisdiction. A justification as to why banishment moved from the "ownership" of the village council, to that of a Court is:

> that the imposition of a banishment order is made fair and reasonable and according to law ... An individual who is dissatisfied with a decision given at the first instance level of the Land and Titles Court also has further (formal) avenues for seeking redress ... as the Land and Titles Court can make a banishment order, so that court can cancel it.

The process of "ownership" is 'that a village council minded towards banishment from the village would be well advised to petition that (the Land and Titles) Court for an order rather than take an extreme course on their own responsibility'. Further, because serious offences such as murder and rape are grounds for banishment 'it is necessary to say that the punishment of (such) offences is a matter for the criminal courts. Serious crime is properly dealt with in the Supreme Court'. This appears to be both a further constraint on the object and purpose of banishment and a limitation over its ownership.

The court concluded:

> Banishment from a village is, at the present time, a reasonable restriction imposed by existing law, in the interests of public order, on the exercise of the rights of freedom of movement and residence affirmed (in the Constitution).

Interestingly the court recognised the dynamic and culture-bound nature of this penalty:

> as Western Samoan society continues to develop the time may come when banishment will no longer be justifiable.

With banishment we have a pre-existing and prevailing custom-based resolution which is 'indigenised by the state and its bureaucratised justice system'. In New Zealand, on the other hand with family group conferencing, we are witnessing the state claiming cultural sensitivity by adopting the structures and discourse of Maori justice practice and philosophies. As Tauri suggests:

> Indigenisation of the justice system...must also refer to the ideological and practical (re)legitimation of the state's own system. This is attempted through the implementation of legislation and justice initiatives that, while appearing on the surface to empower First Nations, merely incorporate their justice philosophies and practices within hybridised judicial forms (1998: 177-178).

This is not integrated criminal justice (see Findlay, 1999: Ch. 6). Nor is it the victory of one form of control over another. It is a process of colonisation, where bureaucratised justice claims legitimacy through assimilation. The integration of justice resolutions requires more than the transaction of benefits and interests, one context to another. The integrity of the original context needs to be retained along with the credibility of any new application (and its context) for integration rather than colonisation to take place.

Integration of Justice Forms

The discussion of criminal justice relocated from the context of custom into formalised criminal justice institutions highlights several problems for integration:

- the structures of sanction on which crime control traditionally lies may be culturally specific
- the structures of community out of which such sanctions emerge may not be compatible with the 'communities' of modernisation
- the delineations between control, tolerance and reintegration in modernised communities may be hard and fast. In custom settings these may more naturally merge, as the behaviours and situations they regulate are not so rigidly labelled

- the interests regulated for in modernised societies are more individual and therefore require more formalised legal protection
- the bureaucracies which construct modernised criminal justice have a large investment in crime control. As such they are reluctant to divest their areas of responsibility in favour of other socialisers
- the state represents the interests of those affected by crime in modernised criminal justice. Therefore, the community consensus and cooption so essential for tolerance and reintegration (and evident in the custom contexts) are removed from more formalised crime control.

Within modernised communities these difficulties necessitate either artificial or imposed integration in place of a natural and evolutionary integrative context for control.

The forces favouring integration will encounter resistance from localised control regimes, where sophisticated bureaucracies monopolise the institutions and processes of crime control. As much as crime is differentiated from other behaviours and situations needing regulation, crime control in these localised contexts is institutionally separate from the broader themes of socialisation.

Despite certain representations of globalised crime which suggest a return to the modes of denunciation common in simpler societies, the preference for adapting and advancing modernised crime control strategies is a feature of global politics. This paradox cannot be explained in terms of a common language of criminal liability, local to global. Globalised crime offends morality, polity and perpetuity rather than the interests of individuals. Victimisation is collectivised. Harm is global. Threats are common. As such, the context of globalised crime seems to be communal, and control arguably should be integrated in order to address a collectivised problem.

To test this suggestion, the transportation of a custom-based control technique into a globalised context may indicate the applicability of integrated control for regulating global crime. Banishment is a control strategy with roots deep in customary socialisation. It depends on consensus, approbation, comprehensive ascription, and total enforcement.[3] Banishment is reliant on community and not state sanction. It grows out of stages of tolerance, and failed situations of reintegration.

A global crime context where banishment would be relevant is corporate crime. For the individual, bankruptcy is banishment from the marketplace. For the corporation "winding up" proceedings may have some regulatory impact but this is limited to where the company against which these are directed is simply an expendable part of a wider corporate entity.

Banishment means exclusion from the community. Essential for its punitive and regulatory significance is separation from those features of community life valued by the banished. The community is more than a referent in that it must maintain the boundaries of exclusion. For instance, international trade sanctions imposed by one nation on another will not have the same impact without multinational endorsement.

Some might see banishment as anything but an integrated control strategy. It appears to depend on segregation and difference. What makes banishment integrative, however, is the manner in which it involves the whole community and a range of socialisation beyond crime control. In addition, banishment is a transitional state, usually imposed for a determinate period, with the expectation that it will create a radical context for reintegration when its time has run.

Banishment's influence within a corporate commercial community would depend on the authority prescribing this penalty. Once the banishment order was determined, the community would be required to achieve the banishment from a series of nominated and valued relationships. These might involve market position, consumer confidence, capital access, and share trading. A schedule for reintegration might be set as part of the banishment strategy.

This mechanism will be far better suited to the corporate entity than individualised penalties such as the fine, or imprisonment. Banishment requires and incorporates responsibilities advocated by the corporate community in its arguments for self-regulation. It has a reintegrative goal, while adopting clearly retributive and deterrent measures in its early stages.

The feature on which the effectiveness of an integrated (local to global) control strategy relies is the scope of community collaboration for its achievement. Collaboration in simple, local communities is obvious and essential to the context of the sanction in question. The restorative consequence of its application is insured through the commitment of the community and the collaboration between the perpetrator, victim and their immediate community. On a global level collaboration is equally essential but more difficult to realise and retain. This is not just a product of a more complex community context. It is a consequence of confusion over responsibility to collaborate, and the state to which the offender and the victim must be restored.

Conclusion - Collaboration rather than Restoration?

It is necessary to examine in more detail the issue of collaboration and its crucial connection with restoration prior to anticipating the successful integration of justice mechanisms at various levels of formalisation. By focusing on harmonisation and collaboration as features of the essential context within which certain less formalised justice resolutions tend to prevail might be more productive than tending to focus on their restorative outcomes. An outcome-driven analysis has the danger of overlooking the possibility of disharmony and domination inherent in the preference for restorative justice.

A re-thinking of the notion of "restorative justice" may facilitate efforts at harmony. In recent justice parlance restorative justice refers to:

> an alternative process for resolving disputes in organisations, to alternative sanctioning options, or to distinctly different new modes of criminal/juvenile justice organised around principles of restoration to victims, offenders, and the communities in which they live (Daly, 1998: 5).

Another way of looking at restoration here is to focus on the process rather than on the participants and the outcome. This will necessarily then require an exploration of traditional or custom-based mechanisms for resolution, mechanisms which have a particular cultural resonance worthy of recognition and protection. In any such consideration, we would be answering Harry Blagg's question; what is being restored in restorative justice? (Blagg, 1998: 8). Blagg's argument away from restoring to the status quo, where this is both 'incomplete and one-dimensional', has some significance for any reflection on the restoration process of custom-based resolution. Only when the full cultural context of such resolutions operating within a contemporary world is considered, will restoration of a 'status quo' be dynamic and transformational. Further, the recognition of context, both initial and transformed, when examining restorative justice mechanisms will automatically highlight the situations and stages where community collaboration is possible or denied.

A new interpretation of restorative justice, (i.e. restoring culturally sensitive custom-based resolutions within and beyond their original context), is possible through recognising the essential significance of collaboration, in any context of its application. More than simply an expectation that alternative, less formalised strategies will likely be restorative, collaborative justice claims that the effective delivery of criminal justice must be both culturally relative and reliant on community cooperation. Even so, certain common themes will tend to invigorate the relevance and impact of particular criminal justice initiatives. In this respect the "collaboration" in justice is not simply an expectation for local communities, but between proponents of custom-based resolution, and those with investments in the rejuvenation of more formalised criminal justice regimes. Collaborative justice relies on an integrative model for criminal justice delivery in transitional cultures, where the state values customary resolutions and the community accepts the state's responsibilities in the area (Findlay, 1999: Ch. 7). Essential to such recognition and acceptance is a program of education and training in which principal participants would be involved. These participants may include victims and their immediate community, perpetrators, police, community agencies, sentencers, and elders. They need initially to be made aware of their mutual interests and potential contributions prior to being invited to explore and apply interactive models for justice delivery.

In societies where state-sponsored justice is weak and customary resolution is widespread or recognised, (such as those in our examples from the South Pacific) the most efficient way in which the legitimate goals of criminal justice are to be achieved is through collaborative models and initiatives. However, in order that collaboration is to emerge and be sustained in a climate of cooperation and ownership, the principal participants in criminal justice must be brought together to identify their expectations for justice resolutions and determine the most effective response to these expectations.

To facilitate collaboration beyond the initial customary context (such as at a global level), participants and stakeholders in the justice process should be provided with collaborative justice models which have been successfully tested in other settings. These must exhibit elements compatible with the characteristics of the 'new communities' in which collaboration is offered (i.e. the mutual obligations which bind multi-national corporate enterprise, as compared with homogeneous village organisation, in the case of banishment). The crude transplantation of culturally specific models into alien settings is neither collaborative nor potentially successful. Rather, collaborative justice models in a context where custom and introduced law intersect, allow for the critical adaptation of effective models of resolution, encouraging original or new participants to own, implement and sustain collaborative justice initiatives which emerge in such an exercise.

Collaborative justice will also ensure custom-based initiatives, presently endangered by the colonisation of introduced law and systems enhance their sustainability through appropriate integration within competing systems. This process of integration, being essentially collaborative and community-based offers a responsive and relevant alternative to the dissection and cooption of some restorative justice agendas.

What distinguishes collaborative justice (and its largely unrecognised potential) from orientalism is:

• recognition of the crucial contextual significance of custom-based justice resolutions;

- acceptance of the legitimacy and integrity of these resolutions in their own right, rather than depending on recognition from bureaucratised justice structures;
- appreciating that in transitional settings custom-base resolutions may need to change and develop along with the dynamics of co-existent competing cultures;
- requiring that incorporations or integrations of custom-based resolutions into introduced justice frameworks contain the essential contextual preconditions that ensure custom-based justice outcomes;
- enunciation of the justice outcomes intended through any such incorporation or integration so that original expectations will add to the legitimacy but fail to survive the transfer;
- good-will on the part of those who advocate collateral or competing mechanisms and notions of justice when collaboration is envisaged;
- realisation of the need to tackle institutional and structural feudalism within bureaucratised justice in order that collaboration will not simply result in subsumption;
- acceptance that collaborative justice initiatives may need to serve and satisfy plurality rather than homogeneity in communities;
- the development of lateral justice terrain wherein several resolution mechanisms and modes may be open for choice in preference to hierarchies of compulsion; and
- the avoidance of a tendency to justify the collaborative endeavour (and directions within it) by unrealistic cultural claims, or through reflection on failure.

The essence of collaboration for the success of restorative justice initiatives explains the recent predominance of restorative over bureaucratised justice forms. Further, effective community collaboration distinguishes those justice resolutions which "work", along with those that survive transplantation from one cultural context or level, to another.

If collaboration is conceded as a crucial characteristic of the restorative justice context, the nature of that collaboration within and between the original and transplanted community requires critical review. Such a review, to avoid contributing to little more than dogma or policy imperialism, can only proceed if immersed in the context of its origins and its cultural translation.

Notes

1   Such as conferencing and Maori culture, reconciliation and Fijian custom, and sentencing circles and First Nation peoples in Canada.

2   I am not comfortable with the suggestion of simple dichotomies between the mechanisms of justice based on degrees of formalism.   It is better to see

formalism as a continuum when analysing justice mechanisms   (See Findlay and Zvekic, 1988).

3   In some situations the alienation of banishment may be modified or ameliorated by expelling the individual to another community with kinship connections.

References

Abel, R. (1995), 'Contested Communities', *Journal of Law and Society*, vol. 22, pp. 113-26.

Beirne, P. (1983), 'Generalisation and its Discontents', in E. Johnson and I. Barak-Glantz (eds), *Comparative Criminology*, Sage, Beverly Hills.

Blagg, H. (1997), 'A Just Measure of Shame?: Aboriginal Youth on Conferencing in Australia', *British Journal of Criminology*, vol. 57, pp. 481-501.

Blagg, H. (1998), 'Restorative Visions: Conferencing, Ceremony and Reconciliation', *Current Issues in Criminal Justice*, vol. 10, pp. 5-15.

Cohen, S. (1985), *Visions of Social Control*, Polity Press, Cambridge.

Cunneen, C. (1997), 'Community Conferencing and the Fiction of Indigenous Control', *Australian and New Zealand Journal of Criminology*, vol. 30, pp. 292-311.

Daly, C. (1998), 'Restorative Justice: Moving Past the Caricatures', unpublished conference paper.

Findlay, M. (1997a), 'Crime, Community Penalty and Integration with Legal Formalism in the South Pacific', *Journal of Pacific Studies*, vol. 21, pp. 145-60.

Findlay, M. (1997b), 'Corruption in Small States: A Case Study in Compromise', in B. Rider (ed.), *Corruption: The Enemy Within*, Kluwer, Deventer, pp. 49-61.

Findlay, M. (1999), *The Globalisation of Crime*, Cambridge University Press, Cambridge.

Findlay, M. and Zvekic, U. (1988), *Informal Mechanisms of Crime Control: A Cross-Cultural Perspective*, UNSDRI, Rome.

Fisse, B. and Braithwaite, J. (1988), 'Accountability and the Control of Corporate Crime: Making the Buck Stop', in M. Findlay and R. Hogg (eds), *Understanding Crime and Criminal Justice,* Law Book Co., Sydney.

Garland, D. (1990), *Punishment and Modern Society*, Oxford University Press, Oxford.

Mann, M. (1986), *The Sources of Social Power*, Vol.1, Cambridge University Press, Cambridge.

Matthews, R. (1988), 'Reassessing Informal Justice', in R. Matthews (ed.), *Informal Justice?*, Sage, Newbury Park, CA, pp. 1-24.

Nelken, D. (1994), 'The Future of Comparative Criminology', in D. Nelken (ed.), *The Futures of Criminology*, Sage, London, pp 220-43.

Nelken, D. (ed.) (1995), 'Legal Culture, Diversity and Globalisation', *Social and Legal Studies*, vol. 4, Special Issue.

Nelken, D. (1997), 'Understanding Criminal Justice Comparatively', in M. Maguire (et al) (eds), *The Oxford Handbook of Criminology*, Oxford University Press, Oxford, pp. 559-73.

Sztompka, P. (1990), 'Conceptual Frameworks in Comparative Inquiry: Divergent or Convergent', in M. Albrow and E. King (eds), *Globalisation, Knowledge and Society*, Sage, London, pp. 140-56.

Tauri, J. (1998), 'Family Group Conferencing: A Case-Study of the Indigenisation of New Zealand's Justice System', *Current Issues in Criminal Justice*, vol. 10, pp. 168-82, at 177-78.

Zedner, L. (1995), 'In Pursuit of the Vernacular: Comparing Law and Order Discourse in Britain and Germany', *Social and Legal Studies*, vol. 4, pp. 517-34.

12 Connecting Philosophy and Practice

JOHN BRAITHWAITE AND HEATHER STRANG

It was Kurt Lewin who famously said there is nothing as practical as a good theory. This was a statement about the impact of explanatory theories on practice in the world. Philip Pettit and John Braithwaite in their contribution to this volume take Lewin a step further. They argue that normative theory is improved by being responsive to good explanatory theory and vice versa. There is nothing as practical as a good philosophy and the best philosophy is informed by practice.

The history of restorative justice in the 1990s illuminates both claims. Restorative practices preceded their philosophical interpretation as restorative justice. Since Kant, Hegel and Bentham made their seminal contributions, the philosophy of punishment has been one of the dullest, least inspired fields within both philosophy and criminology, even though it has attracted contributions from many of law and philosophy's brightest and best – Rawls, Dworkin, Hart, Habermas, Nozick, among others. Restorative justice practice has inspired some creative new thinking, as evidenced in this volume. Yet the volume also indicates that it is early days; philosophy is still lagging behind practice. This is clear in the way the New Zealand courts struggled with the *Clotworthy* case as discussed by Sir Anthony Mason in his opening contribution, and taken up by Morris and Young and Barton in their essays. At the time of writing even greater judicial ferment surrounds the decision of the Canadian Supreme Court in *Gladue* to recognise restorative justice as a more important principle of criminal sentencing for First Nations defendants than for defendants from the rest of the community.

Equally, the volume demonstrates a crying need for practice to be more informed by philosophy. Consider, for example, Christine Alder's warnings about the dangers restorative justice practices might pose to young women – shame as a threat to self-esteem, family members who have sexually abused them having a say in how their offending will be dealt with, community controls that seek to dominate young women into conventional moulds of femininity, and more.

Values

The starting point for confronting these dangers of practice may be to be clearer about what restorative justice values are, a challenge Morris and Young seek to address up front in their essay. What sort of space do these values create for traditional liberal rights? Do they weaken or strengthen them? If dominion, or freedom as non-domination, is a restorative value as Walgrave argues, then dominating young women into conventional moulds of femininity clearly becomes an unacceptable practice. But how tight can the fit between restorative process and restorative values be in the context of such a problem? If a bedrock of restorative process is empowerment of all stakeholders (Barton's essay), where do we stand when it so happens that the stakeholders want to shame in a stigmatising way or hold together family relationships where women are victims of sexual abuse?

It is not good enough to say that juvenile courts sometimes do these things as well. The challenge for restorative justice is to involve value commitments and process commitments that are more explicit than those of contemporary courts in respect of such concerns. And then to move on to empirical research that evaluates different approaches to delivering such commitments in practice. For example, do we achieve less stigmatising processing of girls by training conference coordinators to recognise and reframe shaming that attacks the self, training that distinguishes stigmatisation of the violent girl from the communication of community disapproval of violence? Or do we achieve less stigmatisation by sweeping shame under the carpet – seeing shaming as a bad thing that will pop up but that we minimise by keeping criminal process as demoralised as possible? Walgrave has a hybrid position that would see the courts take the latter path, conferences more the former path. Our main point is that the effects of such policies are eminently empirically testable and that such empirical work is an obligation of both those who advocate the new and those who defend the old.

In a future world when we are clearer about restorative values, they might be enshrined in legislation as principles The hope would then be that programs for which the research showed a failure to deliver on them would be discontinued. Even with "good" programs in terms of these values, when they threw up bad cases courts could invoke the values to strike down the decisions of the conference. Hence, silencing of a young woman by the presence of her sexual abuser, humiliation or degradation as in a conference decision to order the wearing of a T-shirt saying "I am a thief", could and should be grounds for courts to strike down a conference decision.

Much more debate of the kind in this book and more empirical experience with restorative justice innovation and its risks is needed before we are ready to settle any such list of restorative values. As important as it is to settle on cultural and legal commitments to restorative values, more important still is guaranteeing restorative process commitments.

Process

Some of the crucial restorative process commitments have become fairly clear from the chapters in this book: ensuring all stakeholders have an opportunity to attend and have their say; cultural responsiveness to those stakeholders in a particular conference or circle (participant control of process); shouting, violent threats or other forms of domination of speech as out of order; violation of fundamental human rights as out of order; ensuring that the full plurality of relevant voices is heard in the room.

The last of these process commitments is an example of one that may be more important to dealing with the concerns Alder raises than the value commitments. Courts are unlikely to give voice to a homeless young woman's street community. But restorative justice conferences can and should do this. The best assurance against dominating voices in a conference (for example, those who wish to coerce a girl into some hegemonic femininity) is not enforcement of the value of non-domination, because domination inevitably happens. The best assurance is for the process to be so structured that other voices will be raised against the voices of domination. The voice that says there is no harm in the kind of identity the young woman presents, that there is good in it, that the harm is in threatening her freedom to go with it. If there is one thing our empirical experience of conferences and circles has taught us it is that allowing a large number of people into the circle does not produce chaos. Practitioners say they prefer to facilitate conferences with many participants because the process unfolds more easily and naturally. Welcoming plurality is the best way of guaranteeing that there will be someone who will speak up when domination occurs. This is a more practically achievable process objective in a restorative justice conference than in a court where a judge or magistrate, who is the source of the domination, can rely on the law to defend his/her right to call the shots. Such process controls that are available in court – mainly appeal – can be fully available in restorative justice processes where the defendant is advised of a right to walk out of a conference at any time to have the matter settled in a court decision that can then be appealed to a higher court.

Punishment

One of the divides in this collection is over the place of punishment in restorative justice, over values like equal punishment for equal wrongs. The debate around *Clotworthy* (Mason, Morris and Young, Barton) illustrates what a philosophical divide this is among scholars who consider themselves sympathetic to restorative justice. Kathleen Daly and Charles Barton are undoubtedly right that as an empirical matter if you set up processes which comply with any process definition of restorative justice, at times the outcomes will be quite punitive. Certainly punitive values will get a good bit of play during the restorative justice dialogue.

This is one reason why many want restorative justice to qualify as such only if it passes a values test as well as a stakeholder empowerment test. In those cases where the stakeholders turn punitive, stigmatising, disrespectful of difference, dominating the vulnerable, you simply cannot call what happened restorative justice. Valerie Braithwaite's research in this volume shows that support for restorative justice has deep roots in harmony values, as does support for punitive justice have deep roots in security values. Since both harmony and security values have a near universal hold on human beings, at any gathering of mortals, both are likely to be manifest.

The point we wish to make in this conclusion is that while this is a major divide, it has rather less bite at the level of practice than it does at the level of philosophy. This is because most of the protagonists in this debate can agree on two things:

1. Restorative justice processes should be constrained from breaching upper limits on the amount of punishment permissible for a given crime.
2. If we are serious about empowering stakeholders, we cannot rule out of order arguments or outcomes that involve punishing offenders.

On the first point, Lode Walgrave can have a serious philosophical difference with Kathleen Daly on the meaning of punishment when he argues that a community service order may not be punishment. When a community service order is ordered not for the purpose of intentionally inflicting pain but for the purpose of aiding the restoration of community, victim, offender, or all three, then Walgrave wants not to conceive it as retributive. However, we expect Walgrave to yield to Daly when the upper constraint on the amount of punishment that is permissible for a given crime is determined. It would be unthinkable to contend that an onerous community service order should not count here just because it was imposed without punitive intent. Equally, we think Daly would yield to Walgrave when it comes to the practical question of whether to design restorative process so as to put the problem in the centre of the circle (encouraging deliberation around what should be done about the problem) or whether to put the person in the centre of the circle (encouraging deliberation around what is the right punishment of that person). They can agree that what we want to encourage is restorative problem-solving rather than intentions to punish. Parsimony in resort to punishment is a value which, as Walgrave suggests, a social movement for restorative justice might promote. What this means in practice is creativity and active search for non-coercive ways of solving a problem and preventing recurrence. Valerie Braithwaite's data also show that support for restorative justice is predicted by trust. Yamagishi and Yamagishi's (2000) wonderful Japanese research program further shows that trust builds social intelligence. Those who opt not to take the risk to trust never learn how to make correct contextual judgments of trustworthiness, never learn how to forge creative win-win solutions. In the context of schools, we therefore might conceive of restorative problem-solving as education for a socially intelligent democracy.

We also suspect that none of the scholars writing in this volume would be so determinedly anti-punishment as to advocate the prohibition of punitive speech or punitive outcomes in conferences. That is, they all take empowerment of stakeholders as a more fundamental restorative value than movement from punitive to restorative outcomes.

A good analogy is the way we think morally about democracy. Republicans believe in electoral democracy because they think it is more likely to produce freedom as non-domination than despotism by a king. But what do they do when the people elect a worse despot than the king? They do not turn around and argue for displacing democracy with a return to the divine right of kings. They start campaigning for the election of a genuine democrat at the next vote. All process values will at times produce self-defeating outcomes in terms of the outcome values that motivate support for those processes. The democratic election delivers anti-democratic government; the restorative justice conference delivers anti-restoration. So long as this is not consistently so, we must show our sincerity of commitment to processes that empower by honouring their outcomes. But this does not preclude constitutional prohibition of certain outcomes in advance of the empowerment. The elected president is empowered to govern as she sees fit, but that does not extend to dissolving the parliament and dismissing the judiciary. The conference is empowered to solve the problem however it sees fit, including by punishment, but that does not mean it is allowed to punish with a severity that exceeds the legal limit or in a way that breaches fundamental human rights.

Mixing Philosophies

Miller and Blackler argue that retributive, consequentialist and restorative theories are not mutually exclusive. They seek to define rather limited contexts where restorative justice seems the way to go. They would exclude restorative justice from realms such as tort or non-violent school bullying. But why would one not want to deploy all the defining features of restorative process and restorative values in such arenas? Daly seems to suggest a fruitful perspective on the mixing of philosophies question when she says: 'one cannot begin a restorative justice process by announcing "let's reconcile", "let's negotiate", or "let's reintegrate"'. In other words, our intuition about getting the mixing of philosophies right is that it is more a trick of timing than of defining characteristics of the problem to specify what is a restorative justice problem and what is not.

There is no problem so serious that restorative processes and values might not be morally superior to formally retributive processes and values. Nuclear safety, as one of us has argued elsewhere, is most effective when its regulation is restorative (Braithwaite, 1999). Apartheid, mass murder in Timor or genocide in Rwanda are not too serious for restorative justice. In such traumatic cases, however, restorative justice is a disaster if victims and their families are not ready for it, have not been persuaded that it is worth a try, reject the proposition that it could be the most practical way to move forward. Indeed, in cases of mass killing, as Prunier (1995) has shown using the Rwanda case, any kind of legal justice is a disaster if it is attempted before the prevention of further killing is fully effected. Why? Because justice can prevent peace when its selective commencement gives reason to some to keep killing.

A paradox of justice is that the more traumatic the victimisation of a crime, the less is speedy justice the ideal. Angry people must be disarmed, tempers cooled lest hot justice be injustice. But most importantly, we must be patient with victims. They need time for grief. Peace first, grieving second, justice only third. It is in the interests of offenders to give victims all the time they need to grieve, to seek counsel from those who care for their healing and then decide whether they want to opt for a restorative justice process.

Equal Justice?

In the *Clotworthy* case, it can be argued that Mr Clotworthy was lucky that he stuck his knife into a man who wanted the healing available to him in a restorative justice conference.   Sir Anthony Mason points out that inequality of sentencing arises when other serious offenders are not so lucky as to have a victim who wants the grace of waiving the repayment of hurt with hurt.   But why should equal sentences for offenders be a higher value than equal concern for victims?   Where is the justice in denying that grace to Clotworthy's victim and denying him the plastic surgery the offender could no longer pay for in prison?   The theory of proportionality ducks the question of why equal justice for offenders is a higher value than equal justice for victims.   While these two objectives are incompatible, one possible compromise is to constrain unequal treatment of offenders only by a guarantee that none will be punished above a maximum specified for each offence and to guarantee victims a hearing where their needs are considered, where the state and state-supported victims' assistance associations take responsibility for helping them back to emotional and physical health.[1] Thus we might ensure minimum guarantees of justice for both victims and offenders instead of the impossible reconciliation of equal justice for victims and equal justice for offenders.

A Time for Justice

The timing question discussed earlier and the justice question are connected.   With traumatic cases we should certainly privilege the needs of victims over the convenience of courts and the wishes of offenders for a speedy trial.

> To everything there is a season, and a time to every purpose under the heaven:
> A time to be born and a time to die; a time to plant, and a time to pluck up that which is planted;
> A time to kill, and a time to heal; a time to break down and a time to build up;
> A time to weep, and a time to laugh; a time to mourn, and a time to dance;
> A time to cast away stones, and a time to gather stones together; a time to embrace and a time to refrain from embracing;
> A time to get, and a time to lose; a time to keep and a time to cast away;
> A time to rend, and a time to sew; a time to keep silence, and a time to speak;

A time to love, and a time to hate; a time of war and a time of peace. (Ecclesiastes 3, King James version).

We do not read this text as advocating killing, warmaking or hating. We read it as saying that part of the human condition is that terrible things like East Timor or the Holocaust happen. We find ourselves in situations where we feel we must kill or vote for governments that kill. In these situations, it is a mistake to deny hatred, to deny retributive emotions. To try to heal when we have not dealt with our hate is misguided. We read the text as saying that with wise timing it is not misguided to help others to discover the miracle of the transformation of hate into love. This is Kathleen Daly's wisdom too when she says that we do not expect to commence restorative justice processes with "let's reconcile". This will escalate victim anger because victims will believe we are not taking their suffering seriously.

Within existing restorative justice conference processes we think there is considerable genius of design in the way extended talking through of consequences for victims precedes any discussion of restoration. However, we suspect that more often conferences should adjourn at this point to give victims some grieving time, some healing time, after they have expressed all the hurts that matter to them. This is one reason we suspect why First Nations healing circles in places like Hollow Water in Canada have been able to grapple with rather bigger restorative justice challenges than we have risen to in Australia – such as community-wide patterns of sexual abuse of children. People need time for the enormity of something like this to sink in. Retributiveness is a natural first response to such a threat to our being or to the security of those we love. The time to hate in the wise justice system might involve many months of victim-centred work where if healing of the offender is on the agenda at all, it is not on the victim agenda, but dealt with for example in a circle with other abusers.

A second sense in which philosophies of criminal justice need to be mixed across time is provided by the responsive theory of regulation (Ayres and Braithwaite, 1992). According to this theory, less interventionist, more cooperative strategies of regulation are generally preferable, even for very serious wrongs perpetrated by maximally ruthless and exploitative offenders. This implies a presumptive preference for restorative justice. Equally a regulatory system that relies solely on restorative justice will be exploited by the most ruthless offenders. Deterrent approaches are needed when restorative justice repeatedly fails and incapacitation is needed when deterrence fails. An enforcement pyramid of the kind in Figure 12.1 is advocated, where the preference is to start at the bottom and only move up the pyramid when there is failure at lower levels of the pyramid. Part of the implicit explanatory theory of the pyramid is that you don't need consistent deterrence or incapacitation for the law to deliver on its promises. Occasional deterrence in the aftermath of restorative justice failure is quite enough to deliver a minimum level of general deterrence without which, according to the theory of responsive regulation, no system of regulation can succeed.

Figure 12.1:   Toward an Integration of Restorative, Deterrent and Incapacitative Justice

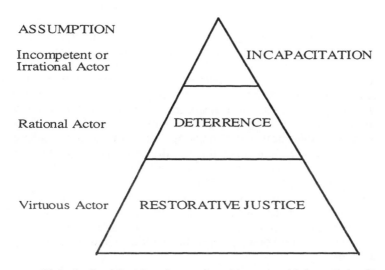

ASSUMPTION

Incompetent or   INCAPACITATION
Irrational Actor

Rational Actor   DETERRENCE

Virtuous Actor   RESTORATIVE JUSTICE

Valerie Braithwaite shows that this pyramidal model of regulation – dialogic problem-solving first and stricter enforcement if this fails – has intuitive appeal to citizens compared to consistent enforcement or consistent restorative justice. Note that this model also implies rejection of the view that restorative justice under the threat of coercion cannot be genuinely restorative. While it is important that threats of escalated enforcement action never be made in a restorative justice process, it is pointless and counterproductive to deny them as a possibility. Any criminal justice encounter involves an implied threat of coercion in the background (see Daly's chapter). It is best they be kept in the background rather than the foreground of deliberation; but if they are not there at all, we are not dealing with a criminal justice matter, nor with a criminal law enforcement process that is likely to afford prudent protection to citizens.

Very occasionally, however, it will be necessary to go for the maximally incapacitative outcome that the law allows – as when the convicted murderer of one member of a family vows to do the same to surviving members.   Under the responsive strategy this does not preclude a restorative justice conference a few years on when offender and family members are ready for a reconciliation that both sides can persuade each other to be genuine.   Release from prison at this point makes no sense under a retributive policy but can make perfect moral sense under a responsive-restorative strategy.   The time to hate has passed.

At the other end of the spectrum, it seems wrong to suggest that there are some kinds of matters that are too trivial for a fully-fledged restorative justice process.   The principle of parsimony outlined by Walgrave certainly justifies rules of thumb like the following – if it is a first and minor juvenile shop-lift, the police should always issue a caution with the parents rather than send it to a conference.   But that is a rule of thumb for the police to follow.   It can make perfect sense for private actors who are victims and perpetrators of a particular kind of harm to agree to an elaborate restorative justice process (one that passes all the value and process tests in a definition of restorative justice) on matters that the rest of us might regard as utterly trivial.   So if two relatives agree to a conference on "nagging" or if two school children agree to one on "putting each other down", that can make all the sense in the world to them.   Indeed it can make all the sense in the world from the perspective of the community's wider interest in crime prevention (but only if the principals want to be in it).   So there is no domain of law or life where what we call restorative justice processes that satisfy restorative values might not be apposite.   As Barton contends, it is for empowered parties to decide whether restorative justice is apposite.

Accountability, Privacy, Effectiveness – Who Should be in the Circle?

Accountability is another issue of concern in most chapters of this volume where we might consider mixing philosophies across time.   A key contest of values here is between accountability and privacy.   Do we conduct restorative justice conferences in private (by invitation only to members of the community of care)?   Miller and Blackler's essay is one that takes a strong line in favour of this.   On the other hand, Alder worries about the accountability question if in these private spaces girls especially are oppressed by their families.   While Australian and New Zealand conferencing practice mostly keeps outside members of the public out of the circle, Canadian healing circles tend to be open to any member of the community who wants to attend and have their say in the justice transacted in the circle.   But this oversimplifies the privacy/community-accountability dichotomy. In Hollow Water, circles dealing with sexual abuse of children were held for months or years in private with selected victims and supporters, selected offenders and supporters, before ultimately a circle was open to the whole community at the final stage of the process. Partly, this is about privileging privacy as a value over community accountability until a final resolution has been worked through by the principals in a way that is ready to be put before the whole community (or at least anyone from the community interested to attend). But it is also about giving everyone time so that there is more chance of a general willingness to acknowledge a degree of remorse and healing that enables ratification of a restorative final settlement.

The contributors to this volume tend to favour a circle or conference process over one-on-one victim-offender mediation. An expanded circle of community accountability is one reason. But the more important reason was mentioned earlier. The more people there are in the circle who deeply care about the principals to the conflict, the more likely it will be that if one of those principals is dominated by the speech of another, someone will speak up to defend against that domination. Often that takes courage; but as soon as one person has the courage to speak against someone who seeks to dominate another, their words will often resonate around the circle if the circle is wide enough. From a democratic theory perspective, the wider circle also assures a more complex plurality of voices so that any specious univocal community morality will come under contest. In a complexly plural circle, imbalances of power are more cross-cutting than they are with the crude imbalances of dyadic mediation between a boss accused of sexually harassing a secretary and his victim, or between a child offender and an adult victim. By this we mean that in the circle there are likely to be adults and children, men and women on both sides of the conflict.

Iris Young (1995) is a feminist critic of theories of deliberative democracy about undominated rational argument leading to moral consensus. Such a conception, that we find preeminently in Habermas's theory of communicative action, does not take emotion and storytelling seriously enough, nor other devices that are alternatives to rational argument. Young is advancing a feminist critique, but one can critique conferencing from an Australian Aboriginal perspective in a similar way. Many aboriginal peoples (not just in Australia) find direct questioning a rude Western practice. Yet conventional conferencing is substantially based on asking questions. At the same time, the deformalised procedure of conferences makes it an easy matter to break out of question-asking scripts. For example, instead of starting by asking a young offender to tell us in their own words what happened, an elder might start with a story about a similar misdeed he did when young. Others in the circle can then be moved to tell similar confessionals about themselves until the contemporary offender is hence moved to self-disclosure.

This is one of many reasons why indigenous peoples often view it as important for the most respected elders to be in the circle even if those elders are not intimates of either the offender or the victim. Justice rituals are important occasions where those with most "mana" (to use the Maori term) can teach others about how to lead with firmness, kindness and grace. Spirituality in both Western and non-Western conferences seems of great importance to many of us who have observed a large number of conferences. Yet we but dimly understand how and why it is important. We simply suspect that when a Mandela appoints a Tutu to head the Truth and Reconciliation Commission, this is wise. The reason has something to do with the spirituality of indigenous elders such as Tutu (or Mandela himself) being infectious. Their grace rubs off on the rest of us. We suspect that every school, every workplace, every local community has people with special gifts of grace. Difficult matters always seem to go better when they are in the room. Contagion of the spirit is a research agenda we do not yet understand how to tackle.

That said, we also know from Nathan Harris's (1999) research that shame or remorse over a wrong we have done is not something normally induced by strangers. Harris measured perceptions by offenders of how much conference participants disapproved of their offence. The perceived disapproval of most people in the room had no power in predicting how ashamed offenders felt of what they had done. The only perceived disapproval that mattered was of those the offenders had an unusually high respect for. This reinforces Miller and Blackler's attack on the potentially counterproductive role of outsiders – community representatives – in Canberra conferences. On the other hand, we might be open to non-intimates if they are elders with "mana", particularly in the case of indigenous offenders or victims who see them that way. And we must bear in mind the work of Inkpen (1999; Mugford and Inkpen, 1995) on another kind of rationale for community representatives for those common kinds of reckless endangerment offences (e.g. drink driving) where there is no victim and where communities of care may see nothing wrong with the behaviour. The problem that must be solved somehow is insufficient plurality of voices in the circle. And there is also as a consequence a community accountability and legitimacy problem when you have a community of care that simply closes ranks around the offender and covers up. Miller and Blackler may be right that this means that restorative justice is not appropriate for offences without direct victims.

But we think this conclusion is premature in light of the research evidence we have at this stage. One reason for pause is the evidence we have found for the remarkable effectiveness of what we would call restorative justice processes without victims in increasing nuclear power plant safety.

A final advantage of a plural circle over dyadic victim-offender mediation is about remorse-induction, which Maxwell and Morris's contribution to this volume shows to be a significant predictor of reduced reoffending. Many offenders are offenders precisely because they have cut themselves off from a capacity to experience remorse over suffering they cause others. One learns how to acquire that capacity (and how to deal with the shame that is induced) through social interaction with others, especially interactions with others who we love or deeply respect – the lesson from Harris's (1999) research.

In Kathleen Daly's contribution to this volume she quotes Braithwaite and Mugford's (1994) unfortunate metaphor of a shaft of shame crossing the floor of a conference as a victim explains the consequences she has suffered. The offender has learnt a callousness that protects him from experiencing any shame in the face of hearing these consequences. This shield deflects the 'shaft of shame' which then pierces like a spear the heart of the offender's mother, who sobs in consequence. It is the mother's tears which then get behind the offender's emotional defences. Through this indirect emotional dynamic the offender experiences remorse – a remorse mediated by letting down a mother he loves, indeed by hurting her. This complex social emotional possibility is not present in a one-on-one victim-offender mediation. Daly's reading of this may not be a productive one: 'offenders should feel a vicarious sense of punishment via seeing the anguish of their mothers receiving a "shaft of shame"'. Doubtless the emotional pain is punishing at that moment for both mother and child. That is clearly a bad thing. Certainly from the perspective of the retributive theory Daly addresses this is a bad thing because mothers do not deserve to be punished. At the same time, from the perspective of a restorative theory, we hypothesise that the emotional connection that induces remorse in this group dynamic tends to redound to the benefit of both mother and child. The benefit has nothing to do with the moral bad of the punishment that occurs in this context, but to do with restoration of connection between parent and child, in turn enabling connection between offender and victim. Until young offenders come to terms with the way they are hurting their loved ones and extend their hand to them in remorse for that hurt, the suffering of those loved ones will not heal. Nor will the full possibilities for the healing of the offender be realised. We read the evaluation research to date as suggesting that those who find restorative justice processes most satisfying, who secure the greatest emotional benefits from them may be the families of offenders (compared with victims for example). It is the kind of group healing dynamic that we are describing here, perhaps one that happens more backstage than on the frontstage of conferences and circles, that we suspect underpins this accomplishment.

Some Research Questions

The Maxwell and Morris results reported in this book will be an influential contribution to the empirical literature. They are results that lend support to a number of influential restorative justice theories. When offenders feel remorse after the family group conference, reoffending is reduced; however, when they feel shame in the sense of being made to feel that they are a bad person, reoffending is increased. Apology and a feeling on the offender's part that they have repaired the damage predicts reduced reoffending, while a feeling that they were not involved in the family group conference decision-making predicted increased reoffending. Note that this last finding supports the key hypothesis of Barton's chapter: '*Restorative justice fails in cases where one or more of the primary stakeholders is silenced, marginalised and disempowered in processes that are intended to be restorative. Conversely restorative justice succeeds in cases where the primary stakeholders can speak their minds without intimidation or fear, and are empowered to take an active role in negotiating a resolution that is acceptable and is right for them*'. Maxwell and Morris's findings about lack of education and employment post-conference predicting reoffending supports Alder's comments on the importance and widespread neglect of developmental issues in restorative justice processes. There is also some support in the Maxwell and Morris findings of the importance of perceived fairness of conferences to the prediction of reoffending.

These papers raise more questions than they answer, however. Morris and Young express concern about victims being used to benefit offenders – victims as props in a production to meet the needs of others. It is surprising that in the conferencing evaluation research of recent years, no one has explicitly asked victims whether they felt this happened to them. What we do know is that victims are more likely to feel better off than worse off as a result of conferences (Strang and Sherman, 1997; Daly, 1996). However, there is a significant minority who feel worse off. Might it be that these are victims who do feel they have been used as props?

Daly asks questions about the value of coerced symbolic reparation in conferences. It would be easy to explore the predictive power of symbolic reparation in conferences under conditions where this is perceived as coerced versus voluntary.

Findlay plays with the idea of graduated corporate banishment to regulate corporate crime restoratively. Bankruptcy and banishment from all commercial activity might be complemented with a schedule for reintegration which could ultimately allow full access to share trading and company directorships. In the case of a struck-off lawyer, graduated reintegration might involve first *pro bono* work only, followed by limited commercial practice of law and ultimately return to a partnership after several years being reintegrated into the profession. R and D on such ideas could first be done experimentally as an innovative order of a pioneering judge.

Findlay's collaborative justice ideas also require an action research frame of the kind that Clifford Shearing (2000) and the Community Peace Foundation in South Africa is pioneering. In part this involves using restorative justice for dealing with specific acts of violence, rape or theft in a community as a catalyst for raising wider agendas of community development, housing and community relationships.

In the aftermath of *Clotworthy* and *Gladue*, new traditions of restorative doctrinal research will open up. The preliminary treatments of the issues in the contributions to this volume by Mason, Morris and Young and Barton show the way.

Perhaps the biggest research question which will keep us busy for many decades involves the tension between restorative justice and transformative justice, to use Ruth Morris's (1995) term. Mark Findlay has a particular concern about the limitations of 'restoration to the status quo'. What if the status quo is unjust? Surely then we want a transformative rather than a restorative agenda? At the other end of this debate we have Miller and Blackler who want restorative justice to work in limited ways in those limited contexts where moral rights have been infringed and there is a need for redress or repair in relation to those specific infringements. Walgrave is on a similar wavelength in contending that the criminal justice system is a sensible vehicle for a restorative agenda, but a dangerous one for a transformative agenda. His Figure 10.1 conceptualises the choice nicely within a republican theoretical frame as a choice between the restoration of dominion or the promotion of dominion.

Our own view is that restorative justice can never be the most important vehicle for social justice. The most important institutional arenas in the modern world to struggle for social justice are the IMF, the World Bank, the World Trade Organisation, the development of international taxation policies in institutions like the OECD, and the like. But what seems equally true is that unless struggles for social justice infect all levels of institutions, from the most global to the most local, then social injustice will prevail. This is because social injustice is insidiously resilient because of the power and self-interest that drives it. Whenever social justice is victorious in one set of institutions, the forces of social injustice seek to use other institutions as vehicles to reestablish power imbalances.

More social structural kinds of research are needed here to reveal how the largely restorative approach to the regulation of tax cheating, stock market manipulation and trade practices are an important advantage to the rich, while the denial to the poor of restorative justice, in particular of indigenous justice, in favour of incarcerative justice, is a central cause of oppression and injustice. As Alder's contribution shows, the criminal justice system is a significant issue in the oppression of women. Again, while it can never be the primary institutional vehicle for sexual equality, there are local things it can do, from helping delinquent girls get back to their education or into jobs, to confronting cultures of exploitative masculinity in a school following a sexual assault in its playground.

Finally, we must remember that we live in a professionalised, managerialised society where opportunities for small groups of citizens to get together and make decisions of any consequence are rare. One of the nice things about restorative justice is that it opens up a little space where a slice of deliberative democracy can occur, where young citizens and old can learn to be democratic perhaps for the first time. This opportunity is particularly rich for all citizens during their school years over problems like bullying, as Valerie Braithwaite's chapter shows. If participatory democratic opportunities are rare in the modern world and if restorative circles are one of those rare opportunities, then we should want citizens to link the personal troubles they confront there to wider public issues, including issues of social justice – calls to governments to take some concrete initiatives about youth homelessness, to reduce school expulsions, even to transform the regulation of the insurance industry as did happen after the Australian Aboriginal insurance cases of the early 1990s (Fisse and Braithwaite, 1993). Very little research has been directed to community-building through restorative justice and to the education for democracy potential of restorative justice, perhaps because this seems so romantic in these early years of a new social movement that is barely finding its feet.

All these questions bubble up from the Chapters with their diverse commentaries and ideas on connecting philosophy and practice. Restorative justice is old, but new for us. We must learn again the philosophical principles that should guide practice; we must develop practice that informs those principles to maximise the possibilities for justice to be delivered and harm to be healed.

Note

1 This implies that for most kinds of financial losses that could not be recovered from offenders, citizens would be expected to take out insurance rather than rely on the state for compensation. The alternative is a fiscally unmanageable moral hazard problem.

References

Ayres, I. and Braithwaite, J. (1992), *Responsive Regulation: Transcending the Deregulation Debate*, Oxford University Press, New York.

Braithwaite, John (1999), 'Restorative Justice: Assessing Optimistic and Pessimistic Accounts', in M. Tonry (ed.), *Crime and Justice: A Review of Research*, vol. 25, pp. 1-127.

Braithwaite, John and Mugford, S. (1994), 'Conditions of Successful Reintegration Ceremonies: Dealing With Juvenile Offenders', *British Journal of Criminology*, vol. 34, pp. 139-71.

Daly, K. (1996), 'Diversionary Conferences in Australia: A Reply to the Optimists and Skeptics', Paper prepared for presentation at the American Society of Criminology Annual Meeting, November 20-23.

Fisse, B. and Braithwaite, J. (1993), *Corporations, Crime and Accountability*, Cambridge University Press, Cambridge.

Harris, Nathan (1999), 'Shame and Shaming: An Empirical Analysis', PhD Dissertation, Law Program, Australian National University.

Inkpen, Nova (1999), 'Reintegrative Shaming through Collective Conscience Building: The Intended and Unintended Consequences of Drink Driving Diversionary Conferences for Offenders and their Supporters', PhD Dissertation, Department of Sociology, Australian National University.

Morris, Ruth (1995), 'Not Enough!', *Mediation Quarterly*, vol. 12, pp. 285-91.

Mugford, S. and Inkpen, N. (1995), *The Implementation of Shaming Conferences as a New Policy Strategy: The Case of Drink Drivers*, Paper to the American Society of Criminology Conference, Boston.

Prunier, G. (1995), *The Rwanda Crisis: History of a Genocide*, Columbia University Press, New York.

Shearing, Clifford (forthcoming), 'Transforming Security: A South African Experiment', in H. Strang and J. Braithwaite (eds), *Restorative Justice and Civil Society*.

Strang, H. and Sherman, L. W. (1997), 'The Victim's Perspective', Paper 2, RISE Working Paper, Law Program, RSSS, ANU, Canberra.

Yamagishi, Toshio (2000), 'Trust as a Form of Social Intelligence', in Karen S. Cook (ed.), *Trust in Society*, Russell Sage Foundation, New York.

Young, Iris (1995), 'Communication and the Other: Beyond Deliberative Democracy', in Margaret Wilson and Anna Yeatman (eds), *Justice and Identity: Antipodean Practices*, Bridget Williams Books, Wellington, New Zealand.

Index